# THE GLUTEN CONNECTION

# THE GLUTEN CONNECTION

## HOW GLUTEN SENSITIVITY MAY BE SABOTAGING YOUR HEALTH—
### And What You Can Do to Take Control NOW

SHARI LIEBERMAN, PhD, CNS, FACN

WITH LINDA SEGALL

RODALE

Book design by Drew Frantzen

**Library of Congress Cataloging-in-Publication Data**

Lieberman, Shari.
  The gluten connection : how gluten sensitivity may be sabotaging your weight and your health-and what you can do to take control now  / Shari Lieberman,  with Linda Segall.
     p.     cm.
  Includes index.
  ISBN-13 978-1-59486-387-5 trade paperback
  ISBN-10 1-59486-387-3 trade paperback
  ISBN-13 978-1-59486-386-8 direct hardcover
  ISBN-10 1-59486-386-5 direct hardcover
  1. Gluten—Health aspects—Popular works.   2. Gluten-free diet—Recipes.   3. Celiac disease—Diet therapy.   I. Title.
  RC862.C44.L54   2007
  641.5'638—dc22                                                    2006029360

**Distributed to the trade by Holtzbrinck Publishers**

  4   6   8   10   9   7   5   3     hardcover
2   4   6   8   10   9   7   5   3   1   paperback

**To my husband, Augusto,**
whose love and support
make monumental tasks
so much easier.

# CONTENTS

When Dr. Shari Lieberman asked me to write the foreword to her book on gluten sensitivity, I paused to think for a moment: I'm a specialist in matters of the heart, not gastrointestinal (GI) disease.

But in addition to being a cardiologist, I am a certified nutrition specialist, and so I am deeply entrenched in the dietary and nutritional issues of my patients. Combining a healthy diet with essential targeted nutrition is perhaps the most important way to prevent disease. Certainly in my specialty (preventive and metabolic cardiology), the Mediterranean diet has proven to be the healthiest dietary approach for preventing sudden cardiac death, as well as for reducing the incidence of subsequent cardiac events. The Mediterranean diet provides an abundance of precious omega-3 essential fatty acids that have a profound impact in reducing inflammation.

Silent inflammation as we know it today is the main factor in the development of cardiovascular disease, gastrointestinal problems, diabetes, cancer, Parkinson's disease, and other neurodegenerative diseases. Although the many causes of silent inflammation include cigarette smoking, heavy metals, microbes, trans fatty acids, and excessive radiation, dietary factors that cause surging insulin levels appear to top the list.

And then, of course, there are the insidious food allergies and intolerances and "leaky gut" type syndromes that cause immune-system dysfunctions that can slowly undermine our health.

I can attest to the fact that problems with indigestion, food allergies, malabsorption, and excessive gas and bloating do, indeed, affect the heart. So, it is not uncommon for someone like me to be intrigued by Dr. Lieberman's book. I see multiple cardiovascular issues, such as heart irregularities, atypical chest pain, and high blood pressure, in people with digestive problems. And, of course, there is the complex issue of gluten sensitivity, which can develop into celiac disease (CD).

Dr. Lieberman's book is about a condition that is reaching epidemic proportions. Although this "malabsorption syndrome" was first identified way back in 1888, it is now believed that it may be the most common *genetic* disorder that sends people like you, looking for answers and relief, to health-care practitioners like me.

While many readers may be wondering what I'm leading up to, those of you diagnosed with this health-threatening disorder—or who know someone who is—have probably figured out that I am referring to celiac disease. Don't worry if you haven't heard of this problem, because that's how uninformed the general public and some medical professionals still are about CD.

This disorder is *not* a food allergy; it is an intolerance. The condition is also known by other multiple names—such as gluten-sensitive enteropathy, celiac sprue, nontropical sprue, and Gee-Herter's disease/syndrome.

Regardless of what label it carries, the problem is consistent: an inability to tolerate the gluten found in wheat, barley, and rye, with or without damage to the villi of the jejunum (upper part of the small intestine). The villi are microscopic, hairlike projections in the small intestine that provide the surface area needed to absorb the nutrients from the foods and supplements you ingest.

The link between this disease and diet wasn't made until 1944, when a Dutch pediatrician observed that children in his clinic started getting better after the Nazi invasion. Symptoms such as bloating, stomach cramping, diarrhea, and generalized fatigue gradually abated as bread disappeared from their diets, even though the children were starving for food.

Despite recent public awareness campaigns, most doctors think CD is a low-incidence problem. And most doctors think *only* in terms of celiac disease—the "ultimate" form of gluten sensitivity.

CD can be, and is, diagnosed at any age, from infancy to the last decade of life, but it may take up to 10 years of symptoms for that to happen in the United States, while the typically affected European is diagnosed by more CD–conscious doctors within a year, on average.

I remember one of my patients, a Catholic nun who was diagnosed as having CD in her late 80s, after years of becoming ill after ingesting the communion wafer. The small amount of gluten in the wafer caused her to develop gas, bloating, and diarrhea. Unfortunately, she suffered for an enormous length of time before someone finally diagnosed her problem.

One year, 10 years, or *any* chunk of your life is a long time to suffer when no one knows what is wrong with you. Dr. Lieberman's book raises public awareness about this terrible condition that afflicts many people—some genetically predisposed, some not. One person in the latter category (not genetically predisposed) is my own son Step, who developed acquired celiac disease after being exposed to toxic molds.

As you can imagine, when my own grown child complained of GI symptoms of bloating, diarrhea, and gas, along with a 40- to 50-pound weight loss, I became concerned. I took him to more than a dozen top doctors and specialists across the country, but the puzzle pieces didn't fall into place. He even went to the Mayo Clinic and saw specialists in endocrinology and neurology and had a muscle biopsy done by the general surgery service.

Although laboratory tests showed multiple laboratory abnormalities, a diagnosis was still uncertain. Finally, he found a physician-expert in environmental biotoxins, who diagnosed him with acquired gliadin allergy.

CD responds well when gluten—the trigger food-product ingredient—is removed from the diet. Now, I'm sure that many people are still undiagnosed and are still suffering, totally unaware about this bizarre form of acquired CD. But people with CD who continue to eat gluten risk tremendous health consequences, including a host of medical and autoimmune disorders and a higher risk of bowel cancer.

Furthermore, the longer they go undiagnosed, the more damage occurs to their intestines and the rest of their body. Clearly, when my son Step takes in *any* gluten, his health takes a step backward. Even though he does not have genetically predetermined CD, the acquired type of CD that he does have still requires the elimination of gluten from his diet.

Whenever making the diagnosis is obscure or difficult for me—whether I'm treating heart disease, psoriasis, GI symptoms, or whatever—I've found that having the individual restrict or eliminate gluten from the diet has resulted in spontaneous improvement. The prescription to eliminate gluten even in the case of cardiomyopathy is well founded on science. Dr. Lieberman, in fact, cites published studies that show the beneficial effects of a gluten-free diet on patients who suffer from cardiomyopathy, as well as a host of neurological, dermatological, and gastrointestinal problems.

Now, you may think that it's cruel to restrict flour and wheat from someone's diet for several months or even for a lifetime. But when you see the remarkable improvement in health a gluten-sensitive person gains when the offending substance is out of his or her system, all the dietary sacrifices are more than worth it!

If you were the person experiencing this for yourself and getting your life back, I'm sure you'd continue a gluten-free diet, just as my cardiac patients who have experienced a heart attack or gone through bypass surgery are motivated to stick to the Mediterranean or Asian–type diet that I insist they try.

Hippocrates was absolutely right when he said that "food is medicine, and medicine is food." We must understand that being aware of food choices is vital to maintaining health, aliveness, and quality of life.

Permit me to tell you about Virginia, because her story is so typical of what I call a celiac sufferer—someone struggling with symptoms of this disease until the diagnosis is made and the triggers eliminated.

Virginia told me that she felt as though she had been in a "brain fog" her entire life. Even now, she reflects on how, as a youngster, she felt like a "bad girl," recalling tantrums when she couldn't manage her irritability. As a teen, she menstruated only three or four times a year, and it's never been unusual for her to go 6 months without a menstrual period.

As an adult, she blamed herself for feeling "out of it." Virginia engaged in years of personal psychotherapy, searching for insight into her mood and behavior, and doctors placed her on antidepressants. Finally, a trusted psychologist, sensing that a physical source for her symptoms must have been overlooked, recommended that she undergo more medical evaluation.

A neurology workup failed to confirm any reason for her exhaustion. It was probably easy enough for physicians to point to her long-standing anemia and single-mom status for her symptoms, but why couldn't they resolve the anemia—or the depression? Virginia continued to actively search for answers for *2 decades,* consulting doctor after doctor, including a gastroenterologist for her peptic ulcer and other GI symptoms.

Then, one day, a lightbulb came on for her doctor during a routine office visit. Her GI physician asked Virginia about her 23-year-old son,

Aaron, who was also under his care for chronic diarrhea. She told him of an incident that had occurred the night before. Aaron was forced to leave work early with an acute respiratory reaction and swollen and tearing eyes. Aaron is a chef. He'd forgotten to turn down a mixer before adding some flour, and the dust that blew up into his face had triggered his immune system into a violent response.

Virginia will always remember how that doctor riffled through her chart on his desk and then proclaimed, "Oh, my God! I know what's wrong with you!"

The doctor didn't wait for tests to be done to confirm celiac disease. Virginia and her son immediately eliminated grains from their diets. It took 2½ years on a gluten-free diet for Virginia's symptoms (including her depression) to remit *completely*. Finally, she had her life back!

There has been an alarming increased incidence of celiac disease in the past decade. Successfully diagnosing more cases than before may be the reason that statistics reflect a higher prevalence of CD. In 1994, we expected about 1 in 10,000 people to be affected by it. In Europe, the condition appears in 1 in every 200 to 300 inhabitants. The University of Maryland's Dr. Alessio Fasano (CD researcher, pediatrician, and gastroenterologist) reports rates in the United States to be as high as 1 in 133. That's downright shocking! Especially when it appears that only about 1 in 2,000 or 2,500 have actually been diagnosed and treated.

What's even more shocking is this: Celiac disease is the end stage of gluten sensitivity. Many, many more people are gluten *sensitive* who do not (and would not) test positive for celiac disease. That's because blood tests (commonly used in a first pass to diagnose CD) do not always detect gluten sensitivity—and because gluten sensitivity masks itself behind symptoms of many other diseases and conditions. Obviously, we have a *long* way to go—and that's why Dr. Lieberman's book is so important. It uncovers all of these truths.

How do you know if you're at higher risk for inheriting this condition, which may be blocking your absorption of nutrients—and damaging your health? Well, because one cause is genetic, those whose blood relatives have celiac disease are clearly at risk. Obviously, many of us could have a genetic predisposition without actually knowing anyone in our family whose CD was ever confirmed. It's also been observed that women are more vulnerable than men.

In one 2001 study of 1,138 responding adults, most weren't diagnosed with CD until late in life, despite an average of 11 years of symptoms. Women predominated over men at a rate of nearly three to one. About 75 percent surveyed had a biopsy to confirm their diagnosis, and 77 percent reported an improved quality of life after their diagnosis was confirmed and they eliminated gluten from their diets.

There may be cultural tendencies, too. Northern Europeans have the highest incidence of CD. African Americans and Asians are least likely to have it. We do know that CD is common in Europeans—particularly the Irish—which is probably why it's diagnosed more quickly in those countries. As an example, I have a now-adult friend who was diagnosed as a "failure to thrive" baby until her mother happened to visit family in Ireland. An Irish doctor quickly recognized the then 2-year-old's CD and put the toddler on a gluten-free diet. That doctor's diagnosis turned her life around.

In our own country, inroads that have been made to enhance awareness during the past several years have tipped off American physicians to notice less-typical symptoms of CD, such as infertility problems, irritable bowel syndrome, and associated autoimmune deficiencies.

But my best advice to you is to read this book and learn how the multifaceted personality of gluten sensitivity affects multiple organ systems, such as the skin, the neurological system, the muscles, and, of course, the GI tract.

Should you discover that you have gluten sensitivity or CD, one thing is for certain: Your body is not absorbing key nutrients. You will need to go on a strict gluten-free diet. And your doctor or nutritionist may decide that you should supplement your diet with an individualized, targeted vitamin and nutrient strategy to restore a state of health and balance.

Important: If your condition is caused by gluten sensitivity, taking a medication will not cure it. For example, if your osteoporosis is due to a malabsorption of calcium because of CD, then you need to correct the basic problem in the bowel—taking a calcium supplement won't help your condition at all, let alone prevent more damage.

Remember: The key to optimum health is the earliest possible identification of a health issue so that intervention can begin as soon as possible. CD is much more common than we think it is. And gluten sensitivity is even more prevalent than celiac disease.

The good news is that the condition can be diagnosed and treated effectively. Dr. Shari Lieberman's book is a great place to learn about this poorly understood condition that could negatively impact millions of people's lives. She defines the problem clearly and provides you with simple solutions.

—Stephen T. Sinatra, MD, FACC, FACN, CNS
*Specialist in Preventive and Metabolic Cardiology,*
*Author of* The Sinatra Solution: New Hope for Preventing and Treating Heart Disease *and* The Fast Food Diet

I am a nutrition scientist. I help people eat right to be healthy. As a private practitioner, I am frequently the professional of last resort. People come to me, often through medical referral, after they have unsuccessfully tried other, often easier, remedies for their health problems.

It was through these cases of last resort that I became intrigued with gluten sensitivity, also known as gluten intolerance. This intrigue eventually led to the writing of this book.

Gluten is a protein found in wheat, barley, and rye. People who are sensitive to gluten have an autoimmune reaction to it: Instead of the body digesting the protein as it should, it recognizes gluten as an enemy and tries to fight it off. If it is a minor intolerance, no symptoms are produced.

But autoimmune reactions are often cumulative: They get worse with additional introductions of the offending substance. Ultimately, in the case of gluten, the autoimmune reaction can lead to celiac disease.

Researchers and doctors have associated gluten with medical problems for more than 50 years. But the problem they most often identified with gluten was celiac disease. They did not grasp (and many still do not, unfortunately) that the culprit behind celiac disease could be causing a myriad of other problems long before it manifests itself as a disease of the gut.

As a nutritionist, I recognize that people eat foods that nature never meant for them to eat. In today's society, this is especially true. Most food we have available to consume is changed from the way that nature made it. Biochemists have changed the seeds from which plants are grown. And food manufacturers have inundated our food supply with gluten, most notably wheat.

The majority of people can tolerate processed foods. But some cannot. They suffer the consequences of these easy-to-use foods.

And it is these "some" people who often come to nutritionists for help. As we work with them, we examine their diets for suspect foods, including milk, eggs, fish, crustacean shellfish, tree nuts, peanuts, wheat, soybeans, and nightshades (peppers, tomatoes, eggplants). Then we work with them to modify their diets, eliminate troublesome foods and their derivatives, and introduce wholesome nutrition, including appropriate supplementation, to make up for possible deficiencies caused by their physical conditions.

It was through this type of course of action that I discovered the powerful effect gluten can have—and the even more dramatic effect that taking gluten out of a diet can have—on a person's health.

The best way to illustrate this power is to share some of my earliest cases with you, because more than 20 years ago, these cases alerted me to the need to awaken people about gluten sensitivity. Here are some of these cases:

**Saved from the knife.** A 14-year-old Canadian girl was brought to me for help. She was suffering from Crohn's disease. (See Chapter 6, Digestive Disorders.)

Pharmaceutical intervention was limited in the early 1980s, and what was available had been ineffective for this girl. The doctors wanted to remove part of her colon; her parents wanted to avoid this last-ditch effort. (Surgery would have removed necrotic tissue, but it would not have halted the disease.)

Unlike most of my colleagues at that time, who only removed wheat and yeast from diets, I recommended eliminating *all* sources of gluten. I put the girl on a gluten-free diet. And within 30 days, *all* of her symptoms resolved.

She is still gluten-free today and has a healthy 3-year-old baby.

**Controlling blood sugar.** A young woman in her early twenties suffered from type 1 diabetes. (See Chapter 5, Other Autoimmune Diseases.) Although she took insulin and watched her diet carefully to avoid sugars, no matter what she did, her blood sugar levels soared, and she experienced diabetes-related problems, including retinopathy, a complication involving inflammation of the retina.

I put her on a high-fiber diet that included beans, lentils, and oatmeal. We discovered that whenever she ate oatmeal (*without* added sugar), her blood sugar would skyrocket to more than 200.

I switched her to a gluten-free diet that also eliminated oats. (Although oats in themselves do not contain gluten, they are often contaminated with gluten, because they are generally processed in the same plants that process wheat and often grow in the same fields where wheat has been grown.)

Within 2 weeks, my patient found that she could go days without taking insulin to regulate her blood sugar. And after several months, even her retinopathy substantially improved.

**Modified ineffective Feingold diet.** A distraught mother brought her 10-year-old daughter to see me. The girl exhibited behavioral problems classic of a child with an attention deficit disorder (ADD/ADHD). (See Chapter 4, Neurological Disorders.) She could not concentrate or sit still, and she was impulsive. Her schoolwork was greatly affected by her inability to concentrate.

The mother had tried everything except Ritalin, a medication that works as a stimulant on the central nervous system and is often prescribed to calm children with ADD/ADHD. The mother did not want to expose her child to the risks involved with pharmaceuticals.

Among her sincere attempts at solving the girl's behavior problems was the Feingold diet, which eliminates foods with artificial coloring and flavoring, synthetic sweeteners, and the artificial preservatives BHA, BHT, and TBHQ.

The diet is effective with many children who have ADD/ADHD, but it was not with this girl. Although she did not have any physical symptoms to suggest a sensitivity to gluten, I put her on a gluten-free diet. Six weeks later, the mother called me. Not only had her daughter "aced" a math test, her behavior and learning were so greatly improved that she was being moved from a special education class to a regular class! The change in the girl was dramatic.

**Overcome developmental delay.** I was the "last stop" for a 4-year-old boy who was developmentally delayed and was diagnosed with a failure to thrive. He could not talk, but he could scream, which he did incessantly. Screaming was how he communicated with the world.

I put the boy on a gluten-free diet, accompanied by a dairy-free diet. Within 2 weeks, the parents called to report his progress. They cried tears of happiness as they told me that not only had his behavior improved, but he had also spoken his first words! And he was already gaining weight.

One "side effect" the parents noticed: The boy was jealous of anyone who approached his "special" food. He knew it was making him normal, and he didn't want it to go away. He no longer felt like he was crawling out of his skin.

That case happened 25 years ago. The "boy" remains gluten-free to this day and is a normal young man.

**Erased mask.** A 30-year-old patient suffering from early-stage lupus (see Chapter 5, Other Autoimmune Diseases) asked for help. One of her primary symptoms was a "wolf mask" (discoloration on the face).

After 1 month of being on a gluten-free diet, her skin cleared up, and she was in full clinical remission.

**Halted MS.** A woman with late-stage multiple sclerosis (MS) came to me for guidance. Although she had neurological damage and her left leg was impaired, she continued to exercise daily, determined to fight the disease that kept progressing, despite all her efforts.

When she went on a gluten-free diet, the neurological progression stopped. Her damaged left leg regained some of its feeling, and her right leg returned to normal function. Even more important, her vision was restored! The diet stopped the MS progression.

**Two-for-one treatment.** A young lady who was diagnosed with ulcerative colitis and who was tired of feeling bad wanted help with her diet. She thought that if she could only eliminate the foods that made her digestive system disruptive, she could live a normal life.

When she came in for consultation, her male cousin, who had Crohn's disease and had already had surgery to remove necrotic tissue in his colon, accompanied her. Both of these young people were in their twenties.

I consulted with the young lady, who was my patient. The cousin—who came in only for moral support—listened as I advised her to start a gluten-free and dairy-free diet immediately.

Four weeks later, she returned, again accompanied by her cousin. Her bloody diarrhea had completely resolved; she felt "normal" and appreciative.

Then came the surprise: Her cousin told me, "I listened to what you said, and I also went gluten-free. It's the first time in my life that I've had normal bowel movements. I wish I had met you 10 years ago!"

**Head-to-toe makeover.** Perhaps one of the most visibly dramatic improvements I've seen was a case of a young man who had been diagnosed with Darier's disease.

Darier's is a rare psoriasis-like genetic skin condition that covers the person with a scaly rash. This young man had the rash from head to toe. The condition was so extreme that he would not wear T-shirts or shorts. He kept as much skin covered as possible to avoid embarrassing stares.

I put him on a gluten-free and dairy-free diet. In less than 6 months, his skin cleared up completely. He even started going to the beach!

The response was so dramatic, and he was so grateful, that he kept in touch with me for 5 years to thank me. His skin lesions never came back.

I must again remind you that these were *early* cases, more than 20 years ago. At that time, there was no research that linked an intolerance to gluten to the conditions these individuals exhibited.

Today, that is changing. Much of the research is *still* focused on celiac disease. Yet, more researchers are recognizing that gluten is a problem long before it causes deterioration of the digestive system.

The unfortunate thing about research into gluten intolerance is that it has not been collected into one place. And because gluten intolerance manifests itself in so many different ways—including skin disorders, neurological disorders, digestive disorders, and disorders that have no apparent cause—the research gets published in too many places for the internists and family physicians who first see patients to know about it.

As a consequence, these doctors attempt to treat symptoms by applying pharmaceutical solutions to the problem. The wrong solution applied to a problem doesn't resolve anything! And their patients are left to cope.

This book is *not* about coping. I wrote this book to create an awareness that the problems you or your loved ones are experiencing may be due to something you ate—and can be resolved by eliminating that "something." It's as simple as that.

This introduction would not be complete without sharing a personal story about "creating an awareness."

As my coauthor was researching the chapter on digestive disorders, she decided to find out what research had been done associating gluten sensitivity with colitis, in particular, lymphocytic colitis. Her husband, JC, had been diagnosed with that particular "brand" of colitis and had been taking mesalamine for it for more than 2 years.

Unfortunately, the drug provided minimal (if any) relief. Some days, he had to take the maximum dosage; other days, he seemed to be able to reduce the number of pills he swallowed. But never did the drug completely alleviate his diarrhea. His gastroenterologist actually told him that the problem could be lifelong and that he would have to cope with it.

My coauthor found a study conducted in 2001[1] indicating that 15 percent of patients with lymphocytic colitis had celiac disease. The authors wrote, "There is a high frequency of celiac disease in patients with lymphocytic colitis. Given the importance of the early detection of celiac disease, it should be excluded in all patients with lymphocytic colitis, particularly if diarrhea does not respond to conventional treatment."

JC showed the study to his internist, who ordered a celiac panel blood test. It came back negative. That meant he did not have celiac disease. But the blood test did *not* rule out gluten sensitivity.

At my urging, he then took a stool-sample test, available only at one laboratory and (unfortunately) not well known among medical doctors, including his gastroenterologist. (See Chapter 10, Are You Gluten Sensitive?)

*The test came back positive.* He went on a gluten-free diet. Within a few days, he reduced the amount of mesalamine he had been taking. And within 2 weeks, he was symptom-free and medication-free!

But there's more to this story! Because her husband was on a gluten-free diet, my coauthor decided that she, too, would abstain from all gluten. She had vaguely wondered if she could be gluten sensitive, although her only "symptoms" were minor colon disturbances and frequent gas that she had not given much thought to.

Two weeks after starting the diet, she realized that she hadn't felt so good in years! Her symptoms were gone—another gluten-free victory.

The discoveries my coauthor made are ones that you can make, too. That is my goal in writing this book—to make you aware that good health may be restored to you just by eliminating a nonessential food from your diet.

I've written this book in four parts:

Part 1 deals with "something you ate"—gluten. You'll learn about its proliferation and the difference between an allergy and an intolerance.

Part 2 explores how gluten sensitivity is often mistaken for other disorders. For doubters (including medical doctors!), we've pulled together scientific proof that gluten is the cause of a myriad of conditions that perplex and plague people. Research aside, I know you will be amazed at the anecdotal evidence and testimonies of medical doctors who have had gluten-sensitive patients—and have successfully treated them by putting them on a gluten-free diet.

Also in the second part, in a chapter devoted to testing, you will read about how you can discover if you are gluten sensitive. (You'll also find out why blood tests don't tell the story about gluten sensitivity.)

If you discover that your condition may be caused by something you ate, what do you do? That's what Part 3 of this book is about. Its goal is to put you on the road to healthy, gluten-free eating.

You'll also discover what to do if eliminating gluten *still* doesn't make you feel better. (Yes, you have more options.)

Finally, Part 4 deals with cooking. When I recommend a gluten-free diet to my patients, their reaction invariably is, "What am I going to eat? Am I going to have to give up *everything*?" This part will show you that you don't have to give up taste or good food to go gluten-free. You'll find recipes for people who don't have much time or interest in cooking, as well as recipes for people who love to cook. And you'll also find a 14-day gluten-free diet.

Are you sick and tired of being sick and tired? Then what do you have to lose? You don't need wheat, barley, or rye to be healthy. You *can* live without them. And as I and my coauthor and her husband have quickly learned, "After a few days, you don't really miss them."

So, pull out your reading glasses, prop up your feet, and find out if gluten is the hidden cause of your problems.

To your good health!

# PART 1

# SOMETHING YOU ATE

It has been said, "Man cannot live by bread alone." But some men (and women, of course) cannot live by *eating* bread. To them, bread is *not* the staff of life. It is a slow-working poison.

As a way of introducing you to the dangers of grain and setting the stage to explore gluten sensitivity, I invite you to take a short quiz, which I hope will jump-start your curiosity:

Q.   *What is gluten? (a) glue (b) something used in making bread (c) a protein found in some grains*

A.   In a sense, all three answers are correct. Most people have heard of gluten in the context of baking bread. Gluten is the stuff that makes dough sticky. In that regard, it *is* a glue—and, in fact, it is sometimes used as a binding agent in the glue found on envelopes and stamps. But in terms of physiological composition, *gluten is a protein,* which is found in wheat, barley, and rye.

Q.   *Is wheat safe to eat? (a) yes (b) no*

A.   This is a "yes, but" answer. Whole wheat, eaten in moderation and used in heat-treated cooking or baking, is safe to eat, *but only if you are not gluten sensitive.* Wheat as a raw grain or even in its processed (flour) form is not safe to eat. That is because the grain contains enzyme blockers and lectin, chemicals that are toxic to animals, including human beings. Heat, however, destroys these toxins to a safe level for consumption.

Q.   *Is the wheat that is grown today the same as wheat that was cultivated 100 years ago? (a) yes (b) no*

A.   No! Bioengineers continually work to produce wheat that has more gluten and "better" gluten, in other words, gluten that is stickier. A search of the U.S. Patent Office delivers hundreds of patents for gluten. Wheat has been genetically altered so that the wheat that is planted and harvested today is considerably different from the wheat that even our grandparents harvested, milled, and used for baking.

Q.   *Which of these grains has gluten?(a) wheat (b) spelt (c) durum (d) semolina (e) rye (f) barley (g) oats*

A.   Spelt, durum, and semolina are all types of wheat, and wheat contains gluten. Rye and barley are also gluten-containing grains. Oats are also a grain, but they do not have gluten.

*However*—oats often become cross-contaminated when they are planted in fields that have grown wheat or when they are processed in plants that refine wheat. So although oats themselves do not contain gluten, they may not be safe for gluten-sensitive individuals to consume, unless certified to be gluten-free.

Q.  *If you are gluten sensitive, should you (a) become desensitized to gluten just as you might with bee venom (b) take a special "gluten pill" before eating bread (c) eliminate all gluten from your diet forever?*

A.  Since gluten sensitivity is not an allergy—it is an intolerance—it is not possible to outgrow it or to become desensitized to it. Most gluten-sensitive people probably wish they could take a pill so that they could eat bread or cake, but no pharmaceutical remedy is available. *The only solution to gluten sensitivity is to eliminate all gluten from your diet.*

In Part 1 of this book, you'll discover:

Chapter 1: Grain Danger. This chapter points out the menace of grains to nutrition today.

Chapter 2: Allergy or Intolerance? In this chapter, you'll see why gluten sensitivity is not considered an allergy and will understand why lifelong abstinence from gluten is physiologically important for gluten-sensitive individuals.

# CHAPTER 1

## GRAIN DANGER

We Americans love food. We love food so much that we make sure we are never far from it.

In every strip shopping center, you'll find at least one fast-food restaurant. In most grocery stores, there is a deli counter. Every 15 minutes on television, commercials for McDonald's, Burger King, Pizza Hut, and Kentucky Fried Chicken bombard viewers. Saturday morning cartoons tempt children with sweet treats and breakfast cereals.

And if viewers fail to satiate their visual appetites with the commercials, they can turn on TV's Food Channel to drool over all types of concoctions, from pastas to French pastries.

Years ago, our grandparents ate a basic diet of meat, poultry, and fish; potatoes and other root vegetables; and a variety of garden-fresh vegetables. Their meat was free from hormone enhancements. The fish came directly from the ocean or from crystal-clear lakes and rivers, which did not experience fertilizer runoff. And their vegetables were exposed to few (if any) pesticides and herbicides.

They ate bread, cake, and pie, of course. But they baked these goods in their own kitchens, using wheat that had not been genetically altered.

What a difference a few decades have made! Today, we eat out more often than we cook in. And we eat fast food more than well-balanced meals.

Food-manufacturing companies have made sure that we can open a box or a can, or pop a frozen entrée into the microwave oven and enjoy, within minutes and without any cooking skill, whatever type of delicacy turns our fancy.

Food nourishes. It comforts. When it tastes good, it makes us feel good.

*But the same food that you enjoy putting into your mouth may be making you sick!*

The culprit? *Gluten.*

If you have heard the word *gluten,* it was most likely in context with baking, as in "kneading dough to develop the gluten." Gluten—a protein—is the stuff that makes dough sticky.

Unfortunately, this chewy, gluey protein that makes bread and bagels taste so good is poison to a large segment of the population who cannot tolerate it. *These people are gluten sensitive.* They suffer from a systemic autoimmune disorder. When they eat *anything* with gluten in it—and that is virtually all processed and prepared foods!—their immune system reacts.

For more than 50 years, doctors have pointed to gluten as the cause of celiac disease (CD)—an autoimmune disorder centered in the gastrointestinal system.

Worldwide, celiac disease has been studied extensively, almost since it was discovered and named. As testing became more sophisticated and as the definition of celiac disease was expanded to include more than individuals who had overt symptoms, researchers have shown that celiac disease afflicts approximately 1 percent of the world's population, or anywhere from 1 in 100 to 1 in 200 worldwide,[1] with much higher rates in some countries.[2]

In the general populations of Western Europe, the prevalence ranges from 0.5 to 1.26 percent (1 in 200 to 1 in 79).[3]

For example: A report published in 2001 said that the prevalence of CD (identified through screening methods) in the United Kingdom was 1 in 112 people; in Finland, it was 1 in 130; in Italy, 1 in 184; and in the Sahara, an astonishing 1 in 70.[4]

In this country, medical researchers and practitioners had believed this disease was confined to a relatively small number of people, primarily children. Within the past several years, those beliefs have been put down.

Researchers have discovered that celiac disease afflicts just under 1 percent of the population in the United States. A large-scale study of 13,145 individuals[5] showed that 1 out of 133 people in the general population has CD.

The odds are even worse that you have this disease if you have a first-degree relative with CD (1 out of 22), if you have a second-degree relative with it (1 out of 39), or if you have digestive-disorder symptoms (1 out of 56). If you are one of these unfortunate individuals and continue to eat gluten, you can waste away from malnutrition and may suffer premature death.

But the gluten problem touches *far more* of the U.S. population than the 1 out of 133 who have celiac disease. Some researchers now speculate that *as many as 29 percent*[6]—almost 3 out of 10 people—are gluten sensitive! And approximately 81 percent[7] of Americans have a genetic disposition toward gluten sensitivity. That's a tremendous number of people in the United States who are gluten sensitive or have the propensity to become gluten sensitive.

If you are gluten sensitive, you can have a low level of intolerance and function for years—perhaps your entire life—without any identifiable symptoms or with symptoms so mild that you pay no attention to them. Feeling less than 100 percent is so normal that you don't know you can feel better.

But many people (most of the 2.9 out of 10 who are gluten sensitive) suffer from a variety of physical problems that you and your doctors have *not* linked to the "killer cause," gluten—problems such as diabetes, multiple sclerosis, lupus, arthritis, osteoporosis, chronic fatigue syndrome, and some forms of dermatitis and psoriasis, to name a few. (Part 2 of this book details the variety of problems that gluten can cause.)

Gluten sensitivity is a *huge* problem contributing to the chronic diseases that plague American society today and cost us trillions of dollars. We are only now discovering its extent.

But, like any other problem, if we understand its origin and its cause, we can fix it. All problems, after all, have a solution. Gluten sensitivity is no different.

## AN EVOLUTIONARY PROBLEM

The problem with gluten can be traced back to the agricultural revolution and the cultivation of grains more than 10,000 years ago. Until that time, Paleolithic man subsisted off the land: He was a hunter-gatherer—getting his needed protein, fat, and carbohydrate requirements by hunting game and fish and gathering fruits, nuts, and vegetables. Nature provided him with all of his needed nutrients; all he had to do was find them.

Although the life span of early *Homo sapiens* was short (his life expectancy was only about 20 years), his health was relatively good, especially when food was plentiful. When food was scarce, early man did suffer from nutritional deficiencies, which contributed to early demise, but death was caused largely by infection, parasitic infestation, and accident.

Enter the age of agriculture. When Neolithic man, a successor to Paleolithic man, discovered how to cultivate and mill grain and how to use fire to cook his food—which destroyed toxins in otherwise inedible foodstuffs—his life changed. No longer dependent on the abundance of nature, he could now control much of his food source. This resulted in allowing more people to exist on a smaller amount of land—a *good* consequence of agricultural technology.

A *bad* consequence was that with the planting, harvesting, and milling of grain—particularly wheat, but also barley and rye—man introduced a new plant protein into his digestive system. *That protein was gluten.*

Many nutritional scientists trace the cause of today's chronic health problems to the advent of the agricultural revolution. Two researchers, James H. O'Keefe Jr., MD, and Loren Cordain, PhD, observed, "Humans evolved during the Paleolithic period, from approximately 2.6 million years ago to 10,000 years ago. Although the human genome has remained largely unchanged…our diet and lifestyle have become progressively more divergent from those of our ancient ancestors. These maladaptive changes began approximately 10,000 years ago with the advent of the agricultural revolution and have been accelerating in recent decades. Socially, we are a people of the 21st century, but genetically, we remain citizens of the Paleolithic era."[8]

Our genetic similarity to Paleolithic man—and our inability to tolerate gluten—began to create a serious problem when we left our agricultural society behind and entered into another significant stage of human development: the Industrial Revolution.

Technology stimulated a change in grain consumption in the United States with two significant inventions:

**The mechanical reaper.** Through Cyrus McCormick's invention of the mechanical reaper in 1831, wheat could be harvested more efficiently than by hand—eight acres a day by the reaper, only two by hand. That resulted in the greater abundance of grain to feed the growing populations of the Western world.

**The roller mill.** Until the Industrial Revolution, milling had been done through stone grinding in a process not dissimilar to that used by Neolithic man (although on a larger scale): The heads of grain were crushed between two big stones to make flour. The flour that resulted was whole-grain flour that included all parts of the wheat kernel.

In 1873, the milling process changed. At that year's World's Fair, the world was introduced to the roller miller,[9] which used steel rollers to mill grain and refined flour better and more cheaply. With the adoption of this technology throughout the United States, the majority of the U.S. population suddenly could afford to buy refined flour. And they quickly acquired a taste for white bread.

Because of the availability of refined flour, as well as the invention of new types of mechanizations, people no longer had to live off the land; the "land" came to them through processed meats, vegetables, and grains. Their hunting and gathering consisted of finding a market and putting cans into a grocery bag.

In the United States, as the 20th century began and the emigration of Americans from the land to the cities intensified, the demand for more-processed foods continued to increase, initially for canned goods, later—once households had electric refrigeration—for frozen goods. In the 1950s, TV dinners became popular, along with frozen bakery treats.

Today, of course, every type of food you desire is available in a convenience form, ready to be popped into a microwave or an oven.

This demand for convenience caused grain consumption to escalate. Records from the Economic Research Service (ERS) of the U.S. Department of Agriculture show that in 1967 (the earliest complete records available), per capita annual consumption of *gluten-containing grains* (wheat, barley, and rye) was 115 pounds. In 2003, this figure had grown to 139 pounds. That's an increase of 24 pounds of gluten-containing grain per person per year in the United States—a *lot* of gluten.[10]

If you think that you don't eat that much grain (and gluten), think again: Much of the gluten that you consume is hidden. You don't know you are eating it! For example:

- Food manufacturers *add* "vital gluten" (gluten that is specifically processed from high-gluten–containing wheat) to wheat flour to give it more binding power.

- Gluten is used in the manufacturing of virtually all boxed, packaged, and canned processed foods to create textures that are more palatable to our taste buds, or is used as binders, thickeners, and coatings. It is even used as glue on envelopes and stamps!

- Even if you were consuming the same amount of grain today as you did last year or 10 years ago, you would be ingesting more gluten. That is because bioengineers continually work to "improve" gluten and make it a larger and more potent part of edible grain. It is estimated that today's wheat contains nearly 90 percent more gluten than wheat did from a century ago!

To get an idea of how much hidden gluten you consume, take a walk down the aisles in your grocery store. Stop to read the labels. You'll find wheat, barley, or rye in products such as:

- Barbecue sauce
- Breaded fish, chicken, and shrimp
- Bread—even "potato bread" or "rice bread"
- Canned and dried soups
- Cereal
- Cookies and cakes
- Couscous
- Crackers
- Flavored potato chips
- Frozen dinners
- Pasta
- Pies
- Rice mixes
- Sauces and gravies
- Some ice creams
- Some salad dressings
- Soy sauce
- Teriyaki sauce
- And many, many more items

## INCREASED JEOPARDY

Have you heard the expression, "Just because you *can,* doesn't mean you *should*"? The expression may well apply to the consumption of grain, especially wheat, barley, and rye.

The danger that grains present to us is probably best evidenced by looking at the effect that modern diet has had on modern-day hunter-gatherers, whose diet is significantly different from ours.

All people require foods that provide energy. According to ERS,[11] the energy sources of Americans in 2000 came from:

- Fats and oils (22 percent)
- Grains (24 percent—that's one-quarter of our diet!)
- Meat, poultry, and fish (14 percent)
- Processed foods (21 percent)
- Sugars and sweeteners (19 percent)

Our diet is considerably different from hunter-gatherers (yes, some tribes still exist today), who consume:[12]

- Fruits, vegetables, nuts, and honey (65 percent)
- Lean game, wild fowl, eggs, fish, and shellfish (35 percent)

Noticeably absent from the hunter-gatherer diet are three types of foods:

- Dairy (Typically, they use only mother's milk, fermented dairy products, or dairy straight from their own livestock—more often goats than cows.)
- Processed foods (They eat off the land.)
- Refined grains (If they eat grains, they eat them as whole grains and in moderation.)

A number of nutritional anthropologists have studied the danger of grains (and remember—grains are the source of gluten!) on society.

### A Dentist's Observations

In the 1930s, Dr. Weston A. Price,[13] a dentist with a passion for nutrition, roamed the globe to study primitive hunter-gatherer cultures. Dr. Price suspected that poor nutrition played a part in physical degeneration, manifested in dental caries and deformed dental arches. To test his hypothesis, he decided to travel the world and observe isolated primitive peoples—those who were largely (although not exclusively) hunter-gatherers.

His travels took him to sequestered villages in Switzerland and Gaelic communities in the Outer Hebrides; Eskimos and Native Americans; Melanesian and Polynesian South Sea islanders; African tribes; Australian Aborigines; New Zealand Maori; and Indians of South America.

Dr. Price observed that people who ate native diets had beautiful, straight teeth; no caries; strong bodies; and a high resistance to disease. One of the key characteristics Dr. Price noted about traditional diets: *These diets did not include refined or denatured foods, such as refined sugar, white flour, and canned foods.*

He contrasted these healthy native people with those who no longer lived in complete isolation but had been introduced to modern diets that included sugar, white flour, pasteurized milk, and convenience foods filled with extenders and additives.

Dr. Price observed that "modern-day" natives experienced more tooth decay and exhibited deformed and narrow dental arches, tooth crowding, and pinched features. He also noted an increase in birth defects and a susceptibility to illness. Diseases that had previously left these societies untouched now took their toll.[14]

Dr. Price recorded the physical changes in the new generations and compared them with the faces of healthy ancestors. He published his photographs in his book, *Nutrition and Physical Degeneration.*

## Diet and Diabetes

A paper published in 2001 in the *Asia Pacific Journal of Clinical Nutrition* reported on the dietary trends of indigenous Fijians. The author stated that the diet of the Fijians changed drastically over 50 years and adversely affected the population:[15] "The total energy derived from cereals and sugar increased dramatically with a reduction in consumption of traditional foods. The prevalence of diabetes among the urban indigenous population in 1965 was very low compared to the 1980 figure, while the National Nutrition Survey of the same ethnic group showed a *433 percent increase* in urban diabetes from 1965 to 1993."

Gluten sensitivity can affect the functioning of the pancreas—the organ that regulates sugar metabolism. When this happens, the symptoms resemble diabetes.

## Grain Damage

In their 2004 paper, medical and nutritionist researchers O'Keefe and Cordain state that historical evidence indicates that hunter-gatherers were generally fit and free from chronic diseases.[16] That condition, however, changed when these primitive peoples transitioned to an agrarian society. Among the effects grain had on them were:

- Diminished stature
- Greater incidence of osteoporosis, rickets, and other mineral- and vitamin-deficiency diseases
- Higher childhood mortality
- More obesity, diabetes, and other diseases of civilizations
- Shorter life spans

## Native American Travesty

North America had its share of hunter-gatherers—the Native American tribes. When the federal government took the land away from these tribes and placed them on reservations—most of which did not have the resources for hunting nor for agriculture—their diet changed.

Regardless of their origination, traditional Native American diets consisted of wild game, berries, roots, teas, and indigenous vegetables. When Native Americans cultivated grain, it was corn—*a non-gluten-containing grain*. Wheat was not a traditional part of their food intake. (As a side note: Although wheat is the third-largest grain crop in the United States today, it is not native to this country. It was first cultivated in the United States as a cash crop around the mid-1830s.)

When the government placed Native Americans on reservations, bureaucrats provided "food" for them—processed food, canned fruits and vegetables, refined flour, and refined sugars.

The diet of Native Americans today remains high in fat and refined starches and sugars.[17] Popular among them is white bread, white flour, and white rice. The change in diet among Native Americans has resulted in some of the highest rates of diabetes and chronic diseases of any groups in the United States.[18]

In fact, the American Diabetes Association reports that 14.5 percent of Native Americans and Alaska natives who receive care from the Indian Health Services have diabetes.[19] The Pima tribe in Arizona has the highest rate of diabetes in the world. About 50 percent of adults between the ages of 30 and 64 suffer from this chronic disease.[20]

## BACK TO GLUTEN

All around the world—from Fiji to North America—a change in traditional diet to the diet "enjoyed" by us today has resulted in chronic health problems that plague 133 million people in the United States, almost half of the population. That number is expected to increase 37 percent by 2030.[21] These chronic problems annually cost the American people trillions of dollars.

It would be ludicrous to assert that *all* of these chronic problems are due to gluten. But it would also be naïve to think that grain (in particular, wheat, which is the number one staple in the Western world) is an "innocent bystander."

Just because we *can* eat more grain—and gluten—doesn't mean we *should*. Too much of a good thing is bad. Perhaps that is what has happened with our love affair with grain (and gluten). Perhaps we just got carried away with it.

So, now we have a situation: Half of the population has a chronic disease. And almost 30 percent of the population has gluten sensitivity. A coincidence? I don't think so.

So, the question remains, "Was it something you ate?"

It just might be.

## UNDERSTANDING GLUTEN SENSITIVITY

Gluten causes problems. That's an understatement. Comprehending *why* gluten causes so many health problems for those who are sensitive to it and how you can ascertain if you are gluten sensitive requires having a basic understanding of what happens in your digestive system.

Digestion, of course, begins when you put food into your mouth. Chewed food passes from the mouth down the esophagus (a tube that connects the throat to the stomach) to the stomach, where it is churned and mixed with some gastric juices to create a very sloppy type of soup.

This soup then passes into the small intestine, where more juices from the pancreas and the gallbladder help break down the food's various components (proteins, carbohydrates, and fats) into their respective amino acids, monosaccharides, and fatty acids. Once the food is broken down into these soluble components, it is absorbed by fingerlike projections called villi in the small intestine. These thousands of villi are composed of capillaries and lymphatic tissue, which pass the nutrients to the bloodstream.

The parts of the food that cannot be broken down into amino acids, monosaccharides, and fatty acids pass on to the large intestine and are eliminated in a matter of hours.

That's what happens when we eat nutritious food. But unfortunately, not everything we take in as food is healthy for us. We sometimes ingest antigens—foreign substances, such as toxins or bacteria, or (for some people) *actual foodstuffs such as gluten*. In childhood, especially, we are exposed to a plethora of food antigens.

When we take in food antigens, the body goes to work to fight them off. The regulatory T-cells (white cells in the blood) in our immune system easily recognize these antigens and destroy them so that they will not cause us any harm.

Sometimes, however, the balance in our immune system is disrupted by infections, medications, stress, and other factors. This disruption causes our T-cells to stop regulating properly.

When this occurs, the antigens from a food we have eaten all our lives can suddenly produce a significant amount of inflammation, which can cause some atrophy (deterioration) of our intestinal villi, thus allowing the food antigens to enter our bloodstream.

The antigens that enter the bloodstream then cause the body to produce antibodies, which attempt to fight the antigens.

Let's bring this home to the problem of gluten sensitivity.

If you are gluten sensitive, your digestive system does not have the ability to break gluten down into soluble proteins (amino acids). Consequently, whenever you eat wheat, barley, or rye in *any* form and *any* amount (not necessarily as a big slice of bread or cake!), your body reacts to the gluten because it interprets the gluten to be an antigen. The gluten fails to be broken down and passes into the bloodstream.

When the gluten gets into your bloodstream in this "raw" form, your body forms antibodies to combat it. These antibodies, which reside in the intestine as long as the villi are functioning properly, may be:

- Anti-endomysial antibodies
- Antigliadin IgA antibodies
- Anti-tissue transglutaminase antibodies

As your body valiantly but unsuccessfully tries to break down the gluten into its component amino acids, and the antibodies fight the invader gluten, the lining of the intestine becomes inflamed. If the inflammation in your intestine progresses to the point of the villi becoming flattened, the antibodies that formed to fight the gluten also pass into the bloodstream.

Gluten sensitivity is not necessarily something you are born with. You may acquire it at any point during your life. Unfortunately, even though the prevalence of celiac disease (the worst case of gluten sensitivity) is higher than anyone ever envisioned, most physicians do not screen their patients for CD. Many doctors still erroneously believe that CD is rare and a disease of childhood, despite the scientific evidence to the contrary.

You may be asking yourself, "How can I tell if I am gluten sensitive?" You have two options:

- You can eliminate gluten from your diet. Grains are not essential foods! You can give them up without any bad effects on your overall health. If you feel better and any suspect symptoms go away, you are probably gluten sensitive.

- You can be tested for gluten sensitivity—but you must ask for the *right* test. The right test can tell you definitively if you are gluten sensitive. (How to test for celiac disease and gluten sensitivity is covered in detail in Chapter 10, Are You Gluten Sensitive?)

Before we get to that important topic, however, we need to look at who really needs to find out if they're gluten sensitive and why. You'll be amazed.

# CHAPTER 2

## ALLERGY OR INTOLERANCE?

Nutritionists are dietary sleuths. We examine health problems in the context of food, and we make recommendations for dietary changes and supplementation to achieve optimal nutrition and health.

Throughout the years, a number of my patients have been individuals whose health problems and symptoms have failed to respond to traditional medical intervention. When I suggest to these patients that they may be gluten sensitive, they typically react, "Does this mean I have an allergy?"

The answer is "No!"

Gluten sensitivity is *not* an allergy. It is a food intolerance. Allergies and intolerances are both reactions by your immune system, but those reactions are completely different. It's important for you to understand the difference between an allergy and an intolerance, because understanding is critical to accepting and subsequently dealing with it.

## WHAT IS AN ALLERGY?

A food allergy is an exaggerated response by your body's immune system to a food that you have consumed. Approximately 2 percent of adults in the United States (and about 5 percent of children, who often outgrow some food allergies)[1] suffer from food allergies.

Although *any* individual may be allergic to *any* food—even the "safest" of foods—90 percent of food allergies result from eating foods belonging to eight categories: milk, eggs, fish, crustacean shellfish, tree nuts, peanuts, wheat, and soybeans.

Normally, when your body senses a foreign invader, such as a dangerous bacteria, a virus, or even an offending food, it calls upon its immune system—specialized white blood cells, chemicals, and pro-teins and enzymes—to defend against the invader. Specialized white blood cells produce antibodies, which attach to a specific antigen (invader), to make it easier for other specialized white blood cells to destroy it.

But sometimes, the "normal" thing doesn't happen, especially if you come from a family with a propensity toward allergies. Instead, you experience an immediate-onset allergy.

When you are exposed to a food to which you are allergic, several things happen:

- Your body produces a food-specific antibody called immunoglobu-lin E (IgE), which is a type of protein.

- One side of the IgE antibody recognizes the allergic food and tightly binds to it in an effort to destroy it.

- The other side of the IgE antibody attaches to a mast cell, which is an immune cell loaded with histamine and found in all body tissues. (Most mast cells are found in your nose, throat, lungs, skin, and gastrointestinal tract.)

- The next time you eat the allergic food, the IgE antibodies immedi-ately attach themselves to the food, and this causes histamine and other allergy-related chemicals to be released from the mast cell.

The allergic reaction occurs within minutes or up to an hour or so after eating the offending food. Depending upon the severity and the particular food, you may experience tingling or itching in your mouth; stomach cramping, diarrhea, or vomiting; or a skin rash or hives.

And in severe cases, as the histamines travel through your blood-stream, your blood pressure may drop. When they reach the lungs, they can cause an asthmatic attack.

It is the histamine released from mast cells that causes the adverse reaction (hives, diarrhea, gastric symptoms, etc.). To stop the reaction, it is necessary to counteract the histamine. A dose of over-the-counter antihistamine medication is usually sufficient to return to normal.

In severe cases, more-drastic measures must be taken.

For example, people who are allergic to peanuts are at high risk for anaphylaxis, a severe type of life-threatening allergic reaction. They must carry a syringe of adrenalin with them at all times, in case they are unknowingly exposed to some form of peanuts. If they don't inject themselves with the adrenalin immediately, their reaction is so severe that their breathing can become completely obstructed and they can die.

Other folks may find that when they eat seafood, their tongue or throat swells, or they get a rash or one or more of the other symptoms rather quickly after eating the offending food. Quick reaction with an antihistamine is necessary to avoid a trip to the hospital or a call to paramedics.

Children often outgrow minor allergies, but adults who have food allergies own them for life. The only way to avoid an allergic reaction is to avoid the offending food.

## FOOD INTOLERANCE

Although many people think they have a food allergy, they actually have food immune reactivity (FIR)—food intolerance, which is a delayed reaction from eating some foods or ingredients. Common types of FIR occur from eating gluten in wheat, barley, and rye; dairy products; nightshades (tomato, potato, eggplant, tobacco, and peppers); and soy products.

FIR is much more complicated than an allergic reaction:

- Symptoms are sometimes similar to those resulting from an allergic reaction, but the cause is not easily identified. Reactions to ingesting an offending food are delayed—by hours or even days, and symptoms generally become apparent over time.

- FIR does *not* involve IgE reactions; no histamines are released. Consequently, antihistamines have no effect. There are no pills, shots, or medications you can take to alleviate the symptoms.

- An allergic reaction can evoke a violent effect (as in the case of anaphylaxis), but it incurs no long-term damage to organs. FIR, on the other hand, is insidious, and its long-term effects on organs throughout the body can be devastating, even leading to premature death.

Let's look at these differences between immediate-onset reaction and gluten-derived FIR more closely.

## Symptoms

The most common symptoms of an allergic reaction, as we have already described, are an immediate reaction to food, which shows up as tingling or itching in your mouth, swelling, or difficulty in breathing; stomach cramping, diarrhea, or vomiting; or a skin rash or hives.

If you are gluten sensitive (cannot tolerate the protein gluten in wheat, barley, or rye), you may also experience any of those symptoms—as well as a number of others that masquerade as symptoms of other physical conditions. (Part 2 elaborates on the symptoms of gluten sensitivity.)

Because of the immediacy of an allergic reaction, it is relatively easy to see cause and effect between an offending food and the reaction to it. But in FIR, especially with gluten sensitivity, the reaction will not be seen for some time. It may take many exposures over a long period of time before any symptoms appear. That makes FIR difficult to diagnose but even more important to identify, because of long-term consequences.

## Different Antibody Production

In an allergic reaction, the body forms IgE antibodies, which cause histamine to be released. That histamine then causes the specific allergic reaction, such as hives or swelling. Taking an antihistamine makes the symptoms go away.

In FIR, specifically gluten-sensitivity FIR, the body may also produce antibodies—but the antibodies are of a different type: antigliadin IgA antibody (AGA), anti-tissue transglutaminase antibody (ATTA), and anti-endomysial antibody (EMA).

These antibodies do *not* trigger histamines. Rather, they cause a chronic inflammation and eventually can lead to the complete flattening of intestinal villi—the fingerlike projections in the intestine that absorb nutrients. When that happens, gluten sensitivity becomes all-out celiac disease.

## Long-Term Effects

Aside from anaphylaxis, which is violent and must be counteracted quickly to avoid death, the effects of an allergic reaction are not long-term. Once you recover from the allergic reaction, your body resumes normal functioning. As long as you stay away from the offending food, you will not suffer any other effects.

Not so with food immune reactivity. The long-term effects can play havoc on your health, especially in the case of gluten sensitivity. Here are some examples:

**Permanent organ damage.** As we already stated, undiagnosed gluten sensitivity can result in celiac disease. But it can also cause other organ damage, such as damage to the pancreas or to the neurological system. Left unchecked, some of the effects of gluten intolerance can be irreparable.

**Severe tissue damage.** When gluten causes FIR, an extreme inflammatory response results. Ingestion of gluten sparks T-cell mediated inflammation and an abnormal increase in the production of nitric oxide, which can result in severe tissue damage if not controlled.

**Hyperactivated immune system.** If you have gluten-caused FIR, any gluten you eat triggers reactions within the body. For example: Gluten stimulates an overproduction of pro-inflammatory cytokines (such as interferon, which regulates immune responses). The result is inflammation.

Gluten may also cause the production of antibodies that affect the balance of inhibitory and excitatory neurotransmitters in the central nervous system, resulting in symptoms of ataxia and neuropathy. (See Chapter 4, Neurological Disorders, for more information on these conditions.)

## ONE SOLUTION FOR BOTH PROBLEMS

Although it is true that you can take an antihistamine to counteract the effects of a food allergy, you can't "cure" the allergy. The only cure is to abstain from eating the offending food.

The same holds true for FIR. In gluten sensitivity, no medications alleviate symptoms. The only treatment is to eliminate *all* gluten (wheat, barley, and rye) from your diet—for life.

The intolerance your body has for gluten remains with you forever. This intolerance is insidious. Don't be fooled into thinking you are cured if you go off gluten for a time and your symptoms go away. The intolerance is just waiting for you to relapse into a gluten-containing diet again! And if that happens, the symptoms and inflammation—resulting in potential bodily damage—will return.

# PART 2

# GLUTEN SENSITIVITY'S MASQUERADE

Gluten sensitivity is a chameleon-like disease. Instead of confining itself to one area of the body—such as the gut, where it was first described by the ancient Greek doctor Arataeos in AD 100[1]—and exhibiting one set of defining characteristics that can be easily diagnosed, it can develop in many different, unsuspected ways.

The condition's ability to hide behind a variety of symptoms makes it difficult—but not impossible—to diagnose correctly. Obviously, without the correct diagnosis, it is impossible for a physician to prescribe the right remedy, which in the case of gluten sensitivity is *one* thing: *a gluten-free diet*. And prescribing the *wrong* remedy (harsh pharmaceuticals) can often cause even more complicating problems than the original disease!

Misdiagnosis, because of gluten sensitivity's ability to masquerade as—and, in some cases, piggyback onto—the symptoms of other diseases and disorders, can have devastating effects. Not only are people who are misdiagnosed relegated to "living with" a disease (when they may be able to be free of it), but living with this condition can lead to severe consequences—such as the irreversible crippling of rheumatoid arthritis, bone loss and breakage, infection, or even death.

In this part, we're going to take a look at a number of different diseases and conditions to see gluten sensitivity's masquerade:

CHAPTER 3: GLUTEN AND SKIN DISEASES. These include dermatitis herpetiformis, psoriasis, eczema, acne, and hives.

CHAPTER 4: NEUROLOGICAL DISORDERS. These include ataxia (loss of muscle coordination), severe headaches, and behavioral problems.

CHAPTER 5: OTHER AUTOIMMUNE DISEASES. These include lupus, multiple sclerosis, diabetes, scleroderma, thyroid disease, osteoporosis, rheumatoid arthritis, and ankylosing spondylitis.

CHAPTER 6: DIGESTIVE DISORDERS. These include the all-encompassing irritable bowel syndrome (IBS), Crohn's disease, ulcerative colitis, proctitis, gastroesophageal reflux, ulcers, and giardiasis, in addition to classic celiac disease.

CHAPTER 7: UNDIAGNOSED DISEASES AND CONDITIONS. These include such catch-all conditions as chronic fatigue syndrome, fibromyalgia, weight loss that cannot be accounted for, anemia, chronic infection, and asthma.

CHAPTER 8: A WORD ABOUT FIDO. As you'll learn, gluten sensitivity affects pets as well as people.

CHAPTER 9: FROM THE FILES OF HEALTH PROFESSIONALS. MDs share their success stories treating gluten-sensitive patients who come to them with a variety of symptoms.

CHAPTER 10: ARE YOU GLUTEN SENSITIVE? We look at the reasons why blood tests cannot tell the story about gluten sensitivity, and we identify two new tests that are highly sensitive for pinpointing this condition.

# CHAPTER 3

## GLUTEN AND SKIN DISEASES

What is worse than an itch? Well, a lot of things. But to someone who has a rash that won't go away, an itch is unbearable, especially if it spreads and refuses to respond to "normal" lotions, ointments, or even steroids.

In this chapter, we'll examine gluten sensitivity and how it expresses itself in skin disorders, often masquerading as other more-common autoimmune dermal problems.

## DERMATITIS HERPETIFORMIS

One of the itches that won't go away (without proper treatment) is the now-recognized and well-accepted form of gluten sensitivity, dermatitis herpetiformis (DH). DH was first described as a distinct *clinical* entity in 1884 by an American dermatologist, Louis Duhring.[1] But it wasn't until 1967 that it was actually linked to gluten sensitivity.

Typically, DH is characterized by small groups of itchy blisters, often on red plaques, located on the back of the elbows and forearms, on the buttocks, and in the front of the knees. But, the rash can occur in other places on the body, including the face, scalp, and trunk. Anyone can get this skin disorder, but its initial outbreak seems to occur more often in younger people.

DH occurs as an immune-system reaction to gluten. Instead of digesting this protein, the body fights it with an antibody (called IgA) that is produced in the lining of the intestines. When IgA combines with ingested gluten, the combined antibody/gluten substance circulates in the bloodstream and eventually clogs up the small blood vessels in the skin. The clog attracts white blood cells brought in by the body to fight the invasion. The white blood cells, in turn, release powerful chemicals that create the rash.[2]

The interesting thing about DH is that although it is caused by gluten sensitivity, affected individuals may not have *classic* signs of gluten intolerance such as distress to the gastrointestinal system. In other words, their gut may *not* be affected. That's why doctors for years did not think to associate the mysterious skin rash, which failed to respond to "normal" protocols, with gluten sensitivity.

If you have DH, you know how bad it is. One sufferer described that it was "…like rolling in stinging nettles naked with a severe sunburn, then wrapping yourself in a wool blanket filled with ants and fleas…"[3]

Imagine suffering from this type of rash and having it misdiagnosed for years! That's what has happened to countless DH sufferers. Here are a few cases of misdiagnoses:[4]

**A 5-year+ problem.** During the year he was an exchange student in Germany, Eric ate a lot of bread and pastry. Shortly after he returned to the United States to finish high school, he developed a small purple blister on his right buttock. Within a year, the rash grew to include his other buttock and each of his knees and elbows.

The diagnosis his doctor made: a strange case of poison ivy, which he treated with prednisone, a corticosteroid that can have serious side effects, such as upset stomach, stomach irritation, vomiting, headache, dizziness, insomnia, restlessness, depression, anxiety, acne, increased hair growth, easy bruising, swollen face and ankles, vision problems, and muscle weakness.[5]

After another year of unrelenting itching and pain and the spreading of the rash, which did not respond to the cream, Eric went to another doctor, who said he had a rare form of pustular psoriasis. The remedy: another type of topical corticosteroid cream.

He used the cream for 5 years, yet the rash continued to spread, and he developed a secondary staph infection. Eric finally found a doctor who was able to diagnose the problem correctly—dermatitis herpetiformis. A gluten-free diet cleared up the condition.

**Not a mite problem.** According to the first doctor Bill consulted, the rash that began to plague him was shingles. Shingles (herpes zoster) is characterized by an outbreak of a rash or blisters on the skin caused by a virus—the same virus that causes chickenpox, the varicella-zoster virus. Anyone who has had chickenpox is at risk for getting shingles, which is described as being intense and unrelenting. The symptoms of shingles can be relieved, at least temporarily, by taking antiviral drugs, but the disease must run its course, usually 3 to 5 weeks.[6] The virus continues to be harbored in the body even after the condition has cleared up.

Bill didn't have shingles, so the treatment the doctor prescribed did him no good, and the rash persisted. He then went to a dermatologist, who told him he had *scabies*!

Scabies is caused by a tiny mite that burrows under the skin and causes severe itching. The effective cure for scabies is a topical insecticide cream, which the doctor prescribed. Of course, the lotion didn't work.

Bill consulted several different doctors over the course of months. More than one gave him the same scabies diagnosis. Frustrated, he finally returned to his original dermatologist, who this time did a biopsy and discovered that Bill didn't have scabies after all! He had dermatitis herpetiformis. He went on a gluten-free diet, and his skin condition went away.

**Cure worse than the problem.** David began to develop tiny water blisters, which burst and left scabs. Because he had been working long hours in a stressful job, his family doctor initially diagnosed stress-related psoriasis. The condition did not clear up.

For *18 years,* David endured the problem, with only periodic, short-term relief. One doctor prescribed a corticosteroid cream. This, however, was a case of the cure possibly being worse than the problem.

As already mentioned, corticosteroid cream can have harsh side effects if used long term on large areas of the skin, especially on raw skin and in skin folds. The particular cream David used, Fucibet, can cause the adrenal glands to decrease the production of natural hormones and also cause the skin to thin.[7] After using the cream daily for 2 years, he began to experience side effects, including sore eyes and dry skin on his cheek bones.

David finally found a new doctor who correctly diagnosed the problem as DH caused by gluten sensitivity. A gluten-free diet cured his 18-year condition.

DH *can* be cured. For immediate relief, doctors may prescribe drugs—Dapsone, sulphapyridine, or sulphamethoxypyridazine. All of these drugs are actually antibiotics that were developed in the 1930s and 1940s. It is not understood exactly *how* they work on DH, but it is known that they do not work as antibiotics; rather, they act as agents to address the skin condition. Although the drugs control the rash within days, DH returns quickly when the drugs are discontinued.

In other words, these drugs are used to produce immediate relief from the itching but do not cure the condition.[8]

The cure for DH, like any other gluten sensitivity, is a gluten-free diet. When the individuals mentioned in the previous cases went on a gluten-free diet, their DH disappeared!

## PSORIASIS

In the mini–case studies we just cited, DH was misdiagnosed as psoriasis, a noncontagious skin disease that afflicts approximately 2.6 percent of adults in the United States. Misdiagnosis is understandable, because psoriasis and DH have two things in common.

**Similar appearance.** The conditions look the same—a recurrent skin condition that appears as raised red patches of skin and is often itchy.

**Caused by an immune-system response.** Both DH and psoriasis are caused by an immune-system response. A number of different things, such as stress, infections, reactions to some medications, and heat, may trigger psoriasis. DH, on the other hand, is triggered by the immune system's response to gluten.

With these similarities, it is no wonder that doctors may assume that a person suffering from psoriasis-like symptoms actually had the more common condition.

However, that assumption is not valid. In one screening study, researchers found that 16 percent of people with psoriasis also had antibodies (IgA and/or IgG) to gliadin (gluten).[9]

In another study, researchers had observed that because gluten antibodies (AGA) were often present in people who had psoriasis, they conducted a study of 130 patients with psoriasis. They found that people who had a higher level of AGA had more-severe cases of psoriasis.[10] Put another way—*some people who have psoriasis also have gluten sensitivity, and the gluten sensitivity aggravates the psoriasis.*

The treatment for psoriasis is considerably different than the treatment for DH. Psoriasis may be treated in a variety of ways, including using creams and ointments to reduce swelling and itching, exposing the affected skin to natural ultraviolet light, and in severe cases, taking drugs or getting injections for systemic treatment.

Despite the variety of treatments for psoriasis, none cures it.

However, people with psoriasis (without arthritis) who have gluten sensitivity recover from their psoriasis when they go on a gluten-free diet. In a 2003 study,[11] individuals showed a clinical improvement in their psoriasis when they went gluten-free for 3 months. When they went back to a regular diet, the psoriasis worsened. The study confirmed that a gluten-free diet can influence psoriasis in people who have gluten antibodies (IgA or IgG).

Unfortunately, a gluten-free diet will not help all people who have psoriasis—only those with gluten sensitivity. A study of 33 individuals who had antigliadin antibodies and six who did not proved that a gluten-free diet helped clear up psoriasis in the gluten-sensitive patients but did not have any effect on those who were not gluten sensitive.[12]

## ECZEMA, ACNE, AND ACNE ROSEA

What about eczema, acne, and acne rosea—skin conditions that are similar in their symptoms to DH and are also caused by an autoimmune response? Doctors know that diet affects these conditions, and some doctors have observed that when some individuals with these conditions go on a gluten-free diet, their skin condition improves, similar to what occurred in the following two cases[13] of pemphigus (a type of eczema), a rare autoimmune blistering disease of the skin:

**Gluten sensitivity late in life.** An 82-year-old woman broke out in blister-like lesions on her trunk and thighs. She had not been taking any drugs that might have accounted for the eczema, and she had been in good health. Laboratory tests showed that the patient had gluten antibodies (IgA). Her physician put her on a gluten-free diet, and 22 days later, the lesions had cleared.

**Sensitivity in a teenager.** An 18-year-old woman broke out in fluid-filled skin lesions on her chest, abdomen, neck, and lower back. The lesions were even present on her arms and legs. She had no other abnormalities. Testing showed the presence of gluten antibodies, and she was placed on a gluten-free diet. Within a month, the lesions disappeared.

# HIVES (URTICARIA)

Urticaria—commonly known as hives—is another condition affecting 15 to 20 percent[14] of the general population. This condition may also be a clue for undiagnosed gluten sensitivity.

Most hives are caused by an allergic reaction to eating certain foods, such as shellfish or strawberries. Usually within minutes or sometimes hours of eating the food, the person breaks out in itchy welts or pimples. Generally, these acute hives last only a short time and go away on their own. If relief from the itching is needed, an oral or ointment antihistamine is effective.

When hives become chronic, however, and the cause is difficult if not impossible to pinpoint, sensitivity to gluten should be considered, as these cases suggest:

**From hay fever to hives.**[15] A 24-year-old woman went to her doctor because she was experiencing hay fever. Pinprick tests showed that she was allergic to pollen. She was successfully treated with antihistamines. Three months later, she returned to the doctor, this time with generalized hives. The doctor took a detailed medical history, which did not reveal any allergies to food, food additives, or medications. She was in otherwise good health, with no other symptoms of any other condition. The doctor treated her hives with an oral antihistamine.

After taking the drug for a month with no improvement, her hives worsened to the point that she was admitted to the hospital. A complete physical exam, including blood tests for antigliadin antibodies, was given. The diagnosis: celiac disease.

The woman began a gluten-free diet. Her hives improved after a month and completely disappeared after 3 months.

**Seven months of itching.**[16] An 11-year-old boy came down with a case of chronic hives that persisted for 7 months. He had wheals on his trunk, face, and extremities that did not respond to conventional therapy.

The doctors took a skin biopsy and found that he had dermatitis herpetiformis. At the time of diagnosis, he had no other symptoms of gluten sensitivity.

If anecdotal case studies are not convincing enough, consider this: In a study published in 2005, researchers found that 4 out of 79 children (5 percent) with chronic hives were gluten sensitive.[17] This represented a much higher incidence than in the control group (0.67 percent). When the newly discovered gluten-sensitive patients were put on a gluten-free diet, their hives went away.

Not all skin disorders are caused by gluten sensitivity, but for those that cannot be traced to specific causes, gluten should be considered a culprit.

# CHAPTER 4

## NEUROLOGICAL DISORDERS

Neurological disorders include such diverse problems as lack of muscle coordination, unexplained severe headaches, and psychiatric problems that are exemplified by bizarre behavior.

Not all of these types of neurological disorders can be attributed to a sensitivity to gluten, of course. But gluten sensitivity can take on the same types of symptoms.

When symptoms persist and medical remedies are ineffective, it may be time to consider gluten intolerance.

## ATAXIA (LOSS OF MUSCLE COORDINATION)

*Idiopathic sporadic ataxia* is a fancy name for irregular loss of muscle coordination (sporadic ataxia) that has no known cause (idiopathic).

People who have idiopathic sporadic ataxia may exhibit a number of symptoms, such as:

- Darting, unfocused vision

- Difficulty walking because of leg-muscle control

- Drooling

- Jerky arm and hand movements

- Slurred speech

- Sporadic leg movements

An estimated 150,000 Americans are afflicted with hereditary and sporadic ataxia.[1] Through testing, doctors can correctly identify and label some forms of this disorder. But when they can't pinpoint a specific cause, such as genetics, stroke, or alcoholism, doctors dub the syndrome "idiopathic sporadic ataxia."

One cause they often overlook but *should* consider is gluten sensitivity.

Idiopathic sporadic ataxia accounts for nearly 74 percent of all patients who have ataxia.[2] That's a lot of people. But even more important—research published in 2002 showed that approximately *41 percent* of people with idiopathic sporadic ataxia have gluten sensitivity, as defined by the presence of circulating antigliadin antibodies![3] *The correct diagnosis for these 41 percent is gluten ataxia.*

Another common ailment similar to ataxia is peripheral neuropathy—damage to the peripheral nervous system, which sends messages from every part of the body to the brain.

More than 100 different types of peripheral neuropathy have been identified, each with its own characteristic set of symptoms, pattern of development, and prognosis.[4] Most commonly, a person having peripheral neuropathy may have muscle weakness, cramps, muscle twitching, and loss of coordination.

Just like ataxia, the condition can have many different causes, ranging from shingles to Lyme disease. But one that should not be discounted—or rather, *should be counted immediately*—is gluten sensitivity.

A review of all reports from 1964 to 2002[5] showed that ataxia and peripheral neuropathy were the most common neurological manifestations observed in people with *established* celiac disease (CD). These were individuals in whom CD had been diagnosed with a biopsy of the small intestine. (*Remember: All people who have celiac disease are sensitive to gluten—gluten intolerant—but only some people who are gluten sensitive have CD, which results from gluten sensitivity gone awry!*) Research was conducted to see the extent of gluten sensitivity in patients with *unknown* neurological causes.

The authors of the study stated, "The evidence was statistical: Patients with neurological disease of unknown etiology [cause] were found to have a much higher prevalence of circulating antigliadin antibodies (57 percent) in their blood than either healthy control subjects (12 percent) or those with neurological disorders of known etiology (5 percent)."[6]

*Translation:* More than 50 percent of people with unknown causes of neurological disorders have a sensitivity to gluten.

The treatment for dermatitis herpetiformis, the severe skin disease that we discussed in the previous chapter, and CD is a gluten-free diet. When this type of diet is introduced, the skin condition caused by dermatitis herpetiformis clears up and the gut heals itself. Would this same diet relieve symptoms in individuals who have gluten ataxia and other similar neurological gluten-sensitive disorders? Research confirmed it would.

In one study, scientists identified 43 people who had gluten ataxia and antigliadin antibodies in their blood. Before putting them on a gluten-free diet, they assessed the extent of ataxia in each individual by using five different neurological assessments:[7]

**Computerized finger-nose test.** People in the study sat at arm's length from a touch-sensitive computer screen. They were asked to put their right index finger on the tip of their nose and were instructed to touch, as quickly and accurately as possible, the center of a flashing cross that appeared on the monitor. When they touched the cross, the picture disappeared. They were told to repeat the task nine more times as the cross changed positions on the screen. The computer recorded the mean response time in milliseconds.

**Grooved pegboard test.** This test measured manipulative dexterity. People in the study had to insert pegs into holes, using only one hand and without additional help from the other hand, as fast as possible. The time it took for them to complete the task was recorded. The task was repeated with the other hand.

**Tapping test.** Study participants were asked to press a button on a counter with their index finger as rapidly as possible for 30 seconds. The task was repeated with the other hand. The total count for both hands was recorded. They then repeated the task using each foot.

**Quantitative Romberg's test.** These individuals were asked to stand with their feet together and their eyes closed. They were then told to stay that way as long as possible. The time to first foot movement or eye opening was recorded.

**Subjective global clinical impression.** Study participants were instructed to mark on a visual analog scale their impression of their symptoms of imbalance over the past month.

The testing established a baseline of the patients' symptoms. After the initial testing, the patients were introduced to a gluten-free diet. During the course of the study, which lasted 12 months (with 6-month and 12-month neurological assessments conducted), 26 individuals adhered to a strict gluten-free direct; 14 refused the diet. These 14 were considered the control group.

The result? Individuals on the gluten-free diet showed a significant improvement in performance in *all* the neurological tests, whereas those in the control group generally worsened. The research confirmed that a gluten-free diet is an effective treatment for gluten ataxia.

## SEVERE HEADACHES

Gluten sensitivity can also cause severe headaches—a symptom that can pop up in other systemic diseases such as lupus (discussed later).

In 2004, a study was conducted to identify the association of celiac disease with "soft" neurologic conditions such as headaches in young adults and children.[8] The researchers found that headaches were the most commonly found neurologic disorder in the 111 patients with CD (confirmed by biopsy) who participated in the study; 64.5 percent (20 patients) with headaches had late-onset symptoms of CD or were asymptomatic (gluten sensitive), and 35.5 percent (11 patients) had the classical early infantile form of celiac disease.

The study further broke down the types of headaches these individuals experienced:

- Migraine, 45.1 percent

- Nonspecific, 35.5 percent

- Tension-psychogenic, 19.4 percent

In 16 patients (nine with migraines and six with nonspecific headaches), a gluten-free diet relieved the symptoms.

*Speculate, if you will, what the results could have been if all the patients who were gluten sensitive—not just those diagnosed with CD—had been placed on a gluten-free diet!*

In an earlier study conducted in 2001,[9] 10 patients who suffered from severe headaches and who had MRI tests suggesting inflammation of the central nervous system were found to be gluten sensitive. When these patients were told to go on a gluten-free diet, *all but one found relief*. Seven of the 10 patients had a *complete* resolution of their headaches, and two experienced partial improvement. The one person who continued to suffer headaches? He refused to try the gluten-free diet.

The following case from that study illustrates the power of going gluten-free:

A 50-year-old man whose medical history did not disclose a disposition toward migraines experienced unexplained headaches for 4 years. When his headaches increased in severity and frequency, he agreed to undergo a blood test, which showed that he had antigliadin antibodies.

When he started on a gluten-free diet, his balance improved and his headaches resolved completely. But 2 years later, his symptoms returned. Upon being questioned, the man confessed: He had fallen off his gluten-free diet. A repeat of tests confirmed a return of antigliadin antibodies.

The tests convinced this man that gluten was the culprit behind his headaches. He went back on a gluten-free diet and has remained headache-free since then.

If this weren't enough evidence to suggest that gluten can be the culprit in headaches, consider this account:[10]

One individual said that he had suffered from migraine headaches for more than 10 years. The problem, for which the neurologists he had consulted could find no cure, intensified to the point that he had to take early retirement. By 2002, his three-headaches-a-week syndrome had escalated to an almost nonstop headache. In 1 month, he was headache-free for only 3 days. Migraine medications did not alleviate the pain.

Then his family doctor suggested a gluten-free diet. The headaches gradually became less frequent, and after several months, he was 98 percent headache-free.

Gluten-free wins again.

## AUTISM

No parent wants to hear the pediatrician say, "I'm sorry. Your child is autistic." But increasingly, that is the message given to parents in the United States. And the situation is getting worse. The number of reported cases of autism is increasing, according to the Centers for Disease Control and Prevention[11] (CDC) and other governmental agencies.

A look at the increase in statistics tells the story: In 1996, data from a large surveillance system in metropolitan Atlanta indicated that autism affected 3.4 per 1,000 children 3 to 10 years old.[12] That number increased to 6.7 per 1,000 children 3 to 10 years old according to a 1998 community study.[13]

A report issued in May 2006 by the CDC suggests that at least 300,000 school-age children nationwide had autism in 2003 to 2004.[14]

Autism and related conditions are lifelong developmental disabilities. They are characterized by repetitive behaviors and social and communication problems. Individuals who have autism tend to have unusual ways of (or difficulty in) learning, paying attention, or reacting to different sensations.

Although scientists speculate about the reasons for the increase in autism, the exact cause is not yet known. Doctors and parents have reached out for a number of different treatments, among them dietary control—more specifically, the elimination of gluten and casein (from dairy products) from the diet.

When parents discover that they have an autistic child, they often take desperate measures, including using drugs to control or counteract the autistic patterns. The Autism Research Institute (ARI) collected information provided by more than 23,700 parents who completed a questionnaire. ARI wanted to find out which remedies were most effective in treating the autism.

One of the most effective treatments was special diet: removing gluten and casein from the child's diet, with 65 percent of parents reporting that their child got better.[15]

Parents themselves report excellent results from a gluten-free, casein-free (GF/CF) diet.[16] (Casein is the major protein found in milk.)

**Nine years of noncommunication.** A 9-year-old boy was diagnosed as autistic when he was 3. He never learned to talk, had difficulty focusing, and had trouble responding to communication. At the age of 7, he finally started saying words spontaneously. When he was 9, however, his parents put him on a GF/CF diet at the urging of some friends. Within *4 months,* the boy was potty-trained, started reading, began talking in long and sophisticated sentences, and was able to interact with other children and adults.

**Tantrums and more.** A 10-year-old boy who had been diagnosed as autistic at age 4 had typical autistic behavior: temper tantrums, biting himself, kicking, pushing, and screaming. His mother put him on a GF/CF diet on her own. Within *3 weeks,* the boy started to talk clearly in long sentences. His temper tantrums diminished, and he became friendly and lovable.

**A 2-year trial.** A mother reported that her baby boy seemed entirely normal at birth, and for the first 5 months, his development was "by the book." Then, by 6 months old, he stopped developing and actually regressed in his behavior. He did not even move around on his own until he was almost 11 months old and did not walk until 18 months. At that age, he had only one word in his vocabulary: dog. The mother heard about the benefits of a GF/CF diet shortly after her son's second birthday. *Ten days* into the diet, the boy started talking, and his development has continued from that day on. Now, at age 4, he is enrolled in regular preschool and "fits in fine." He is potty-trained, speaks conversationally, has a sense of humor, and plays games.

How do these miracles happen? Researchers have found that autistic children excrete more opioid peptides—naturally occurring peptides that have pain-relieving and sedative effects—than nonautistic children and that some of these peptides are derived from gluten, gliadin, and casein.[17]

The implication of this discovery is that the presence of these peptides may cause the signs and symptoms of autistic disorders[18] and that excessive peptides from undigested casein and gluten exert significant toxicity.[19]

A 2004 study[20] found that children with autism had significantly higher levels of gluten antibodies in more than 80 percent of the cases. The researchers concluded: "The results of these studies further support dietary intervention, including a gluten-, gliadin-, and casein-free diet, in children with autism."

## BEHAVIORAL PROBLEMS

Imagine not being able to sit still, always needing to be on the go—actually being compelled to move. That's what happens to children and adults with attention deficit disorder (ADD), also known as attention deficit hyperactivity disorder (ADHD).

The difference between ADD and ADHD is mainly that of labeling: According to the Attention Deficit Disorder Association, the "official" clinical diagnosis is ADHD. In turn, ADHD is subcategorized into three types: combined type, predominantly inattentive type, and the predominantly hyperactive-impulsive type.[21] Most people use ADD as the generic term to refer to all types of these conditions.

It is estimated that approximately 2 million children in the United States—about 1 in every classroom of 25 to 30 children—have ADD.[22] The condition usually persists into adulthood, affecting between 4 percent and 6 percent of the U.S. population.[23]

Some research has been conducted that shows an association between celiac disease and ADD. Mind you, the research has concentrated on diagnosed celiac disease—not gluten sensitivity.

One study, for example, published in 2004,[24] showed that people with celiac disease were more prone to develop neurologic disorders (51.4 percent) compared with control subjects (19.9 percent). The researchers included a number of different neurologic disorders in the study: hypotonia, developmental delay, learning disorders and ADHD, headaches, and cerebellar ataxia.

Of special interest, however, is the comparison of people with learning disabilities and ADHD with controls: Twice as many of the celiac patients (20.7 percent) had learning disabilities/ADHD than the control group (10.4 percent).

Again: I cannot emphasize enough that these studies showed dramatic results with celiac patients. The results would have been even more dramatic if gluten sensitivity had been included.

Another type of behavior problem that afflicts both children and adults is obsessive-compulsive disorder (OCD). It is estimated that approximately 3.3 million adult Americans have this disorder, with one-third of adults stating that they began having OCD symptoms as a child.[25]

People with OCD can't stop performing rituals. If they do, they become anxious and may become plagued with persistent, unwelcome thoughts or images. They may be obsessed with germs and dirt, order, or symmetry.

It is not known how many people with OCD may be gluten sensitive, but gluten does play a role in the obsessive behavior of some individuals. A case study illustrates:[26]

From the time that Tom was a child, he exhibited behavior problems. By age 13, his problems had become so pronounced that he met the criteria for OCD.

At age 14, he was tested for CD because both of his parents had been diagnosed with the disease. At that time, the tests showed an elevated level of antigliadin antibodies—suggesting gluten sensitivity—*but no action was taken at that time.*

At age 15, however, Tom's mother insisted on another CD test. The test showed that his gluten sensitivity had progressed to the point of celiac disease.

Five months after starting a gluten-free diet, the boy's depressive tendencies remitted, his sleeping problems subsided, and he was able to attend school normally. His school performance improved, and he learned to control his obsessive thoughts and fears.

The gluten-free diet worked to free this boy of OCD. Too bad he didn't start the diet when gluten sensitivity was discovered.

The power of gluten—and a gluten-free diet—can be seen in these reports:[27]

**New toddler in town.** A mother reports that her toddler is like a new child since he went on a gluten-free diet. "I had been told he was autistic. He did all the classic things autistic kids do—screaming, biting, spinning, and not looking you in the eye. Since going gluten-free, his behavior is nothing less than miraculous."

**Accidents happen.** A parent says that her daughter behaved so badly that they took her to a psychologist, who then wanted to refer her to a psychiatrist who could prescribe a pharmacological solution. The parents discovered that gluten might be the culprit and put her on a gluten-free diet. But gluten accidents have happened. The parents say: "She has had a couple of accidents—eating something with gluten—and her behaviors come right back. She gets moody, cries, and clings."

**A bad transformation.** Another mother relates to accidents: "After being totally accident-free for 3-plus months, gluten totally transformed my sweet baby girl into a different child. I would not have been surprised to see her head spinning around. She threw things, hit the wall, and pulled her hair. The reaction lasted about a week."

Powerful stuff, gluten. Bad stuff for people who are gluten sensitive.

# CHAPTER 5

## OTHER AUTOIMMUNE DISEASES

Remember the television commercial that asked, "Is it real, or is it Memorex?" We might ask, "Is it (*fill in the name of your favorite autoimmune disease*), or is it gluten sensitivity?" Gluten sensitivity looks like a lot of other autoimmune diseases, which by themselves create a variety of symptoms. This makes it difficult for doctors to correctly diagnose and treat the real disease.

### LUPUS

To this point, we have been examining symptoms of neurological disorders exhibited by individuals who have gluten sensitivity. Once the sensitivity is discovered, a gluten-free diet resolves the problem. However, that discovery is not always easy, nor is it fast, because, as we have stated several times, gluten sensitivity is a chameleon-like disorder. It mimics the characteristics of other autoimmune diseases or may actually piggyback on those diseases. One such disease is systemic lupus erythematosus, more commonly known as lupus.

Lupus itself is a chameleon. As a systemic disorder, it manifests itself in different parts of the body and mimics symptoms of many other diseases, making it difficult to diagnose.

This disorder can affect a number of different parts of the body concurrently or at different times, including the joints, skin, kidneys, heart, lungs, blood vessels, and brain. When people come down with lupus, they may suffer from extreme fatigue, painful or swollen joints (arthritis), unexplained fever, skin rashes, and kidney problems[1]—and they may have any, some, or all of these symptoms. Consequently, the 1.5 million Americans who have lupus[2] may appear to be suffering from diseases ranging from arthritis to dermatitis or kidney disease.

One disorder that should be considered early when such symptoms appear is gluten sensitivity. A study conducted in 2001 showed that 23 percent of people with lupus tested positive for antigliadin antibodies.[3] That means that almost one in five individuals with lupus is gluten sensitive. Those one in five may be misdiagnosed as having lupus, just as these patients were:[4]

**From toddler to teen.** The 17-year-old girl's symptoms first started when she was a toddler of 20 months—poor weight gain, eczema, and a facial rash that her parents attributed to sun exposure.

She was treated with steroids, from which she developed side effects, including badly formed tooth enamel.

At 17, suffering from a psoriatic skin rash on the palms of her hands, she was sent to an adult lupus clinic, where doctors decided to consider gluten sensitivity. Testing confirmed antigliadin antibodies, and she was placed on a gluten-free diet.

Six months later, the symptoms she'd had for nearly 15 years went away. She got off drugs, her tests were normal, and the skin rash disappeared—all because she excluded gluten from her diet.

**Recurrent neurological symptoms.** From the time she was 20, a 53-year-old woman had suffered from periodic headaches, blurred vision, and general weakness. The symptoms would be severe, then would spontaneously clear up. When the symptoms began to persist, however, doctors ran her through a gamut of tests, including MRIs, CT scans, cerebrospinal fluid exams, and blood tests. When she was 23, the doctors decided she had lupus.

Her symptoms would come and go for years at a time—typical of lupus. Finally, when symptoms returned in full force and she began to suffer from wobbliness (ataxia), doctors ran an immunological profile. It showed she had antigliadin antibodies.

She went on a gluten-free diet and *in 6 months,* she was able to discontinue her medications. Her headaches subsided, and she was symptom-free after nearly 30 years of suffering.

**A variety of symptoms.** At the age of 40, a woman began to have severe headaches, as well as a number of other complaints. Headache was the chief concern, however, so her doctors ran a CT scan to see if she had any brain abnormalities. She did not.

Nine years later, she complained of severe itching around the anal area (pruritus) and intermittent facial edema (swelling). That condition was diagnosed as hives. Her main complaints, however, continued to be bad headaches and abdominal discomfort. The doctors diagnosed lupus.

Her complaints did not go away. Finally, at age 54, a gastroenterologist who performed a colonoscopy on her reviewed her history and suggested she might be gluten sensitive. Immunological tests confirmed the diagnosis. The woman began a gluten-free diet, and her headaches and gastrointestinal symptoms disappeared.

## MULTIPLE SCLEROSIS

Another disease that is difficult to diagnose, because it has many symptoms and unknown causes, is multiple sclerosis (MS).

Multiple sclerosis is thought to be an autoimmune disease, the same as gluten sensitivity. This disorder, however, affects the central nervous system, which consists of the brain, spinal cord, and optic nerves.

A key part of the nervous system is a fatty tissue called myelin. This tissue helps nerve fibers conduct electrical impulses, which control muscles. In MS, myelin is destroyed in many (multiple) places. It is replaced with scar tissue, known as sclerosis—hence, the name multiple sclerosis.

Individuals who come down with MS can display a number of different symptoms, including some shared with gluten sensitivity. Some of these symptoms include fatigue, problems with balance and coordination, spasticity, and headache.[5]

MS typically follows one of four different clinical courses, each of which might be mild, moderate, or severe:[6]

**Relapsing–remitting characteristics.** People with relapsing-remitting MS have clearly defined relapses (attacks), in which they suffer an acute worsening of neurological functions. These relapses are followed by partial or complete recovery periods that are free from the disease progression. Relapsing–remitting MS is the most common type of MS, affecting about 85 percent of those who have the disease.

**Primary-progressive characteristics.** Individuals with the primary-progressive form of MS experience slow but continuous worsening of the disorder from the onset, with no distinct relapses. The rate of progression varies, however. About 10 percent of those with MS fall into this category of characteristics.

**Secondary-progressive characteristics.** People with secondary-progressive MS have an initial period of relapsing-remitting disease, which is followed by steadily worsening of conditions. About 50 percent of people with relapsing-remitting MS develop this form of the disease within 10 years of the initial diagnosis.

**Progressive-relapsing characteristics.** People with the progressive-relapsing form of MS—a relatively rare form (about 5 percent of those who have the disease)—have a steady worsening of symptoms from the onset. However, they also experience clear acute relapses with or without recovery. In contrast to relapsing-remitting MS, the periods between relapses are characterized by continuing disease progression.

Sensitivity to gluten is most likely not a cause of MS.[7] However, researchers have found cases of people who fall into the primary-progressive or atypical MS–like illnesses who also had gluten sensitivity. In five such cases, the doctors reported that the primary feature was ataxia (lack of muscle coordination), although other neurological symptoms were also present.

The conclusion of the authors: Gluten sensitivity may be considered the cause of "atypical" primary-progressive MS, especially if ataxia is the prominent feature. In those cases, a gluten-free diet can result in a stabilization of neurology. In other words, the symptoms will not get worse.

Perhaps more important to keep in mind, however, is that *it can be impossible to distinguish between the symptoms of MS and those of gluten sensitivity.* For people who have MS symptoms, a gluten-free diet is worth trying.

## OSTEOPENIA AND OSTEOPOROSIS

Did you break your arm when you were a kid? If you did, you know that the novelty of a cast soon wears off. You couldn't wait to get the cast off and get back to normal again. The bones of children (at least children who don't have celiac disease [CD]) heal fairly rapidly. Those of adults may not, especially if the adult has osteopenia or osteoporosis.

The difference between osteopenia and osteoporosis is essentially one of degree: Osteopenia is a mild thinning of bone density, a precursor to osteoporosis. Osteoporosis, by definition, means "porous bones." It is a disease characterized by low bone mass and structural deterioration. This can lead to bone fragility and an increased risk of fracture, especially of the hip, spine, and wrist. Fractures are painful and may not heal fully, leading to disability.

According to the National Osteoporosis Foundation,[8] an estimated 10 million Americans already have osteoporosis, while another 34 million have low bone mass (osteopenia), which puts them at risk of developing osteoporosis. At increased risk are women over age 50 who are menopausal.

Other risk factors include:

- Being thin or having a small frame

- Drinking too much alcohol

- Having a family history of the disease

- Not getting enough calcium

- Not getting enough physical activity

- Smoking

- Using certain medications, such as glucocorticoids

Significantly, some autoimmune diseases such as rheumatoid arthritis can cause osteoporosis. *So can gluten sensitivity.* In a study published in 2005,[9] researchers evaluated 266 individuals with osteoporosis (and 574 without the condition) to identify the prevalence of celiac disease. They discovered that almost 5 percent of people with osteoporosis had a positive blood test for CD—a number significantly higher than those without osteoporosis (just 1 percent). Their findings were dramatic enough that the researchers recommended blood tests for gluten antibodies in *all* patients with osteoporosis.

As we consider this statistic, as amazingly high as it is, we need to keep in mind that blood testing for celiac disease misses a significant number of individuals who are gluten sensitive. And these individuals may be on the way to losing bone density. (For more information on testing for gluten sensitivity, see Chapter 10, Are You Gluten Sensitive?)

Osteopenia and osteoporosis can often be reversed—but the condition must be treated with the proper remedy. That does not always happen, because of misdiagnosis, as the following case illustrates:[10]

Because osteoporosis ran in her family and because she was thin and small-boned, Willow, a postmenopausal woman, had her first bone scan in 1991. She was not surprised that she was diagnosed with osteoporosis. In an attempt to curb and reverse the disorder, her family rheumatologist tried the medications available at that time—Fosamax and Actonel. They failed to help her.

Several years passed, and the disease progressed. In 2003, her osteoporosis specialist prescribed another medication (yet another bisphosphonate). Despite her diligence in taking this course of treatment, it also failed to stop the degeneration of her bones.

It was either by luck or by instinct that the woman demanded to be tested for celiac disease. Her husband had been diagnosed with CD in 1982, so she had kept up-to-date on CD research. Although she had not experienced any symptoms of CD—she did not have diarrhea, weight loss, anemia, or other symptoms—she asked her family physician to run a tissue transglutaminase blood test—a test for gluten sensitivity. The doctor and laboratory were unfamiliar with the blood test, but they learned how to do it.

To everyone's surprise (except possibly Willow's), the tests came back positive. She went on a gluten-free diet, gained 15 pounds, and has continued to see an improvement in her bone density. A gluten-free diet came to her osteoporosis rescue.

This woman's experience is not an anomaly. As far back as 1996, research showed that going on a gluten-free diet would reverse bone-density loss, even in patients who did not show symptoms of malabsorption—the primary reason why osteoporosis occurs among people with celiac disease.[11] (In cases of malabsorption, the body does not absorb minerals and other nutrients necessary for bone growth. Porosity then results.) In that study of 63 patients, *all* of them improved when they followed a gluten-free diet.

The improvement is not short-term. Authors of a 5-year follow-up study of celiac patients who had adhered to a gluten-free diet said, "According to our results, bone disease in celiac patients is cured in most patients during 5 years on a gluten-free diet. The improvement in BMD (bone mineral density) mostly occurred already within the first year after the establishment of a gluten-free diet."[12]

The lesson to be learned: If you have been diagnosed with osteopenia or osteoporosis, and you haven't seen improvement with all you have tried, go gluten-free. The diet may save you from pain and suffering.

## OSTEOMALACIA

Soft bones. That's what osteomalacia is. Like osteoporosis, this condition weakens the bones and makes them more susceptible to breaking. In osteoporosis, however, bone breaks down faster than it can be replaced. In osteomalacia, bone forms but does not become dense and hard.[13]

In children, this condition is called rickets. In both children and adults, osteomalacia is a serious condition. It is a metabolic bone disease directly caused by a lack of vitamin D.

People may lack this vitamin because they do not get enough sun exposure or because their diets are deficient and they do not take supplements for it. But the condition is often caused by the lack of absorption of the vitamin into the body's system. That lack of absorption may be caused by gluten sensitivity or celiac disease.

People who have osteomalacia may experience diffuse bone pain, muscle weakness, and bone fractures. Muscles in the upper arms and thighs may become very weak, causing elderly people to have difficulty getting up from chairs or climbing stairs.

Doctors first reported an association between celiac disease and osteomalacia in 1953[14] (long before today's sensitive testing for gluten intolerance). Some cases illustrate:

**One constant symptom.** A 59-year-old male[15] suffered from 2½ years of osteomalacia caused by severe malabsorption. His doctor finally tested for celiac disease and found that his malabsorption was the only symptom he had. The doctor wrote, "It seems that patients with gluten-sensitive enteropathy [disease] who undergo little exposure to the sun are at particular risk of developing overt osteomalacia. Unrecognized [gluten sensitivity] should always be considered in the differential diagnosis of osteomalacia."

**Many symptoms for 20 years.** A 67-year-old woman had a 20-year history of recurrent abdominal pain, diarrhea, and diffuse bone pain.[16] Her doctors had labeled her condition "iron absorption disorder," "osteoporosis," and "hyperparathyroidism." However, none of the treatments for these diseases alleviated her symptoms, and she eventually required constant care.

Finally, her doctor diagnosed her with celiac disease. She was placed on a gluten-free diet, supplemented with high doses of vitamin $D_3$ and oral calcium, and within 3 months, she improved to the point that she could take care of herself again.

**Back pain.** A 43-year-old premenopausal woman complained of pain in her spine and back muscles for more than a year.[17] She was of normal height and weight and did not report any other symptoms.

At first, the doctors thought she might have fibromalagia, but tests discounted that diagnosis. She was then given a test for gluten sensitivity (an anti-endomysial antibody test). It was positive. A biopsy confirmed the diagnosis of gluten intolerance. She went on a gluten-free diet and started taking vitamin D supplements, and her symptoms promptly went away. Her small bowel tissue tested normal after 4 months.

Ah, the power of going gluten-free!

## ARTHRITIS

What comes to mind when you think of arthritis? Older people who complain of aches and pains? Middle-aged actors in TV commercials who have difficulty remaining active enough to play with their grandchildren? Elderly individuals, especially women, bent over and crippled with a dowager's hump?

Whatever your image, all of them are correct. Arthritis is a term that describes more than 100 rheumatic diseases and conditions affecting one out of five adults in the United States.[18] (Rheumatic diseases are those characterized by inflammation or pain in muscles, joints, or fibrous tissue.)

Arthritis affects the joints, the tissues that surround the joints, and other connective tissue. It is a painful condition and can result in disability. In fact, more than 16 million of the 42.7 million adults diagnosed with arthritis say that the condition limits their life activities in some way.

Even worse—some arthritic (rheumatic) conditions can affect a number of internal organs of the body.

Arthritis is often thought to be an inevitable consequence of growing older. This is not true. Many forms of arthritis are associated with old age and extraordinary wear and tear on the joints such as through repetitive motion. However, individuals of any age—even very young children—can come down with arthritis that is caused by a faulty immune system. In fact, in the United States, more than 300,000 children between the ages of 6 months and 16 years experience juvenile rheumatoid arthritis,[19] an autoimmune disease.

One type of arthritis triggered by the immune system and affecting 1 percent (2.1 million) of the U.S. population is rheumatoid arthritis (RA).[20] In its first stages, RA causes swelling of the synovial lining of the joints. (The synovial lining is the membrane that surrounds the joints.) Later, the synovial lining thickens and loses its protective characteristics. And finally, the inflamed cells in the synovial lining release enzymes that may digest bone and cartilage. This causes the involved joint to lose its shape and alignment. It also causes a great deal of pain and loss of movement.[21]

Rheumatoid arthritis is chronic and systemic. Not only does it persist, but it may also affect other organs and glands in the body. For example, RA can affect the glands around the eyes and mouth, causing a decreased production of tears and saliva (Sjögren's syndrome), or it can cause serositis—inflammation of the lining around the heart or lungs.

The disease is treated pharmaceutically, often with the use of glucocorticoids. Unfortunately, the treatment can lead to osteopenia and osteoporosis. *And the treatment may not be necessary.*

A 1995 study found that 68 percent of people with celiac disease had joint inflammation.[22] Conversely, celiac disease was found in 26 percent of 200 individuals in a study designed to identify the prevalence of celiac disease in arthritic patients.[23] (Keep in mind: These studies were conducted in the late 1990s. The studies were done on celiac patients—those who had celiac sprue of the gut, confirmed by biopsy. The statistics *do not* reflect patients who might have tested positive for gluten sensitivity without overt symptoms of celiac disease if today's sensitive testing had been available!)

It should not surprise you to learn that going on a gluten-free diet can reduce or eliminate RA symptoms. Doctors have suspected for a long time that diet may affect RA symptoms.

For example: In 2001, one study confirmed that going gluten-free clinically benefits RA patients.[24] In this study, 66 patients with active rheumatoid arthritis were randomly assigned to either a vegan gluten-free diet (38 patients) or a well-balanced nonvegan diet that included gluten (28 patients). The test subjects participated in the study for 12 months and were assessed at the start of the test, as well as at 3-, 6-, and 12-month intervals, using criteria established by the American College of Rheumatology. Researchers also measured levels of antibodies against gliadin.

Mind you: These were individuals who had rheumatoid arthritis. *Prior to the study, none of them had been diagnosed with gluten sensitivity.*

The results of the study? Twenty-two individuals in the gluten-free group and 25 in the non-gluten-free group completed 9 months or more on the diet regimens. Of those who completed the study, 40.5 percent (nine patients) in the gluten-free group experienced significant improvement in their RA symptoms, compared with 4 percent (one patient) in the non-gluten-free group. And—not to minimize its importance—the antigliadin antibody levels decreased in the gluten-free group but not in the other group.

Going gluten-free may also help individuals who have osteoarthritis (OA), the oldest and most common type of arthritis.

Osteoarthritis exists as two different types: primary OA and secondary OA.

Primary OA is the "wear and tear" form of osteoarthritis. As each of us gets older, it is likely that we will have some degree of primary OA. Although OA is widespread and can be traced to the dawn of human-kind (Ice Age skeletons showing OA have been found), its causes are not known. It is thought to be genetically linked, and some researchers speculate that it may also be autoimmune in origin.

Secondary OA is arthritis that has an apparent cause, such as injury, heredity, obesity, or something else. That "something else" might easily be gluten sensitivity.

Whatever researchers have to say, individuals with osteoarthritis who have tried a gluten-free diet give testament to its effectiveness:

**An active life restored.** At the age of 66, one woman's OA became insufferable. She could hardly climb stairs, and she had lost the grip in her hands. The OA significantly altered her lifestyle, which had been extremely active. Failing to find relief from the medical community, she decided to try something she had read about—an alkaline diet to neutralize acidity in her body. The alkaline diet helped, she said, but she was still plagued with pain. She then decided to change to a gluten-free diet. Within a short time, her pain subsided. She credits both of these diets with almost completely alleviating her symptoms. Now at age 73, she is able to climb stairs, walk up hills, and even jog.[25]

**Relief for a nursing mother.** A young woman who was nursing her infant son went gluten-free because the child had a wheat allergy. The woman had been suffering with OA for some time. Within a week of going gluten-free, she says her symptoms disappeared.[26]

Although rheumatoid arthritis and osteoarthritis are the most studied rheumatic diseases relative to gluten sensitivity, other rheumatic diseases deserve mention.

**Ankylosing spondylitis.** This is an arthritis that is similar to rheumatoid arthritis but affects the spinal joints, especially the joints at the pelvis. These disorders are related: Both are triggered by an autoimmune response in the body.

Does it not stand to reason that if some of these disorders or their symptoms are actually caused by an intolerance to gluten that others would be, too?

**Scleroderma.** This is a chronic connective tissue disease, generally classified as one of the autoimmune rheumatic diseases.[27] (This classification connects it to rheumatoid arthritis, which we have seen is linked to gluten sensitivity!)

Approximately 300,000 people in the United States have scleroderma, which is described as a hardening of the skin. The disease affects more than the skin, however. In fact, about 75 to 90 percent of all patients have their digestive system affected by this disease. All organs of the digestive system can be affected—the esophagus, stomach, small intestine, and large intestine.

**Sjögren's syndrome.** This autoimmune disease is also an arthritis-related disorder that can affect a number of different organs.[28] Its most common manifestation is in the moisture-producing glands, such as the eyes and the mouth, causing dry eyes and dry mouth. Sjögren's occurs in both primary and secondary forms. It is considered primary when it occurs alone, and secondary when it occurs along with other autoimmune diseases, *such as rheumatoid arthritis or lupus*. The secondary form is most common. Affecting approximately 2 million to 4 million Americans, this disease has no cure—unless, of course, it is caused by gluten sensitivity. Then, as we have seen, a gluten-free diet will relieve symptoms.

Arthritis, as I have said, manifests itself in more than 100 different ways. Not all types of arthritis are associated with gluten sensitivity, but researchers recommend that when the symptoms cannot be resolved, gluten should be suspected.[29]

## DIABETES

Gluten sensitivity is also associated with another common condition—diabetes, especially type 1 diabetes and perhaps type 2 diabetes as well. It is estimated that approximately 18.2 million people in the United States—6.3 percent of the population—have diabetes, medically known as diabetes mellitus.[30] Of these, about 5.2 million are undiagnosed.

Diabetes mellitus refers to a group of diseases characterized by high levels of blood sugar (glucose) because of defects in insulin production, insulin action, or both. Individuals who have diabetes fall into one of several different types:

- **Type 1 diabetes.** Previously called insulin-dependent diabetes mellitus or juvenile-onset diabetes, type 1 diabetes is an autoimmune disease. It develops when the pancreas stops producing insulin, which regulates blood glucose. Type 1 diabetes, accounting for 5 to 10 percent of all diagnosed cases, most often appears in children and young adults, although its onset can actually occur at any age.

- **Type 2 diabetes.** This type was previously called non-insulin-dependent diabetes mellitus, or adult-onset diabetes. Accounting for about 90 to 95 percent of all diagnosed cases, it usually begins with insulin resistance, a disorder in which the cells do not use insulin properly. As the body's need for insulin rises, the pancreas (which produces insulin) gradually loses its ability to produce the hormone. Type 2 diabetes was formerly called adult-onset diabetes because it typically began at an older age. It is more likely to affect individuals who are obese, have a family history of diabetes, have a history of gestational diabetes, have impaired glucose metabolism, are physically inactive, or are of African American, Hispanic, Native American, or Asian American racial or ethnic origin.

- **Gestational diabetes.** This is a form of glucose intolerance that is diagnosed in some women during pregnancy. After pregnancy, 5 to 10 percent of women who have gestational diabetes develop type 2 diabetes. Women who have had gestational diabetes have a 20 to 50 percent chance of developing diabetes in the next 5 to 10 years.

- **Other types of diabetes.** Some other types of diabetes can result from genetic conditions, surgery, drugs, malnutrition, infections, and other illnesses. These types of diabetes may account for 1 to 5 percent of all diagnosed cases.

To what extent is gluten sensitivity associated with diabetes? Consider these facts:

- The prevalence of celiac disease in people with type 1 diabetes is an astounding 10 to 30 times that found in the normal population![31]

- Studies have shown that about 3 to 8 percent of individuals who have type 1 diabetes have celiac disease, and at least 5 percent of individuals who have celiac disease have type 1 diabetes.

- About 1 in 20 people with type 1 diabetes have celiac disease with *no symptoms*[32]—that is, they are gluten sensitive but have not developed CD symptoms of the gut.

What about type 2 diabetes? Recent studies have shown that 5 to 30 percent of people who were originally diagnosed with type 2 diabetes actually have type 1![33] That may mean that even more people with diabetes potentially have gluten sensitivity. We could speculate that individuals who have forms of diabetes that fall into the "other" category may also be susceptible to gluten sensitivity, especially those who suffer from malnutrition (a symptom of classic celiac disease).

*Regardless of the type of diabetes,* individuals with diabetes who have gluten sensitivity benefit from a gluten-free diet. For example: In one study of children with type 1 diabetes who also had celiac disease, a gluten-free diet resulted in a significant increase in growth and weight gain. In other words, they became healthier.[34]

Studies are not available concerning the effect of a gluten-free diet on adults with diabetes; however, in some diabetes centers, especially in Europe, doctors routinely screen diabetic patients for celiac disease and recommend a gluten-free diet when results come back positive.

## THYROID DISEASE

The thyroid is a butterfly-shaped gland that wraps itself around the front part of the windpipe, just below the Adam's apple. This small gland has a long reach: It produces hormones that keep the body's metabolism running right and maintains proper organ functioning. The hormones affect virtually every cell in the body—which is why, when the thyroid's production of hormones is out of balance, the body has a serious reaction.

Autoimmune thyroid disease (thyroiditis) does throw hormone production out of kilter. The two most common types of thyroiditis are Hashimoto's disease and Grave's disease. It is important not to ignore the association of these diseases with gluten sensitivity.

Hashimoto's disease is *hypothyroidism*—inflammation of the thyroid, resulting in the thyroid working inefficiently and failing to produce enough thyroid hormones. Hashimoto's disease is characterized by an enlarged thyroid, although the enlargement may not be noticeable to the untrained eye. Individuals who have the disease typically cannot tolerate cold. They gain weight, experience unexplainable fatigue, become constipated, have dry skin, and lose their hair or have brittle hair. They may also become depressed and experience difficulty concentrating or thinking. Females have heavy menstrual cycles.

Grave's disease is *hyperthyroidism*—an overactive thyroid that produces too high a level of thyroid hormones. The effect of a hyperactive thyroid is virtually the opposite of an underactive thyroid. The excessive amount of thyroid hormones speeds up the body's metabolism and causes nervousness and increased activity, a fast heartbeat, fatigue, moist skin, increased sensitivity to heat, anxiety, increased appetite, weight loss, shakiness, and sleeping disorders. The disease is characterized by an enlarged thyroid (goiter) and bulging eyes.

The association of gluten intolerance to autoimmune diseases has been well established in many different studies. In 1994, one of the earliest studies showed that a significant number of people who have celiac disease also have autoimmune thyroid disease;[35] 14 percent of celiac disease patients had autoimmune thyroid disease. Of that number, 10.3 percent had Hashimoto's disease (hypothyroid), and 3.7 percent had Grave's disease (hyperthyroid).

In 2001, scientists wanted to see the prevalence of celiac disease in people with autoimmune thyroid dysfunction.[36] They tested blood from 200 individuals with autoimmune thyroiditis, 50 who had normal thyroid functioning but had thyroid nodules, and 250 blood donors.

The results of their tests: The prevalence of celiac disease in patients with autoimmune thyroiditis was 3.2 percent, compared with only 0.4 percent in blood donors. Because of this high incidence rate, the study's authors concluded that patients with autoimmune thyroiditis should be tested for antigliadin antibodies. (Again, a reminder: These researchers tested for *celiac disease*—gluten sensitivity at its worst! Today, more-sensitive tests can identify gluten sensitivity long before it causes celiac disease.)

The association between CD and autoimmune disease is well established. But does exposure to gluten *cause* autoimmune disease? Some researchers hypothesize yes. In 1999, a study showed that the longer that children and adolescents ate a diet containing gluten before they were diagnosed with celiac disease, the more autoimmune diseases they came down with later in life.[37] Even more important: In this same study, when the children with celiac went on a gluten-free diet, their insulin-related antibodies disappeared, and their antithyroid antibodies decreased!

The same type of results occurred in a 2001 study,[38] which included 241 untreated celiac patients and 212 controls. The first thing this study found was that thyroid disease was three times more prevalent in celiac patients than in the controls—12.9 percent of celiac patients and only 4.2 percent of controls were diagnosed with hypothyroidism. (Again, remember: These were patients who were diagnosed with *classic celiac disease*—not just gluten sensitivity!)

These individuals were put on a gluten-free diet. Remarkably, *almost all patients* who followed a strict gluten-free diet for 12 months experienced normalization of their thyroid function.

A gluten-free diet works. How much more can we say?

# CHAPTER 6

## DIGESTIVE DISORDERS

As anybody who has ever had them can attest, diarrhea, flatulence (gas), and bloating are not "fun" conditions. Fortunately, these conditions are generally mild and short term.

Most diarrhea, flatulence, and bloating can be traced to either food poisoning (caused by bacterial infection) or a "flu" (caused by a viral infection). By their nature, these infections are generally self-limiting and of a short-term duration. So, while you feel bad for perhaps 24 to 72 hours, your body successfully fights the infection, and the symptoms go away. Miraculously, it seems, you wake up and feel like your old self again.

But sometimes that doesn't happen. Sometimes, diarrhea, flatulence, and bloating (among other symptoms) don't go away by themselves. That's when you generally consult with a medical doctor to find and treat the causes.

Unfortunately, a number of different diseases can hide behind these symptoms. And the cause of the symptoms is not always known—which means that the doctor can treat only the symptoms. Meanwhile, the condition becomes chronic—something you have to live with.

A cause that doctors *infrequently* consider is gluten sensitivity. To illustrate, in 2001, a study showed that the average length of time that people suffered with the most severe form of gluten intolerance—celiac disease (CD)—before it was accurately diagnosed was an astounding 11 years![1]

We can hope that that period of time is decreasing, because by removing gluten from your diet, the digestive disease may disappear. Let's consider the various types of digestive problems and the symptoms that may mask gluten sensitivity.

## CELIAC DISEASE

It's appropriate for us to begin a discussion about digestive diseases by first learning about celiac disease—the "ultimate" in gluten sensitivity. I need to emphasize: Everyone who has celiac disease has a sensitivity to gluten, but not everyone who is gluten sensitive has celiac disease!

Celiac, a full or partial destruction of the intestinal villi (the tiny vascular projections of the small intestine that absorb nutrients) was once thought to be a rare disease in the United States. But in 2003, researchers discovered that, although they may not exhibit symptoms, about 1 out of every 133 people have this disease,[2] which is also known as celiac sprue, nontropical sprue, and gluten-sensitive enteropathy. And interestingly, only about 35 percent of newly diagnosed patients have chronic diarrhea.

The 2003 study, which screened more than 13,000 individuals in 32 states, also showed that 1 out of 22 people who have a close relative—a parent or sibling, for example—with the disease also has it. And 1 in 39 people who have a grandparent, cousin, aunt, or uncle with celiac disease has it, too. Furthermore, 1 out of 56 people who have gastrointestinal symptoms also has CD.

Although it is estimated that about 1.5 million Americans have this disease, only about 3 percent have been diagnosed, probably because celiac disease successfully mimics many other diseases. Also, the medical community is still unaware of its prevalence and fails to consider it when diagnosing symptoms.

When a person who has celiac disease eats food containing gluten—a protein found in all forms of wheat, rye, and barley—the body sets off an autoimmune reaction that damages the small intestine. The result is that the food is not properly digested, and malabsorption occurs. You may not only exhibit symptoms—including diarrhea, flatulence, bloating—you may also become severely malnourished and anemic and ultimately suffer from a number of other autoimmune disorders. The disease may also leave you vulnerable to some types of cancer.

Left untreated, celiac disease causes a greater likelihood of premature death.[3] With that said, let's look at how full-blown celiac disease and gluten intolerance often become confused with other digestive diseases.

# IRRITABLE BOWEL SYNDROME

If you experience persistent diarrhea or constipation, flatulence, bloating, and general malaise, and you can't trace your sick feelings to the more common sources, your doctor may say that your problem is irritable bowel syndrome (IBS), previously known as colitis or spastic colon.

IBS— which affects about 20 percent of the population,[4] generally people in their twenties and thirties—is considered a functional bowel disorder. That's because it is an abnormality of a physiological function, rather than being caused by some outside force. IBS is generally characterized by the rapid movement of food through the intestinal tract. This rapid movement occurs because the muscles of the intestine are out of synch. When food passes through too quickly, it does not get digested, and gas, bloating, and diarrhea are produced.

IBS itself is not an *organic* disease. Doctors treat the condition by treating the symptoms. That is, they try to make you comfortable. They may prescribe antispasmodic drugs, to be taken in conjunction with fiber, to reduce uncomfortable spasms. And because stress is sometimes a trigger for IBS, doctors may also prescribe antidepressants.

But are these palliative therapies necessary? The individuals in the following cases would say no.

**A digestive roller-coaster ride.** When she was still a teenager, Charlene[5] began to experience extreme bloating and indigestion. It seemed to happen after eating spicy or greasy foods, so she began to avoid them.

After she gave birth to her first son, in her early twenties, the condition worsened. She again avoided foods that seemed to trigger the condition, but she periodically suffered from constipation and diarrhea.

At age 26, after giving birth to her second son, her condition got worse. This is when her doctor finally gave her a diagnosis of IBS. For a while, as she watched her diet, she was fine. But then she began to experience other symptoms: itchy rashes, fatigue, pain in her joints, irritability, and pain in the colon. Tests did not find a cause.

Again, she managed her diet more closely, and the symptoms subsided—until her early thirties. She came down with a case of bronchitis. The antibiotics the doctor prescribed triggered severe, explosive diarrhea. This time the doctor tested for parasites.

The tests were negative.

Charlene took charge of her condition and began researching on the Internet, where she found information on gluten intolerance. Suspecting this might be the cause of her IBS, she asked two doctors to test her for celiac disease. *They mocked her for her Internet research and refused to administer the tests.* She took matters into her own hands, went on a gluten-free diet, and is now symptom-free. Her digestive roller-coaster ride finally came to an end.

**Kandee's story.** In 1980, Kandee came down with a severe case of hives. After the usual treatments with antihistamines failed to help, an allergist did a blood test for antibodies and found that she was allergic to wheat. She stopped eating wheat (but not other gluten-containing foods) and used daily doses of a prescription antihistamine. After several years, she gradually tried eating some wheat again and found she could tolerate about two slices of bread a week without any reaction.

She lived with this condition for 20 years. Then, one day she suddenly came down with what was later diagnosed as IBS. She began to experiment with different diets and settled on a diet that was wheat-free (but not gluten-free). The diet relieved her symptoms.

A year later, she went in for a checkup. Because she knew she had a wheat allergy, she asked about getting a test to see if she had inherited a gene for celiac disease from her parents. The doctor ran the blood test and discovered that although she did not have celiac disease, she *was* gluten-intolerant.

She now eats a gluten-free diet and has no problems.

Anecdotal evidence aside, research proves the close association of irritable bowel syndrome and celiac disease.

One 2003 study[6] set out to show the association of celiac disease with IBS. The study included 300 people with IBS and 300 who were healthy. All were given blood tests to determine if they had IgA and IgG antigliadin and anti-endomysial antibodies—tests that would prove the existence of celiac disease. Those who had positive antibody results were offered a biopsy to confirm the possibility of classical celiac disease—flattened villi in the intestine. (Remember: The researchers were testing for celiac disease—not gluten sensitivity. CD is full-blown gluten sensitivity.)

The study found that 66 individuals in the IBS group were gluten sensitive, and 14 of them had celiac disease as confirmed by biopsy. Only two people in the control group had celiac disease.

The authors of the study said, "Compared with matched controls, irritable bowel syndrome was significantly associated with celiac disease...Patients with irritable bowel syndrome...should be investigated routinely for celiac disease."

In another study, also published in 2003,[7] researchers wanted to find out the prevalence of IBS-type symptoms in adult celiac patients and then see what would happen if those people went on a gluten-free diet.

They randomly selected 150 patients with confirmed celiac disease from a computerized database. The control group consisted of 162 individuals with no history of celiac disease.

Of the 150 celiac patients reviewed, 30 (20 percent) met the criteria for having IBS, compared with eight (5 percent) of the controls. Celiac patients with IBS-type symptoms reported a lower quality of life than did those without the symptoms. The patients who later adhered to a gluten-free diet improved their quality of life in 50 percent of the criteria assessed during the study.

Finally, in another interesting project aimed at identifying the frequency of celiac disease among patients with IBS,[8] researchers enrolled 105 patients with IBS. The control group consisted of 105 siblings who did not have any symptoms of IBS. As in other studies, the individuals underwent testing for celiac disease, followed by a duodenal biopsy for those who tested positive.

Individuals who were diagnosed with CD were placed on a gluten-free diet and then were retested in 6 months.

Researchers found 12 cases of celiac disease in the IBS patients and none in the controls. Eleven of the CD cases adhered to a gluten-free diet. After 6 months, all of them had significant improvement of symptoms, and three were totally asymptomatic. Six of these individuals even allowed another biopsy. Five of the six showed improvement in the condition of their intestinal villi.

The researchers concluded that celiac disease is a common finding among patients labeled as having IBS. *And, significantly, a gluten-free diet leads to improvements in symptoms.*

## INFLAMMATORY BOWEL DISEASE

Despite a similarity in names and initials, inflammatory bowel disease (IBD) is not the same as irritable bowel syndrome. Both, of course, affect the digestive system. And many of the symptoms are the same, but the conditions are different.

IBD primarily refers to two chronic diseases affecting more than 1 million people in the United States that cause inflammation of the intestines: ulcerative colitis and Crohn's disease. It may also include other disorders such as ulcerative proctitis.

According to the American College of Gastroenterology,[9] the most common symptoms of both ulcerative colitis and Crohn's are diarrhea, rectal bleeding, urgency to have bowel movements, abdominal cramps and pain, fever, and weight loss. Do these sound familiar? They are symptoms commonly experienced by celiac patients!

What's the difference between the two IBD diseases? In ulcerative colitis, inflammation occurs only in the large intestine (colon) and is limited to the inner lining of the intestinal wall. The inflammation almost always starts in the lowest part of the colon (the rectum) and then extends upward in a continuous pattern. (When ulcerative colitis affects only the lowest part of the colon—the rectum—it is called ulcerative proctitis. When it affects only the left side of the colon, it is named distal colitis.)

In Crohn's disease, inflammation can occur in any part of the intestinal tract, from the mouth to the anal area. Crohn's commonly affects the lower part of the small intestine (the ileum) and the colon. Whereas ulcerative colitis has a continuous pattern of inflammation, Crohn's may skip sections of the intestine, leaving healthy sections between inflamed areas.

Important to note: The exact cause of IBD (regardless if it is colitis or Crohn's) is unknown. But scientists believe it is caused by a *malfunction of the immune system:* The body's immune system in the digestive tract gets turned on to fight an infection but then does not turn off as it should, thus causing inflammation.

Another important fact to note: IBD has a tendency to run in families (just like gluten sensitivity). About 10 to 20 percent of IBD patients have one or more family members affected with IBD.

Since symptoms of IBD may be essentially the same as those of gluten sensitivity or celiac disease, and since IBD and gluten sensitivity both involve the immune system, and since IBD and gluten sensitivity seem to run in families, would it not make sense to consider gluten sensitivity in these types of digestive cases?

Actually, doctors *have* observed an association between CD and IBD for many years:

- A 1977 paper[10] reported a case involving a teenage boy with Crohn's disease. The teen was not growing properly, had intractable diarrhea, and was experiencing a delay in developing secondary sexual characteristics. A biopsy showed he had celiac disease. He went on a gluten-free diet and gained 17.6 pounds in 4 weeks. After 2 years on the diet, his intestinal villi exhibited only minor abnormality.

- A 1982 paper[11] described six people with celiac disease and IBD. Two of those with CD had dermatitis herpetiformis (which we now recognize as resulting from gluten sensitivity!) and ulcerative colitis. Three had CD and ulcerative colitis, and one had Crohn's. The authors wrote, "There seems to be an association between celiac disease without dermatitis herpetiformis and ulcerative colitis. The possible combination of celiac disease and inflammatory bowel disease deserves more attention than it has hitherto received."

- In a 1987 study,[12] researchers studied the association of ulcerative colitis (proctitis) to celiac disease. The authors wrote, "Proctitis as seen in [the] celiac patients had no unique features to differentiate it from proctitis caused by other disorders…Proctitis is common in patients with celiac disease presenting with diarrhea/steatorrhea. This study supports the finding of an increased association of celiac disease and ulcerative colitis and is, to our knowledge, the first rectal biopsy study of a celiac population."

- In 1990,[13] researchers deduced from a study of 182 people with celiac disease that the risk of ulcerative colitis is five times greater for first-degree relatives of people with celiac disease than for the general population. They said, "There is a clear association between celiac disease and ulcerative colitis, which may point to factors involved in the etiology [cause] of colitis."

As we review and consider the impact of these early studies, we must always remember that these researchers were making conclusions based *only on celiac disease as confirmed by biopsy.* It was not until 1993 that serological testing was made available to detect gluten antibodies. And it was not until recently that testing for gluten sensitivity (through stools and saliva) was developed. (See Chapter 10, Are You Gluten Sensitive?)

Doctors distinguish between CD and IBD, but they now recognize that the prevalence of celiac disease is high among people affected by Crohn's disease. A 2005 paper showed that correlation.[14] The authors wrote, "The prevalence of celiac disease seems to be high among patients affected by [Crohn's], and this finding should be kept in mind at the time of the first diagnosis of [Crohn's]. A gluten-free diet should be promptly started."

When properly diagnosed, individuals with IBD-like symptoms do respond to a gluten-free diet. A 2004 paper[15] described three women who had celiac disease, as well as IBD symptoms:

- One woman had a 6-month history of abdominal pain and weight loss. Testing showed that she had hypothyroidism, as well as iron-deficiency anemia. A biopsy revealed lesions consistent with celiac disease and proctitis. She went on a gluten-free diet and is presently well.

- A second woman suffered for 10 years from ulcerative colitis. She failed to gain weight, despite a good diet and control over her lower gastrointestinal symptoms. Testing showed that she was anemic. With further endoscopic examination, doctors found that she had celiac disease. She went on a gluten-free diet and has improved.

- A third woman was not so fortunate, but her misfortune might, in fact, be due to her lack of adherence to a gluten-free diet. This patient had been diagnosed with celiac disease at the age of 6. She did not experience any problems until the age of 33. Then, she suddenly showed symptoms of colitis, which required surgery. (Severe cases of colitis can be treated with surgery.) After the surgery, the woman was still unable to gain weight. She also continued to have abdominal pain. The doctors discovered that she had *not* followed a gluten-free diet, despite knowing that she was gluten intolerant.

Whether gluten sensitivity masquerades as IBD or whether it occurs concurrently with IBD, the fact remains: If you experience symptoms common to IBD, you and your physician should consider gluten sensitivity. A gluten-free diet may remove your chronic discomfort—and save your life.

# GASTROESOPHAGEAL REFLUX (HEARTBURN)

Almost everyone has had heartburn at some time. It can occur after meals or when the stomach is empty. And it feels like a burning sensation in the chest or throat or around the breastbone. When you have a bout of heartburn, you may even taste bile in the back of your mouth.

Occasional heartburn is nothing to worry about. But when it occurs several times a week, it becomes known as gastroesophageal reflux disease (GERD), the term used to describe a chronic backflow of acid from the stomach into the esophagus, the tube through which food passes from the mouth to the stomach.

GERD can affect anyone—including infants and children, as well as adults. Left untreated, GERD can cause esophagitis (inflamed esophagus), which can result in more serious consequences, such as bleeding and esophageal ulcers.

How many of the estimated 60 million Americans who experience heartburn once a month or the 15 million who have it every day have gluten sensitivity, we may never know. But what we have known since 1998[16] is that adults with celiac disease have a high prevalence of esophageal symptoms. That early study also showed that a gluten-free diet controlled these symptoms.

A 2003 study along the same lines[17] as the 1998 research came to the same conclusions. The researchers evaluated whether untreated adults with celiac disease experienced an increased prevalence of reflux esophagitis, and if they did, whether a gluten-free diet would help alleviate GERD symptoms.

The researchers enrolled 205 celiac patients and 400 nonceliac patients who had GERD in the study. Esophagitis was found in 19 percent of the celiac patients and just 8 percent of the people with GERD only. A gluten-free diet decreased the relapse rate of GERD symptoms in those with celiac disease.

The authors wrote, "Celiac patients have a high prevalence of reflux esophagitis. That a gluten-free diet significantly decreased the relapse rate of [GERD] symptoms suggests that celiac disease may represent a risk factor for development of reflux esophagitis."

Do you have frequent and chronic heartburn? Perhaps you ought to think "gluten-free."

## ULCERS

Ulcers are open sores that can develop anywhere in the digestive system—in the mouth (aphthous stomatitis), esophagus (because of GERD, as described earlier), stomach (peptic ulcer), and upper small intestine (duodenal ulcer). All of them are painful. And all of them can be associated with gluten sensitivity.

For years, doctors have been advised to screen for celiac disease in patients with recurrent bouts of mouth ulcers, also known as canker sores (aphthous stomatitis)[18, 19] because of the strong association of this disorder with celiac. Scientists believe that canker sores are caused by an autoimmune disorder. A 2002 study indicated that recurrent and nonhealing mouth ulcers were one of the symptoms of celiac in 31 percent of 48 patients with celiac disease.[20]

But canker sores have been associated with gluten sensitivity even when celiac disease has been ruled out. In 1980, researchers selected 20 people who suffered from recurrent canker sores[21] for a study on the effects of a gluten-free diet on their condition. *None* of these individuals had celiac disease—but they *were* gluten sensitive. And 25 percent responded favorably to gluten withdrawal! The researchers concluded that a gluten-free diet helps a significant number of people who have chronic mouth ulcers.

The common thinking until the 1990s was that digestive-tract ulcers were caused by too much stress or hot and spicy foods. Scientists now know that most peptic ulcers (one of the most common types of ulcers) are caused by the *Helicobacter pylori* bacteria and some strong anti-inflammatory medications. But forward-thinking physicians do not rule out celiac disease or gluten sensitivity, especially when they see patients with the painful symptoms of gastric ulcers.[22]

A 1996 case[23] illustrates:

An obese woman complained of nighttime abdominal pain, common to duodenal ulcers. Medication to treat the ulcer was ineffective, so the treating gastroenterologist performed an endoscopy and a biopsy. The doctor expected to find an ulcer but was surprised to find an active case of celiac disease, although the patient did not have any of the classic symptoms of the disease—just pain identical to that generated by ulcers.

The woman was put on a gluten-free diet. Her ulcerative condition cleared up—and she lost weight. A nice ending for a serious problem.

# GIARDIASIS

I am sure you have heard of "Montezuma's revenge." It's the illness world travelers—especially those who visit countries that do not have sanitary standards and sewage systems like those in the United States—pick up. The illness is characterized by acute diarrhea and nausea.

One form of this illness is caused by bacterial infection. But another form of this traveler's diarrhea--giardiasis—originates from a single-celled, microscopic parasite called *Giardia lamblia*. This parasitic infection is now recognized as one of the most common causes of waterborne diseases in humans in the United States.[24]

This parasite lives in the intestines of human beings and animals and is passed in their stools. Although people traveling abroad often come down with giardiasis, you don't have to go far from home to get it. The parasite is commonly found in drinking water, as well as in recreational water areas, such as public (and even private) swimming pools, hot tubs, lakes, and ponds.

When you go swimming, don't swallow the water! That's one way you pick up this parasite. You can also get it by drinking from seemingly unpolluted mountain streams (infected animals defecate in streams) or eating uncooked food that is contaminated with it. (In some countries, fields are often irrigated with contaminated water. Consequently, eating unwashed fruits and vegetables can be risky. That's why your mother told you to wash your apple before you ate it!) You can even pick up giardiasis from diaper pails or changing tables if you touch the contaminated surface and then touch your mouth!

The symptoms of giardiasis are the *same* as those of celiac disease: diarrhea, gas or flatulence, cramps, and nausea. This makes diagnosis difficult, as the following cases illustrate:[25]

**Giardia and celiac disease.** A 23-year-old woman was diagnosed with malabsorption syndrome. She had iron deficiency anemia, severe diarrhea, and blood-positive stool samples. She was also underweight.

Doctors performed a number of different tests and found that she had a mild giardia infection. They also discovered elevated levels of antigliadin antibodies and the presence of anti-endomysium antibodies—both indications that she had celiac disease.

They prescribed no treatment for the giardiasis. But they put her on a gluten-free diet. Her diarrhea resolved, she gained weight, and her blood tests were normal after 2 months on the diet.

The doctors wrote, "The significance of giardia duodenalis (GD) in the presence of celiac disease is not clear. Association of these two pathologic conditions has been described...In this patient, it can be speculated that a mild, self-resolving acute GD infection may have unmasked a poorly symptomatic gluten enteropathy."

**A traveler's tale.** A young woman who worked for the United Nations[26] had been stationed in East Timor in Southeast Asia for an extended period. When she returned home, she complained of persistent traveler's diarrhea and was convinced that she was harboring a parasite.

Her doctor, however, took a careful history and ordered laboratory tests that showed she had classic celiac disease. Once she started on a gluten-free diet, her symptoms completed resolved.

The lesson is clear: If you still are experiencing symptoms from a recurring parasitic infection such as GD, the medication you're taking or the infection itself may have triggered gluten sensitivity. Try going gluten-free and see what happens.

# CHAPTER 7

## UNDIAGNOSED DISEASES AND CONDITIONS

Not every disease or condition has a scientifically proven cause, yet the symptoms or syndromes can play havoc with your body. It is possible that gluten sensitivity may be the culprit.

## CFS AND FIBROMYALGIA

Are you tired? So tired that you can hardly function? Is your tiredness accompanied by muscle aches and pains and possibly flulike symptoms, such as headache and perhaps abdominal pain and diarrhea? And does your fatigue never seem to go away, perhaps even worsening if you exercise?

It's possible that you may have chronic fatigue syndrome (CFS) or fibromyalgia.

CFS and fibromyalgia are similar syndromes. To be diagnosed with CFS, an individual must satisfy two criteria:[1]

- **Severe chronic fatigue that lasts 6 months or more.** The fatigue must not be a result of another known medical condition.

- **Four or more of the following symptoms:** substantial impairment in short-term memory or concentration; sore throat; tender lymph nodes; muscle pain; multiple joint pain without swelling or redness; headaches of a new type, pattern, or severity; unrefreshing sleep; and postexertional malaise lasting more than 24 hours.

Doctors often confuse CFS and fibromyalgia because of their similar symptoms. The dominating symptom of fibromyalgia is widespread pain and tenderness in the soft tissues. The pain is described as "aching, exhausting, and nagging, and the tenderness is readily felt at certain points around the body, particularly the joints and multiple organ regions."[2]

Just as people with CFS must exhibit certain symptoms to be diagnosed, so do those with fibromyalgia. Doctors cannot detect the syndrome with laboratory tests, but the American College of Rheumatology has issued guidelines for diagnosis. The guidelines state that for fibromyalgia to be diagnosed, patients must experience tenderness in 11 or 18 "tender points" on the body.

How does all of this relate to gluten sensitivity? Consider:

**Linked to the same conditions.** For example, people who have certain rheumatic diseases—rheumatoid arthritis, lupus, or ankylosing spondylitis—may be more likely to have fibromyalgia.[3]

Does this sound familiar? In an earlier chapter, we discussed gluten sensitivity's association with these same conditions!

**Common symptoms.** As we have said many times, people who have gluten sensitivity may—or may not—experience symptoms. And those symptoms may vary. Individuals who have classic celiac disease (CD), however, generally have one symptom in common: They are "tired all the time."

Researchers decided to investigate the prevalence of celiac disease among people who visited the doctor because of CFS. They tested the blood from 100 consecutive patients who met the criteria for CFS.[4]

They discovered two cases (2 percent) of previously undiagnosed celiac disease among the CFS patients. The researchers wrote, "Given our prevalence of 1 percent and the fact that there is a treatment for [celiac disease], we now suggest that screening for [celiac disease] should be added to the relatively short list of mandatory investigations in suspected cases of CFS."

We should emphasize that this particular study was done in 2001 and *only* used blood tests. We now know that serum testing misses a significant percentage of gluten-sensitive individuals. (See Chapter 10, Are You Gluten Sensitive?) Had today's more-sensitive testing been available for this study, in all probability, researchers would have found a much higher rate of CFS sufferers who were gluten sensitive.

Another study, published in 2003,[5] identified a rate of misdiagnosed fibromyalgia in people with celiac disease. The study found that although 82 percent of people who ultimately were diagnosed with CD complained of fatigue, doctors initially diagnosed 9 percent of these patients with fibromyalgia!

Why the confusing or missed diagnoses? Probably because people with gluten sensitivity *are* tired, and that tiredness may well result from iron deficiency anemia.

## ANEMIA

Iron deficiency anemia is the most common type of anemia.[6] Iron is an essential component of hemoglobin, the oxygen-carrying pigment in the blood. Normally, your blood gets iron through the food in your diet and by recycling iron from old red blood cells. When an insufficient amount of iron is absorbed, or there is too little iron in your diet, you become anemic. And if you are anemic, you become easily tired, fatigued, and prone to other illnesses.

Long before today's sensitive blood tests, which can detect gluten sensitivity, as well as celiac disease, some astute doctors recognized that iron deficiency anemia *might* be caused by previously unsuspected celiac disease. A 1994 case illustrates:[7]

A 40-year-old woman suffered from iron deficiency anemia for 2 years because her doctors could not pinpoint its cause. A number of endoscopic exams had not revealed any abnormalities of the gastrointestinal system. She had taken oral iron supplements, with no effect.

Her doctor finally performed a biopsy, which revealed that she had celiac disease. She went on a strict gluten-free diet, and the iron level in her blood increased. Her anemia went away.

In 2001, researchers reported that celiac disease was diagnosed in 13.7 percent (26 out of 190) of people who had iron deficiency anemia![8] These individuals were put on a gluten-free diet and were tested at 6, 12, and 24 months to see their progress toward health.

At 6 months, 77.8 percent of the patients recovered from anemia, although only 27.8 percent reversed from iron deficiency. At 12 months, all but one patient (94.4 percent) recovered from anemia and 50 percent from iron deficiency. And after 24 months on a gluten-free diet, *only one individual was still anemic.*

The researchers concluded that screening for celiac disease should be done in adults with iron deficiency anemia. A gluten-free diet, they observed, allows the intestine to heal. As a consequence, the anemia goes away after 6 to 12 months.

A later study, published in 2004, showed a different prevalence rate of celiac disease—2.8 percent of 105 people with iron deficiency anemia[9]—than the earlier study. But the authors make a similar conclusion, stating that because celiac disease is treatable, it should be suspect as a cause of unexplained iron deficiency anemia.

So, are you tired and possibly achy all of the time and can't figure out why? Go gluten-free (GF) and see what will happen.

## ASTHMA

Imagine trying to breathe deeply, and the result is coughing and wheezing, with little air taken into your lungs. Not only is this frightening, it is life threatening. Yet, it occurs frequently to more than 5 percent of the population in the United States[10] who have asthma, a chronic inflammatory disorder of the airways.

Although scientists have not isolated a gene for asthma, they believe that it is an inherited condition. Children are most affected by asthma, but it may affect adults also. In fact, more than 2.5 million Americans age 65 and older have asthma, and in 2002, more than 970,000 older adults suffered an asthma episode.[11]

Asthma is typically described as an allergic reaction to environmental factors, such as poor air quality, tobacco smoke, smoke from wood-burning stoves, volatile organic compounds, pollen, molds, dust mites, cockroaches, and pet dander.

Gluten sensitivity, however, may also cause asthmatic attacks. A 2001 study showed the prevalence of asthma in children with celiac disease.[12] The authors wrote, "The cumulative incidence of asthma in children with [celiac disease] (24.6 percent)...was significantly higher than in children without CD (3.4 percent)."

Another study, also published in 2001, showed that people with wheat-dependent, exercise-induced anaphylaxis (a severe form of allergic reaction), reacted after eating wheat.[13] Individuals who followed a gluten-free diet remained free of symptoms.

In a similar case report,[14] a 19-year-old student was plagued with chronic hives (urticaria) and asthma for 5 years. Initially, the outbreaks occurred after major exertion during soccer matches. However, after a couple of years, he noticed that they occurred daily. Despite treatment, he continued to experience both hives and asthma.

The doctors had the young man complete a food survey, which showed that he had a diet rich in wheat flour. His mother was a chef's assistant, and every day, he ate cakes that she baked.

Doctors tested this patient for wheat allergy through pinprick tests. The tests were negative. Despite this, the doctors put him on a wheat-elimination diet (not gluten-free). His chronic symptoms disappeared.

Clinical studies and reported scientific cases are strong evidence that gluten sensitivity is linked to asthma. But to me, the most compelling proof is in the stories people tell. Here are some:[15]

**No more inhalers.** Before he went on a gluten-free diet, a child had to use two inhalers in the spring, along with eye drops, nasal spray, and Zyrtec (an antihistamine). His mother reports that since he went gluten-free, "the decrease in asthma symptoms has been remarkable."

**No more medicine.** A gluten-free diet eliminated a number of allergy symptoms for a young woman—including her asthma. She had been using 250 milligrams of Advair (an asthma medication) twice a day. Now she uses none.

**Lifelong asthma a thing of the past.** Joan reported that she had had severe asthma her entire life. "My memories of childhood were the loneliness of being awake in the night with asthma, unable to lie down because that made it worse, unable to sleep, and not wanting to call my parents because there was little they could do."

She had asked her doctor to test her for food allergies, but the doctor declined, saying that since she was allergic to so many things, it would not make a difference to eliminate certain foods.

She took matters into her own hands. She went gluten-free 16 months ago because of neurological symptoms. But the unexpected result was that her asthmatic symptoms disappeared. She has been without symptoms—or asthma medication—for more than a year, even during spring and fall, when pollen is significant.

This lady writes, "My theory is that there is a cumulative effect on your body. My gluten intolerance was stressing my body—causing a heightened response to all allergens. Once the stress was removed, the other allergens have not been able to trigger the allergic reaction."

Is her theory right? Does it matter? What does matter is that because of her gluten-free diet, she now leads a normal life. No more asthma.

## UNEXPLAINED WEIGHT LOSS (OR GAIN)

Americans are obsessed with weight—sometimes to the detriment of their health—and often take glee in announcing that they have lost unwanted pounds.

Losing weight intentionally is one thing. Losing weight *unintentionally* is another and should raise a flag that a medical condition may be at fault.

Many different conditions, of course, can account for unintentional weight loss, such as:[16]

- Acute infection

- AIDS

- Chronic diarrhea

- Chronic infections, such as tuberculosis

- Conditions that prevent the easy consumption of food, such as painful mouth ulcers, newly applied orthodontic appliances, or loss of teeth

- Depression

- Drug abuse and smoking

- Hyperthyroidism

- Loss of appetite

- Malignancy

- Malnutrition

- Parasitic infections, such as giardiasis

- Some medications, including over-the-counter drugs

- Undiagnosed anorexia nervosa or bulimia

We should add one more cause to this list of conditions: gluten sensitivity.

We have already seen that classic celiac disease presents itself with chronic diarrhea and can be confused with parasitic infection (giardiasis) and hyperthyroidism. Left undetected, CD also leads to malnutrition— and that means loss of weight.

Case studies and research repeatedly point to weight loss as a symptom of gluten sensitivity:

- In Denmark, 44 percent of 50 celiac patients indicated that they had had weight loss. This was one of the key symptoms that helped doctors identify the disease.[17]

- Ten of 15 patients who were diagnosed with celiac disease after being examined for hypocalcemia (deficiency of calcium in the blood), skeletal disease, or both had experienced unexplained weight loss—a clue that led to the CD diagnosis.[18]

- In a survey of 414 members of the Ottawa Chapter of the Canadian Celiac Association, 64 percent said that they had experienced unexplained weight loss prior to their diagnosis.

In many of these cases, the patients did not exhibit any other symptoms—no diarrhea, no skin eruptions, no bloating, no flatulence—just loss of weight.

These studies clearly show that if you experience unintentional weight loss, the problem could be attributed to gluten sensitivity—especially if it is accompanied by other symptoms.

Check it out.

## CARDIOMYOPATHY

Approximately 50 million Americans have a type of heart condition known as cardiomyopathy—a serious disease in which the heart muscle becomes inflamed and does not work as it is designed to do.

Cardiomyopathy occurs in three different forms:[19] dilated, hypertrophic, and restrictive. The most common of the three types is dilated cardiomyopathy, a condition in which the heart becomes enlarged, weakened, and does not pump normally. People generally develop congestive heart failure if they have dilated cardiomyopathy.

When cardiomyopathy is caused by infection or as a result of autoimmune disorders, it may be known as myocarditis.[20]

Some of the symptoms of cardiomyopathy and myocarditis include shortness of breath, swelling of the ankles, palpitations (fluttering) in the chest, and chest pain. Once it is identified, doctors generally treat the condition with drugs.

Dilated cardiomyopathy, a form of congestive heart failure, is a recognized atypical symptom of celiac disease.[21] In fact, one study found that 5.7 percent of individuals with idiopathic dilated cardiomyopathy have celiac disease.[22]

If you are gluten sensitive and have cardiomyopathy, however, it is possible that going on a gluten-free diet may reverse the condition, as the following cases illustrate:

**Two winners, one loser (who failed to go GF).** Three individuals with idiopathic dilated cardiomyopathy and celiac disease were instructed to follow a gluten-free diet.[23] Two of the three patients were faithful to the diet. After 28 months on a gluten-free diet, they showed improvement in their echocardiogram tests, as well as in a cardiological questionnaire and the Gastrointestinal Symptom Rating Scale questionnaire. The third patient stubbornly refused to eat gluten-free. He experienced a worsening of symptoms.

**GF wins again.** An account published in 2005 described the case of a 70-year-old man who was experiencing symptoms of cardio myopathy (congestive heart failure).[24] He experienced classic symptoms of nonexertional chest pain. The patient had been diagnosed with dermatitis herpetiformis 20 years before but had not followed a gluten-free diet. When he was examined, he had a dermatitis herpetiformis rash, and, of course, the exam showed cardiomyopathy. The patient was put on a strict gluten-free diet. He also continued with his drug treatment of losartan. After 10 months on a gluten-free diet, he had gained close to 19 pounds, his night sweats had resolved, and he had not experienced further episodes of chest pain.

Another form of cardiomyopathy—myocarditis—also responds to a gluten-free diet. In a study published in 2002,[25] researchers screened the serum of 187 patients with myocarditis and found that 4.4 percent had celiac disease. All of the individuals responded to a gluten-free diet. The authors of the study wrote, "Patients with biopsy-proven myocarditis, especially in the presence of clinical findings of malabsorption, should be screened for CD. In fact, if CD is associated with autoimmune myocarditis, a gluten-free diet alone or the diet in combination with immunosuppressive agents can significantly improve the clinical outcome."

## CHRONIC INFECTIONS

Do you seem to come down with sinusitis, colds, sore throats, ear infections—even urinary tract infections—more often than others? Do you have a problem shaking them off—they seem to linger long after they should be gone? Those chronic infections may be related to an auto-immune disorder such as gluten sensitivity.

Studies have shown that some people who have gluten intolerance also have a deficiency of the IgA antibody.[26, 27] Researchers have found a clear link between IgA deficiency and celiac disease, with 2.6 percent of individuals with IgA deficiency having gluten intolerance.[28] These individuals are clinically undistinguishable from patients with normal IgA levels.

Studies have shown that autoimmunity and recurrent infection are more prevalent in IgA-deficient individuals.[29]

More-recent research presents another theory of the relationship between autoimmune disorders and chronic infection. Researchers at Rice University[30] believe that chronic illnesses may trigger auto-immune responses. They explain that one of the primary functions of the immune system is to generate antibodies when an antigen (bacteria or alien substance) invades the body. Each antibody has a chemical signature that allows it to bind with only one particular sequence of amino acids found on a particular antigen. But sometimes antibodies become cross-reactive and bind with something other than the antigen they evolved to attack. This cross-reactivity, they say, causes some auto-immune diseases.

So, does having an autoimmune disease such as gluten sensitivity cause you to come down with chronic infections? Or does a chronic infection cause you to trigger an autoimmune response when you ingest gluten?

While the scientists decide, you might want to go gluten-free.

# CHAPTER 8

## A WORD ABOUT FIDO

Poor Fido. He gets blamed for all sorts of things, including passing smelly gas. He's usually oblivious to what he has done. But sometimes, even *he* knows the smell is so noxious that he sulks off, banishing himself from the coveted company of humans.

Some flatulence is normal, both in ourselves and in our pets. But when the condition is chronic and the smell is extremely offensive, it's time to look into its causes.

Veterinarians agree that flatulence can be caused by several different conditions:[1]

- Dietary intolerance
- Eating foods that are high in soybeans or fiber
- Eating spoiled foods
- Infections
- Overeating
- Swallowing air too quickly—usually from gulping food

The first source of flatulence (dietary intolerance) may also be the cause of other problems. Dietary sensitivity or intolerance in pets is well documented. Most cases show up in dogs and cats as skin or gastrointestinal disorders, with the majority of dietary hypersensitivity reactions caused by proteins.[2] And the most common of offending proteins? The researchers list:

- Beef
- Dairy
- Eggs

- Lactose

- Other meat proteins

- *Gluten*

That's correct. Dogs and cats can suffer from gluten sensitivity, just like you.

This shouldn't come as a surprise. Dogs and cats are closely related to human beings, genetically speaking, and are susceptible to many of the same types of chronic diseases that we get.[3]

Veterinary scientists have actually observed gluten sensitivity in pets for some time. They are alerted to the condition through a variety of symptoms, most often gastrointestinal. For example:

- One study of 22 cats that had diarrhea and vomiting showed that 4 percent were gluten sensitive.[4]

- A 1992 study showed that gluten was toxic to dogs that had diarrhea and other gastrointestinal symptoms.[5] The toxicity was proven by biopsy that showed flattened villi.

- A study of 55 cats with chronic idiopathic (from an unknown cause) gastrointestinal problems showed that 29 percent were food-sensitive, with wheat, beef, and corn gluten pinpointed as the most common "allergens."[6]

Just as it is known that removing gluten from the diet of an individual who is gluten sensitive will mitigate the problem, eliminating gluten from an animal's diet also alleviates the problem. In the same 1992 study previously mentioned, flattened villi showed improvement when the dogs were placed on a gluten-free diet and relapsed when they were tested after feeding them gluten.

In another study, when 11 dogs with idiopathic, chronic colitis were treated for 4 months with a commercial diet containing protein sources limited to chicken and rice (in other words, a gluten-free diet!), within 1 month, 60 percent of the dogs required either no medication or a reduced dosage.[7] Their condition had cleared up.

As a scientist, I, of course, trust research. But I also place considerable faith in anecdotal evidence when it comes from a credible source.

My friend GC went on a gluten-free diet in 2002 and found relief from the symptoms of Crohn's disease, from which she had been suffering for 18 years. (For more details on her recovery, see Chapter 14, Why Didn't My Doctor Tell Me about This?) GC has a little Maltese dog that suffered from irritable bowel syndrome. The poor little pooch had gas so bad that the room had to be aired out when he passed it!

Since eliminating gluten had given GC a new lease on life, she wondered if it could have the same effect on her pet. She investigated the dog food she had been feeding her pet for years.

I'm not sure of the brand, but GC cares very much for her pet, and I am certain she had purchased a high-end brand of dry food for him, one touted to have all the nutrients a dog needs for a long and healthy life.

Here is the list of ingredients for one of these dog foods:[8]

"Ground yellow corn, chicken by-product meal, corn gluten meal, *whole wheat flour,* beef tallow preserved with mixed tocopherols (source of Vitamin E), rice flour, beef, soy flour, sugar, sorbitol, tricalcium phosphate, water, animal digest, salt, phosphoric acid, potassium chloride, dicalcium phosphate, sorbic acid (a preservative), L-Lysine monohydrochloride, dried peas, dried carrots, calcium carbonate, calcium propionate (a preservative), choline chloride, vitamin supplements (E, A, $B_{12}$, $D_3$), added color (Yellow 5, Red 40, Yellow 6, Blue 2), DL-Methionine, zinc sulfate, glyceryl monostearate, ferrous sulfate, niacin, manganese sulfate, calcium pantothenate, riboflavin supplement, biotin, thiamine mononitrate, garlic oil, copper sulfate, pyridoxine hydrochloride, folic acid, menadione sodium bisulfite complex (source of vitamin K activity), calcium iodate, sodium selenite. F-4090."

Those ingredients are quoted from a high-end brand that you can buy in any grocery or pet store. But what if she had bought the pooch a less expensive, store-brand canned food?

Here are the first six ingredients listed on a can of store-brand dog food whose label says "no added preservatives, formulated for healthy skin and coat, highly digestible, soy free."[9] The dog food lists "chicken, meat by-products, ground rice, wheat flour, wheat gluten, carrageenan" as its top ingredients. (To learn more about the ill effects of the additive carrageenan, see Chapter 13, What If Going Gluten-Free Doesn't Work?)

Keep in mind: Just as in "people food," pet-food ingredients are listed in order of volume. These dog foods are loaded with wheat. (So is cat food.)

After GC discovered that the main portion of her dog's diet had been wheat cereal, GC took him off commercial dog food and began to feed him home-cooked chicken, carrots, and rice. She occasionally mixes in other vegetables and even fruit. The Maltese licked his chops after every meal.

The result: No diarrhea, no bloating, no smelly flatulence. On the dog's final checkup, the veterinarian could not believe how old he was. He died at the ripe old age of 17.

One pet-food manufacturer defends its practice of using wheat in dog and cat foods by saying, "Wheat is a grain used as a high-quality carbohydrate source...It provides energy for daily activity...Iams research has shown that including wheat in a complete and balanced diet resulted in a moderate glycemic response in dogs and cats, lower in general than that observed when a rice-based diet was fed."[10]

The company also states that "gluten...is responsible for wheat-sensitive enteropathy [intestinal disease], occasionally found in Irish setters from the United Kingdom....This condition is very rare, and the reason some dogs develop it is not yet clear."

It's clear why people develop gluten sensitivity. What is the mystery about dogs? And while it is true that much of the study of gluten sensitivity has been done on Irish setters, the studies previously cited show that other dogs, and cats, can also become gluten sensitive.

What's in *your* can or bag of pet food? Is your pet suffering from arthritis? Passing a lot of gas? Having diarrheic accidents on the carpet? Or experiencing any of the symptoms of the disorders discussed in the preceding chapters? Maybe it's time to put him on a gluten-free diet.

But is it possible to buy gluten-free pet food? If you live in Europe, the answer would be an unequivocal yes. Pet foods are advertised as "all wheat and maize gluten free—perfect for all dogs, especially those with gluten intolerances."

In this country, just as with people food, you will have to read the labels. But read them carefully. You may find hidden sources of gluten in pet food (even premium food) such as "brewer's yeast," a by-product of the brewing industry. (Unless brewer's yeast is prepared from a sugar molasses base, it contains gluten.)

Your best bet to guarantee a gluten-free diet for your pet is to do what GC does: Cook the food yourself.

You'll have a healthy and happy pet. And you probably won't need to air out the house nearly so often.

# CHAPTER 9

## FROM THE FILES OF HEALTH PROFESSIONALS

Are you still a skeptic? Do you doubt that gluten could be a problem in your life or the life of a friend or family member?

If science is not enough, if anecdotes told by people who have recovered from their symptoms by eliminating gluten from their diets aren't enough—well, I invite you to consider the experiences that four distinguished health-care professionals and I have had with our patients.

The health-care professionals are:

**Kenneth Bock, MD,** cofounder and codirector of the Rhinebeck Health Center in Rhinebeck, New York, as well as the Center for Progressive Medicine in Albany, New York

**Jeanne Drisko, MD,** associate professor at the University of Kansas Medical Center and program director for the Program in Integrative Medicine

**Ronald Hoffman, MD,** medical director of the Hoffman Center in New York City and the host of *Health Talk* on WOR radio network

**Betty Wedman–St. Louis, PhD, RD, LD,** a licensed nutritionist and environmental health specialist who provides individual nutrition counseling and nutrition consultation

To start you off, I'll share with you one of my own cases, drawn from the many that I have had over the years working as a nutritional counselor. (For several more of my "miracle" cases, please read the Introduction.)

## AN ANSWER TO SUDDEN-ONSET SYMPTOMS

For many people, gluten sensitivity comes on slowly, perhaps because of a genetic propensity, or perhaps because of a growing intolerance to gluten.

For others, however, the onset is rapid. AC's case demonstrates this.

AC is a 24-year-old woman. In 2004, when she was 22, she was diagnosed with pneumonia. To cure the pneumonia, the doctor prescribed a very strong antibiotic—Augmentin—that she took for 10 days, followed by Cipro for another 10 days. She took acidophilus supplementation while on the antibiotics as a preventive measure against side effects from the antibiotics.

Immediately upon completing the antibiotic regimen, AC suffered bad stomach cramps, nausea, dry heaving, and diarrhea. Trying to find the cause of her problems, the doctor ran numerous blood tests (including one for celiac disease [CD], which was negative) and a stool test for parasites.

The tests did not reveal the cause of her symptoms.

After she completed this battery of tests but refused a colonoscopy, her physician suggested that her symptoms were stress-related and that she should "learn how to control her stress and work on her diet." (No one really understood what he meant by that.)

Desperate to get rid of the problem, AC tried numerous products from the health food store, including fiber supplements and colon cleansers. None worked.

Approximately 4 months after trying these natural products, she came to me for help. At my recommendation, she went on a gluten-free diet. AC had already eliminated dairy in high school, since she found it made her congested and caused her face to break out. (She is able to use goat- and sheep-milk products, as well as almond, rice, and soy milks.)

Within a few weeks, AC started to feel well. She stayed off all gluten for 6 months and experienced no symptoms at all.

AC discovered that when she deviates from a gluten-free diet, she feels the effects almost immediately.

For example: If she eats any gluten in the evening, the next day, she wakes up with nausea and dry heaving. When she eats it during the day, her stomach almost immediately becomes bloated and she experiences diarrhea.

She remains on a strict gluten-free diet.

## DR. BOCK'S MIRACLE CHILDREN

Dr. Kenneth Bock has been prescribing gluten-free (GF) and casein-free (CF) diets for many years, in particular for children with autism, pervasive developmental delay (PDD), Asperger's syndrome, attention-deficit disorder, and attention-deficit hyperactivity disorder.

Because the response of these special-needs patients has frequently been so dramatic and because the frequency of celiac disease is no greater for them than in normal children, he no longer finds the need to test for antigliadin antibodies on a routine basis.

Dr. Bock's comprehensive evaluation for each patient focuses on identifying biochemical and metabolic imbalances, dysbiosis (an imbalance between the good and bad bacteria in the intestinal tract) and/or maldigestion, and immune imbalances in order to fine-tune their nutritional program.

Dr. Bock describes three of his patients who have had these almost-miraculous results:

**PDD boy "awakened"—almost overnight.** MR is a 2½-year-old boy who was diagnosed with pervasive developmental delay (PDD). Prior to becoming Dr. Bock's patient, he had seen a number of specialists and was being treated with various therapies to improve his speech and address other aspects of his developmental delay.

Characteristic of a child with PDD, MR had problems with fine motor coordination, speech, and severe drooling. He had no expressive language and was unable to play appropriately.

He had a history of colic until he was 5 months old but now was experiencing constipation.

Dr. Bock immediately put the boy on a GF/CF diet. After a few days, his astonished parents noted that MR "woke up."

MR's dramatic progress has included improved motor skills, eye contact, and awareness of surroundings, as well as elimination of constipation.

Through his nutritional therapy, he also experienced great improvement in language skills and attention. His drooling, which was severe, is almost completely gone, and he is no longer speech-delayed.

His pediatric neurologist, astounded by the results achieved with this young boy, reported that he had never seen anything like this in his entire career. MR's therapists, who work with many PDD and autistic children, also state that they have never seen such dramatic improvement in a child with PDD.

MR is almost back to normal. And perhaps the most miraculous part of this story is that *the turnaround occurred in just a matter of months.*

Dr. Bock commented on the parents' observation that MR "woke up." He said that a fascinating biochemical abnormality occurs with children who have PDD and autism: These children actually experience a withdrawal that can only be described as the same type of withdrawal experienced by drug addicts!

According to Dr. Bock, these children frequently don't just have an immune reactivity to gluten and casein; their condition goes far beyond reactivity. They are unable to digest peptides into amino acids. This inability to digest peptides can cause inflammation and immune reactivity, as well as produce morphine-like compounds. These compounds, called gliadomorphine and caseomorphine, exert effects similar to those of morphine itself! These effects cause an opioid addiction similar to the addiction that occurs from the use of any drug containing morphine.

This opioid addiction explains why these children often have an incredibly high tolerance for pain and why many experience withdrawal symptoms similar to those of drug addicts.

When they come out of the withdrawal, they "wake up."

The Autism Research Institute[1] has found more than 65 percent of children with autism improve with a GF/CF diet. These results are so dramatic that researchers at the University of Rochester School of Medicine in Rochester, New York, are currently conducting a double-blind, placebo-controlled trial to study the effects of this diet restriction with a large group of autistic children.

**No more head-banging.** SW is a 3½-year-old autistic boy who had a very mild speech delay. That condition changed when he received his vaccinations.

According to his parents, 2 months after receiving vaccinations, he experienced a total loss of speech, loss of eye contact, loss of interest in his surroundings, pica (an abnormal craving or appetite for nonfood substances, such as dirt, paint, or clay), toe walking, and a constant glazed look.

He also started banging his head, showed an increased tolerance to pain, and had corrosive diarrhea, which was so severe that it caused lesions on his buttocks.

Prior to bringing their son to Dr. Bock, his parents researched GF/CF diets and started the boy on them. Convinced that nutrition would play a key role in helping their son, they sought nutritional help from Dr. Bock for SW's problems.

Shortly after putting the boy on the diet, the parents saw a significant improvement in his behavior. SW completely stopped head-banging and pica. His motor skills, toe walking, speech, pain threshold, and diarrhea all improved—all to the amazement of SW's therapists.

Dr. Bock fine-tuned the boy's nutrition to achieve even greater improvement. He evaluated SW's biochemistry and metabolism and recommended specific dietary supplements that caused further improvement in his interest, eye contact, and overall functioning.

SW is left with some expressive language delay, but even that continues to improve as he adheres to his dietary regimen.

**Setback, then dramatic improvement.** BG is a 2½-year-old boy diagnosed with mild autism. He suffered speech delay, self-stimulation (eyes moving in a certain way while following the motion of his own hands), flapping, looking at lights, and other signs common to autism.

Like SW's parents, BG's parents also did considerable research about his condition, particularly on the Internet, and started BG on a GF/CF diet a few months before their first visit with Dr. Bock.

With 48 hours of starting the diet, BG experienced severe withdrawal symptoms. Then the child became severely autistic, showing no eye contact and using bizarre behavior. Because of their research, however, his parents were prepared for these conditions.

The setback was temporary. *Within 2 weeks of beginning the diet, BG spoke his first words!*

Although improvement continued, the parents sought Dr. Bock's guidance to fine-tune their son's nutrition through a biomedical approach.

After starting his nutritional therapy, BG began to socialize and play with other children. He surpassed academic goals and was learning almost normally. His improvements continue.

Dr. Bock, as well as my other colleagues, emphasize that it is important to maintain a gluten-free diet for at least 3 months. He also suggests giving a casein-free diet at least 3 weeks to experience its benefits.

He explains that he uses these diet restrictions in patients with other autoimmune diseases, such as autistic enterocolitis and Hashimoto's thyroiditis, as well as inflammatory bowel disease (IBD) and other illnesses that do not respond to conventional treatment.

# DR. DRISKO'S "MARVELOUS" ADULTS

Dr. Jeanne Drisko is a conscientious physician who does a full and comprehensive workup on each patient. Part of that workup is blood tests for IgG food hypersensitivity. However, she has found (as I have) that results from laboratories are inconclusive and often wrong.

To prove that point, she sent several samples of her own blood to five top-rated laboratories. Each lab reported different results—and even the same laboratory gave different results when a sample was sent again for testing!

Upon investigating the cause for these inconsistencies, Dr. Drisko discovered that many labs use open containers for samples. These containers are easily cross-contaminated by foreign substances in the air.

However, in her quest to find a laboratory that was consistent with reproducible results, she finally found IBT Reference Laboratory. (See Helpful Resources for Gluten-Free Living, on page 275, for more information.) She uses this laboratory to determine gluten, casein, celiac disease, and other food hypersensitivities.

Dr. Drisko shares her experiences with three of her adult patients who experienced marvelous recoveries.

**The power of gluten.** MZ is a 19-year-old woman who for several years had suffered from severe chronic fatigue syndrome, as well as irritable bowel syndrome (IBS). Despite being under the care of a number of different physicians throughout her disability, her condition had not improved.

MZ's condition was so severe that she had been homeschooled because of fainting, severe fatigue, brain fog, and an inability to concentrate.

Dr. Drisko's IgG testing showed that MZ had sensitivities to gluten and gliadin. She put MZ on a gluten-free diet.

Within a few months, all of her symptoms (including her IBS) resolved. She was able to attend college and lead a normal, healthy, and vibrant life.

Then something unusual happened. MZ invited some friends to her home. They brought wheat products—chips and bread. She did not eat any of it.

However, she was in the proximity of the opened foodstuffs, most likely breathed in aerosols from them, and she *might* have touched them. *She immediately had a moderate relapse.*

She had her friends remove all of these products from her house, and she fully recovered once again.

MZ's extraordinary episode is an excellent demonstration of just how powerful gluten and gliadin can be to someone who is extremely sensitive.

**Spontaneous dermatitis herpetiformis.** SR is a 21-year-old college student with many food sensitivities and gut disturbances. Prior to becoming Dr. Drisko's patient, she had been seen by many different specialists who had not been able to help her.

Dr. Drisko's testing (IgG test) showed that SR had a hypersensitivity to gluten and gliadin. She went on a gluten-free diet, and her condition cleared up.

One day, she was making loaves of bread (which she had no intention of eating) for a party. As she worked with the flour, she broke out in sores all over her body that looked like poison ivy. Despite Dr. Drisko's medical treatment, the rash continued to spread. Dr. Drisko then correctly diagnosed the skin lesions as dermatitis herpetiformis.

SR immediately cleared her home of all gluten-containing products, and the skin lesions resolved.

This case once again demonstrates how hypersensitive an individual can be without even eating gluten.

**A gluten challenge.** ML is a 50-year-old businessman who had suffered from IBS and back pain for many years. Despite numerous medical interventions by specialists, his conditions had never improved.

Dr. Drisko found that he had elevated IgG antibodies to gluten and gliadin and put on him on a gluten-free diet. His IBS quickly resolved.

His story does not end here, however. ML found that not only had his IBS resolved, so had his back pain! To see if the back pain was related to gluten, he was given a food challenge in which he ate toast and crackers (lots of wheat!) in the morning.

His back pain immediately came back. Gluten reared its powerful head again.

## DR. HOFFMAN'S SUCCESS STORIES

Dr. Ronald Hoffman is the medical director of the Hoffman Center in New York City and has hosted *Health Talk* on WOR radio network since 1987. His clinic, established in 1985, delivers comprehensive and innovative health care, with a special emphasis on nutrition and metabolism. He and his staff work with patients who have bounced from doctor to doctor without success in dealing with their ailments.

Dr. Hoffman has witnessed the miraculous effect of eliminating gluten from the diets of individuals plagued with a variety of symptoms. Here is just a small sampling of the patients who have responded dramatically to a gluten-free diet.

**Multiple problems and overweight condition—resolved.** GS was a 40-year-old registered dietitian who complained of gas, bloating, rheumatoid arthritis, multiple allergies (mold, dust, etc.), bad sinusitis, and exhaustion. She was also overweight.

Because she worked in a hospital, she had access to the top doctors in their fields. Consequently, an endocrinologist, rheumatologist, and allergist were all prescribing medications for her various ailments—but without any success.

Many people who have symptoms pointing to gluten sensitivity are reluctant to give up their lifestyles and go on a gluten-free diet without "proof" from tests. GS was one of these individuals.

Consequently, Dr. Hoffman ran a blood test—the more sophisticated tests were not available at the time of these particular cases—for anti-gliadin IgA antibodies (AGA), anti-tissue transglutaminase (ATTA), and the anti-endomysial antibody (EMA).

He anticipated that she would test positive to AGA (showing gluten sensitivity), but to everyone's surprise, the tests came back positive for all three antibodies, indicating that she had full-blown CD.

What was most unusual about this case was the fact that she had gained around 50 pounds since her symptoms had started about 5 years before diagnosis. With CD, the most common presenting symptom is *weight loss*—not weight gain.

After several months on a gluten-free diet, all her symptoms disappeared. She went off all her medications and has maintained good health using dietary supplements instead. Most surprising (and perhaps rewarding to her) was that she has lost all the weight she had gained. She continues to be gluten-free.

**Progressive idiopathic ataxia—stopped.** AH, a 45-year-old woman, came to see Dr. Hoffman with severe ataxia. Over the course of 5 years prior to visiting Dr. Hoffman, she had had a full workup by many well-respected neurologists, who diagnosed that she had a type of idiopathic (of unknown cause) ataxia with symptoms similar to those of Friedreich's ataxia.

Friedreich's ataxia is a slowly progressive disorder of the nervous system and muscles. Named for the physician who first identified it in the early 1860s, Friedreich's ataxia results in an inability to coordinate voluntary muscle movements (ataxia). This condition is caused by degeneration of nerve tissue in the spinal cord and of nerves that extend to peripheral areas, such as the arms and legs. People with this condition have a drunken, stumbling gait when they walk.

Dr. Hoffman was familiar with the well-known link between idiopathic ataxia and gluten sensitivity and tested the woman for gluten sensitivity. He found AGA and EMA both to be positive through blood tests—*tests that her neurologist had never ordered.*

Despite the results of the blood tests and the fact that her disorder was progressive and she could end up wheelchair-bound, the woman was highly resistant to going on a gluten-free diet.

She was finally convinced to give the diet a try after she was given a number of articles and research studies to read, many of which are cited in this book.

The gluten-free diet completely halted the progression of her disease. She also experienced some improvement in her muscle coordination. Unfortunately, the gluten had inflicted some permanent damage to her nervous system.

It is sad that her gluten sensitivity had not been discovered earlier.

**Chronic conditions and allergies—gone.** Dr. Hoffman sees at least 50 patients each year with chronic sinusitis, asthma, gas, bloating, and common allergies, such as mold, dust, and pollen, who test positive for AGA but negative for all the other antibodies. When these patients are taken off gluten, they are able to wean off all their medications that controlled their symptoms.

**Other conditions—improved.** Dr. Hoffman has also found that patients with thyroid disorders often respond to a gluten-free diet, as well as those with IBS, who are often on medications to control their illness.

These IBS patients do not have celiac disease; they simply have gluten sensitivity as the cause of their problem. Dr. Hoffman does not wait for CD (characterized by villous atrophy of the small intestines) to develop. If patients come in with a large-intestine biopsy that even shows inflammation, he puts a patient on a gluten-free diet—even if AGA does not show up positive in a blood test.

Dr. Hoffman recognizes the limits of blood tests to identify gluten sensitivity. (See Chapter 10, Are You Gluten Sensitive?), but unfortunately, the state of New York restricts the use of testing to those labs licensed under its rules, even if a laboratory is certified by the U.S. Department of Health and Human Services. The two laboratories that have developed more-sensitive testing procedures for gluten sensitivity are not recognized to do testing in New York.

## DR. BETTY WEDMAN–ST. LOUIS'S WONDERS

Dr. Betty Wedman-St. Louis is a nutritionist who provides individual nutritional counseling. The individuals she advises are as likely to come to her on their own as they are to be referred by a medical doctor.

**No more tummy aches.** In mid-summer 2003, 9-year-old MJ began to suffer stomachaches, bloating, and cramping. Every time she consumed her favorite foods, such as cheese on toast and watermelon, she experienced a stomach pain so bad that she escaped to bed and sleep, and she would refuse to eat those foods again.

After 6 months of stomachaches (and then refusal to eat the offending foods), MJ's mother took her to see a pediatrician at All Children's Hospital in St. Petersburg, Florida. Her specific complaints included stomachaches, weight loss, dark circles under her eyes, and a skin rash.

The pediatrician concentrated on the weight loss and stomachaches, and ordered blood tests. Then he told MJ to go home and drink Boost and Resource (milk-based weight-gain drinks that are loaded with sugar, artificial flavor, and fat) to regain the weight she had lost from her self-imposed restricted diet.

Two days into consuming these drinks, MJ became extremely ill. She experienced such intense stomachaches that she was admitted to the hospital.

At the hospital, doctors ordered more blood tests, which mistakenly showed that she had diabetes. (The hospital mixed up her laboratory results with another patient's!) It took 2 days for the hospital to sort out the mistake, after which she was discharged with no diagnosis for her stomachaches.

One month later, her pediatrician finally ordered a blood test for celiac disease. It came back negative. Approximately 3 weeks later, because she was still not doing well, her pediatrician ordered an endoscopic exam for CD. It, too, came back negative—no flattened villi.

The doctor then ordered another blood test for CD. This one showed slightly elevated antigliadin IgA antibodies at a level of 18.2 (normal is less than 10) with normal ATTA. Even though the antigliadin IgA antibodies fell outside the normal range, the pediatrician still insisted the CD panel wasn't specific enough for CD and ignored the results.

He did not consider a diagnosis of gluten intolerance. Instead, he concluded that *MJ required psychological counseling and needed to learn how to eat.*

Fortunately, MJ's mother took her to see Dr. Wedman–St. Louis shortly after the last blood test. Dr. Wedman–St. Louis suggested getting an IgG food antibody profile from Metametrix Clinical Laboratory. (See Helpful Resources for Gluten-Free Living, on page 275, for more information.) This laboratory tests for food antibodies by using 90 substances that might trigger a reaction (antigens).

The profile indicated either a severe or moderate reactivity to almost every food MJ had been avoiding. She showed a severe reactivity (+5) to casein, milk, egg, wheat, and peanuts and a moderate reactivity (+4) to soy, rye, and barley.

*As a side note:* Immunoreactivity tests are limited in what they can identify. If an individual is not in a good nutritional state and has nutritional depletion, the test may show a sensitivity to something that wouldn't be identified if the patient were adequately nourished.

The test may also show severe reactivity to a food that the patient eats daily, whereas it might not produce that level of severity if the patient were eating a variety of foods.

In MJ's case, the immunoreactivity test showed that MJ had both a gluten and a casein intolerance, as well as a soy reactivity.

Dr. Wedman–St. Louis started MJ on a gluten-free/dairy-free diet (which eliminates casein). She recommended excluding eggs as well.

It didn't take long for the diet to work. Within 2 months, MJ's personality changed, she had regained weight, and she was a happy, normal, and active girl who no longer suffered from stomach pain or bloating. The dark circles under her eyes and her skin rash—both of which were ignored by her pediatrician—also completely cleared.

To help MJ achieve optimal health, Dr. Wedman-St. Louis recommended nutritional supplements in addition to changing her diet. These nutrients included a multinutrient formula (providing vitamins, minerals, and antioxidants), medium-chain triglyceride oil, fish oil, amino acid capsules, and other dietary supplements to improve her immune system and enhance gastrointestinal health.

Dr. Wedman-St. Louis also recommended that MJ take *Primadophilus reuteri* as an acidophilus supplement. MJ preferred having capsules emptied into an almond milk smoothie as an easy way to take the supplement.

MJ is not annoyed that she cannot eat the same foods as other kids. Instead, she dutifully checks all labels, because she knows that if she eats the wrong things, she will get a stomachache—something she doesn't want again. She is very thankful to Dr. Wedman-St. Louis. Her mom remains completely supportive and is thrilled with the results.

**No more myasthenia, despite the doctor.** When SW was 63 years old in 2002, she was diagnosed with myasthenia gravis, a neuromuscular disorder.

Prior to the diagnosis, she had experienced a number of medical issues: thyroid disease, diabetes, a partial hysterectomy for fibroid tumors in 1965, surgery for ovarian cancer (followed by chemotherapy) in 1995, and colon cancer, which resulted in the removal of 70 percent of her large colon in 2002. All of these problems were under control when her diagnosis for myasthenia gravis was made.

The myasthenia was clearly interfering with her life, because it was causing severe and very frequent diarrhea. After 3 years of planning her life around being near a bathroom, SW came to see Dr. Wedman-St. Louis to see what could be done about her "rapid transit time" (diarrhea). Because SW refused to have blood tests done, Dr. Wedman-St. Louis put her on a specific nutritional repletion that included acidophilus, alpha-lipoic acid, zinc, and folate. She also started SW on an elimination, hypoallergenic diet that excluded all grains, dairy, eggs, and soy and emphasized drinking a lot of water.

The "gluten-free+" diet was effective. In 1 month, SW's bowel movements decreased from six per day to three. Even more important, she no longer experienced diarrhea but had normal stools.

The diet also cleared her sleep disorder, allowing her to sleep through the night. And she no longer had droopy eyelids (a symptom of myasthenia gravis). Some friends accused her of having plastic surgery! She loved the compliments. The diet also gave her more energy, and her chronic fatigue lessened. At this point, SW, who initially did not want to take supplements, agreed to take a multinutrient formula supplement for more nutritional repletion.

Prior to seeing Dr. Wedman-St. Louis, SW had been under the care of a gastroenterologist who wanted to schedule a colon resection for her diarrhea. After working with Dr. Wedman-St. Louis for a period of time, SW returned to the gastroenterologist for a follow-up visit that she had previously scheduled. She explained to the doctor what she had done and how well she was doing. Rather than supporting her, her physician said that she was just having "passing improvement."

The improvement didn't pass; SW continued to get better. Over the next 2 months, her bowel movements decreased to normal at two per day. She continued to feel better, her skin was better hydrated, and she looked great.

She went back to her physician again, since he had scheduled another 2-month follow-up. She expected him to give her a clean bill of health. Instead, he told her she would need surgery at a future time, since her improvement might not last. However, since she was better now, she wouldn't need the bowel resection at this time. But, if her symptoms returned…

SW thought her doctor would be interested (maybe even delighted) in how well she was doing. Instead, he seemed completely disinterested in her improvement. He didn't even acknowledge her happy disclosure that she was now sleeping well and that her chronic fatigue had gone away.

Dr. Wedman-St. Louis discussed the possibility of reintroducing some of the foods SW had eliminated (such as eggs), but SW has no desire to add any of the foods back into her diet, since she is afraid her symptoms might be triggered. Although she used to love the foods she has given up, she doesn't want to risk getting sick again.

## TREATMENT PROTOCOLS

All of these doctors (and many of my colleagues) use similar treatment protocols with patients they suspect may have autoimmune diseases, such as gluten sensitivity:

**Identification of targeted nutritional needs.** Workup methods vary, but the end result is a comprehensive understanding of the patient's nutritional deficiencies.

**Gluten-free diet.** Even in the absence of blood tests or other tests that definitively point to gluten sensitivity, they put patients who have been unsuccessful with other treatment protocols on a gluten-free diet. And they keep patients on this diet for at least 3 months to see its results.

**Casein-free diet.** Depending upon the patient, the doctors frequently recommend a casein-free diet, especially for those individuals suffering from gastrointestinal disorders, such as IBD or IBS.

**Paleolithic diet.** In addition to having patients go gluten-free, they often put patients with autoimmune disease on a "Paleolithic diet," which is essentially grain-free, with fresh, natural foods as recommended in this book. They believe, as I do, that our ancestors did not eat the way we do today, and genetically, we are not able to adapt to the drastic changes in our diet that have occurred over thousands of years.

**Dietary supplementation.** All of the doctors use dietary supplementation—either orally or intravenously, or both, to help the patient be restored to health faster.

**Detoxification.** In addition to providing dietary supplementation, the doctors use supplements specifically selected to help rid the body of toxic elements.

# CHAPTER 10

## ARE YOU GLUTEN SENSITIVE?

Throughout this book, we've shown that gluten causes problems in a great number of people. If you suspect you may be one of these people, the easiest thing to do is to eliminate gluten from your diet. If your body responds, you will know it. You will feel and be healthier.

Perhaps, though, you want definitive proof to show that you are gluten sensitive. You are in luck. You can ask your doctor to test for gluten sensitivity. The key, though, is to ask for the *right* test.

Before we look at the right tests for gluten sensitivity, let's consider the wrong tests—tests for celiac disease (CD). Remember that celiac disease is gluten sensitivity gone awry! The tests that doctors use to tell if you have celiac disease *cannot* tell them if you are gluten sensitive.

## BLOOD TESTS

In the digestive process, if you are gluten sensitive, your body produces antibodies to gluten. The gold standard for confirming a diagnosis of celiac disease is a positive blood test for antigliadin IgA antibodies (AGA) *plus* anti-tissue transglutaminase (ATTA) (two of the three antibodies produced if you are gluten sensitive). Even more definitive—if a blood test is positive for AGA, ATTA, *and* anti-endomysial antibody (EMA) (the third antibody), doctors are almost 100 percent certain you have celiac disease.

But blood tests are inadequate to detect gluten sensitivity, for a couple of reasons:

**Partial atrophy is ignored.** You can *only* be guaranteed to test positive for AGA, ATTA, and EMA if *total* villous atrophy has occurred—that is, only if the villi are *completely* flattened.

If you have partial, subtotal, or infiltrating villous atrophy, you may *not* test positive for AGA, ATTA, or EMA. The atrophy and inflammation of the villi may not be severe enough to allow all these antibodies to easily pass through your intestinal barrier. Only some of them—or even none of them!—may be in your bloodstream, depending upon the condition of your villi and the progression of your gluten sensitivity.

Despite the fact that you are having a problem with gluten (that's why the antibodies show up in your bloodstream in the first place!), if the other tests are negative, you'll need to wait until *total* villous atrophy has occurred to achieve a positive test that confirms celiac disease.

Unfortunately, by the time that total villous atrophy occurs, you are also one sick puppy, with symptoms that could include diarrhea, gas, bloating, nausea, vomiting, fat in the stool, malabsorption, and significant weight loss. You may even experience periods of constipation as well.

**Laboratory tests are incomplete.** Another reason why blood tests are not accurate is because typical laboratory tests do not identify all the antibodies in your blood.

When a laboratory tests for antibodies, it first creates a buffer agent and then introduces a blood sample into the agent to see what types of antibodies are produced.

The most common antibody that a gluten-sensitive individual produces is antigliadin. The agent laboratories use for this antibody test is wheat mixed into a water solution.

The problem with a wheat-based solution? Gliadin does not dissolve in water. As a result, more than 30 gliadin peptides (molecules) are not evaluated by this test. Your body may be reacting to gliadin peptides that are not picked up by these blood tests.

## BIOPSY

Some doctors are not satisfied with the blood tests—or, if the blood tests come back negative for AGA and ATTA but you still have symptoms, they decide to take a look—literally. They do a biopsy through an endoscopic procedure.

But unless significant structural damage has occurred to the villi of the small intestines, physicians rule out celiac disease and gluten sensitivity.

Without total villous atrophy, doctors consider a biopsy negative—even if early inflammatory changes are seen!

However, research has shown that the brunt of the immune reaction to gluten can affect the function of the intestines and cause symptoms *without* structural damage.

Since the minority of gluten-sensitive individuals actually develop celiac disease, a biopsy that confirms only significant damage means that the vast majority of those reacting to gluten remain undiagnosed and untreated for years.

## GENETIC TESTING

Genetic testing is another way to find out if you may be gluten sensitive. It is estimated that 90 percent of patients in North America who develop celiac disease test positive for a gene called HLA-DQ2.[1] Virtually all remaining patients test positive for another gene, HLA-DQ8. Testing for these genes is done by swabbing the inside of your mouth to gather mucosa.

If the mucosa tests positive for one or both of these genes, there is a high probability that you have gluten sensitivity and may develop celiac disease. But the test is inconclusive. Of the general population that does *not* have CD, 20 to 30 percent test positive for these genes. So without positive blood tests, genetic screening cannot tell if you are gluten sensitive.

Researchers are investigating other genes (such as histocompatibility class 1–related genes) to diagnose more-atypical forms of CD, but these tests are not in use yet.

## INVASIVE BUT SENSITIVE TESTING

Earlier, we said that when a gluten-sensitive person ingests food containing gluten, the gluten becomes an antigen that is attacked by antibodies (AGA, ATTA, or EMA). If the villi are flattened because of pronounced inflammation, these antibodies escape into the bloodstream. But if the villi are not atrophied or are only partially atrophied, antibodies may not (cannot) get into the bloodstream.

Regardless of whether you have antibodies in your bloodstream, if you are gluten sensitive, you *still* have AGA. Although these antibodies are not in your blood, they *are* in your intestine, according to cutting-edge research conducted in the 1990s.[2]

Researchers measured AGA in blood and intestinal fluid by having people in the study swallow a long tube that migrated into the upper small intestines. The research found that *untreated* CD patients had AGA present in both their blood *and* their small intestine.

CD patients who had followed a gluten-free diet for a year and had substantially healed their villous atrophy no longer had AGA present in their blood. However, they still had mild inflammation, and they had a measurable amount of AGA inside the intestine.

Another study investigating rectal installation of gluten (a gluten enema) found an abnormal immunological reaction in 20 percent of children with type 1 (insulin dependent) diabetes. But blood tests for antibodies were negative, and their intestinal biopsies were normal.

What was found was substantial infiltration of lymphocytes—a localized inflammatory immune response. When these children were put on a gluten-free diet, they experienced improved growth and better blood-sugar control.

(As a side note: Early cow's milk consumption before 1 year of age has also been associated with type 1 diabetes in children. If these children had been screened early for gluten and dairy sensitivity or had simply been started on a gluten-free diet as soon as the first symptoms of growth failure and/or poor blood sugar were evident, it is highly probable that the actual destruction of their pancreatic cells that produce insulin could have been avoided.)

The results of these research projects made convincing arguments that more-conclusive tests for gluten sensitivity could be developed, forgoing blood tests and biopsies in favor of tests that examined intestinal fluids.

The late Dr. Anne Ferguson, a researcher from the University of Edinburgh Department of Medicine, pioneered the development of such a test: Patients swallowed a tube, through which many gallons of nonabsorbable fluid were poured, in order to achieve a complete lavage (emptying) of all their gastrointestinal contents. These contents had to be passed by rectum and collected into a large vat and then analyzed for the presence of AGA and ATTA.

The test was clearly far more sensitive for testing for gluten intolerance than the conventional blood testing, but it was not embraced by the medical community because of the arduous procedure that had to be performed to collect the intestinal contents for analysis. And, while it wasn't exactly noninvasive, it was less than pleasant for patients.

## CONCLUSIVE TESTS FOR GLUTEN SENSITIVITY

Fortunately, there are a number of tests that are likely to reveal gluten sensitivity in anyone who has it.

### Stool Testing for Antibodies

Two medical researchers, Drs. Kenneth Fine[3] and Aristo Vojdani, are among many current scientists who concur that better tests are needed to assess gluten sensitivity in individuals who do not have villous atrophy.

Because of the shortcomings of blood tests, the inconclusive evidence of biopsies, and the invasive nature of lavage tests, these researchers agree that evidence of immunologic reaction to gluten has to come from a test for antibodies located where the food comes into direct contact with the tissue, such as inside the intestinal tract or the mouth.

Dr. Fine recognized the value of Dr. Ferguson's work and took up where she left off. His cutting-edge research on microscopic colitis led him to the discovery that stool analysis is an excellent and noninvasive way to assess gluten sensitivity. This also means that it would be able to diagnose gluten sensitivity years before celiac disease develops.

Dr. Fine explained his incredible discovery to me:

Microscopic colitis is a common chronic diarrheal syndrome and accounts for 10 percent of all cases of chronic diarrhea. It is the most common cause of ongoing chronic diarrhea in treated celiac, affecting 4 percent of all celiac patients.

However, from his published research, despite the presence of the HLA-DQ2 gene (the gene that suggests gluten sensitivity) in 64 percent of patients with microscopic colitis, few got positive blood tests or biopsies consistent with celiac disease, because total villous atrophy had not occurred. The biopsies did, however, reveal varying degrees of inflammation and mild villous blunting in 70 percent of the patients.

Negative tests for celiac did not rule out the possibility of gluten sensitivity. He decided to see if the antigliadin IgA antibodies were present in the stools of the research subjects.

His initial data was nothing short of astounding: In people with untreated celiac disease, stool analysis showed a positive presence of the antibodies in 100 percent of the patients. The standard blood test showed a positive presence of antibodies in 76 percent of the patients.[4]

Since that time, Dr. Fine has compared hundreds of tests on people with microscopic colitis. He found that only 7 percent of these individuals test positive for antibodies in blood tests, while 76 percent test positive through the stool test.

Furthermore, he has found that 79 percent of family members of patients with celiac disease have a positive stool test, 77 percent of patients with any type of autoimmune disease test positive, and 57 percent of people with irritable bowel syndrome and similar symptoms test positive.

Fifty percent of people with chronic diarrhea of unknown origin test positive, out of which only 10 to 12 percent test positive on the blood tests—the same as normal volunteers.

From this and other data, it appears that the stool test for AGA is far more sensitive than standard celiac-panel blood tests. His data has also shown that 29 percent of the normal population of this country, almost all of whom eat gluten, show an immunological reaction to gluten in their intestines, even with the absence of any illness or symptoms!

This is not so far-fetched, considering that 11 percent of these "normals" still display positive blood tests, and according to more recent analysis, as many as 42 percent carry the HLA-DQ2 or DQ8 celiac gene.

Dr. Fine also measures the DQ1 and DQ3 genes, which also predispose many people to gluten sensitivity. Positive tests to any one or more of these genes further raise the probability that an individual is gluten sensitive.

All of these genetic markers are easily evaluated by a simple buccal smear, which is a gentle scraping of the inside of the cheek with a small spatula that collects the cells for analysis.

As a further confirmation that the stool tests conclusively indicate gluten sensitivity, individuals who test positive respond to a gluten-free diet. For example: Dr. Fine has treated 25 patients who had refractory (not improving) or relapsing microscopic colitis with a gluten-free diet. Nineteen resolved completely, and the other five were noticeably improved. He has also added a dairy-free regimen, as I do when I suspect gluten sensitivity, and found even greater improvement in some patients.

Dr. Fine continues to study the problem of gluten sensitivity. In the meantime, he has applied his research to a testing facility (www.enterolab.com), where individuals or medical doctors (except those in New York State) can order stool or genetic testing.

## Salivary Testing for Antibodies

Dr. Aristo Vojdani[5] was extremely disappointed with the conventional blood-analysis testing for celiac and was well aware that it would not reveal sensitivity to gluten unless the intestinal villi were totally destroyed.

He was also familiar with research in animals that demonstrated that when a bacterial oral antigen (from milk or gluten, for example) was orally consumed, AGA and ATTA antibodies could not be detected in the blood. However, the antibodies could be detected in the animal's stool and saliva.

He (like Dr. Fine and me) was also aware that a gluten-free diet was therapeutic for a host of illnesses and that an individual could respond to a gluten-free diet for an illness when there were no intestinal symptoms.

Dr. Vojdani determined to prove to skeptics that the positive response to a gluten-free dietary intervention was not a placebo effect.

Thus, he developed a sophisticated salivary assay for testing for AGA and ATTA:

- Patients who have AGA in their saliva are considered to have gluten sensitivity.

- A positive test for both AGA and ATTA confirms celiac disease.

- A positive test for only ATTA, which shows up in type 1 diabetes, for example, demonstrates an autoimmune disease.

His laboratory also provides the buccal testing for the genetic markers for gluten sensitivity and celiac disease.

Dr. Vojdani feels it is important for someone with a positive salivary ATTA to try a gluten-free and dairy-free diet for several months, since these foods are immunoreactive in many people with autoimmune disease.

Like Dr. Fine, Dr. Vojdani has applied his research to a laboratory setting (www.immunoscienceslab.com), where doctors can order these assays. Their laboratories are licensed by the U.S. government's Department of Health and Human Services to do interstate testing in all states except New York.

# PART 3

# GOING GLUTEN-FREE

Life is full of choices. From the moment you get up in the morning, you have a choice:

- Should you get up at 6 a.m., or stay in bed?
- Should you read a book, or watch TV?
- Should you ride your exercise bicycle, or surf the Internet?
- Should you order a salad or a burger for lunch?

Even when you think you are making *good* choices—such as eating a diet based on recommended nutrients—you may *not* be making the *right* choices! Not if you are gluten sensitive.

In 1992, the U.S. government introduced the Food Guide Pyramid to Americans. This nutritional guide encouraged people to eat 6 to 11 servings of grains each day. In 2005, the Department of Agriculture replaced the old Food Guide Pyramid with MyPyramid.com, an interactive nutritional guide.

The new guidelines turn the pyramid on its side and put more emphasis on eating whole grains instead of refined grains. Grains—especially wheat—are a key part of the American diet.

But grains can make you sick if you are among the estimated 29 percent of Americans who are gluten sensitive.

So, if you want to eat healthy foods, you are faced with *new* choices. This part helps you make those decisions.

CHAPTER 11: SETTING YOURSELF FREE. In this chapter, you'll learn how to start and follow a gluten-free lifestyle.

CHAPTER 12: SUPPLEMENTING YOUR HEALTH. Severely gluten-sensitive individuals need an extra boost to make sure they are getting all the nutrients their body needs. This chapter tells what types of supplements you should take—and why.

CHAPTER 13: WHAT IF GOING GLUTEN-FREE DOESN'T WORK? Sometimes going gluten-free is not enough. You'll find out why—and what you can do next.

CHAPTER 14: WHY DIDN'T MY DOCTOR TELL ME ABOUT THIS? The world outside of the United States has understood the problem of gluten sensitivity since 1976—and has acted on it. Why have we lagged behind? This chapter will throw some light onto medical politics that affect your health.

# CHAPTER 11

## SETTING YOURSELF FREE

No pills. No shots. No medical or surgical solution. The only way to treat gluten sensitivity is to eliminate gluten from your diet.

If you are plagued by the chronic symptoms of conditions we described in Part 2 and suspect you are gluten sensitive, a gluten-free diet may make you well again. You have *nothing* to lose (except your symptoms) by trying it for at least 2 weeks. If your symptoms are severe, however, it may take up to 3 months to feel the positive effects of the diet. Isn't your health worth a 90-day investment?

The decision to go gluten-free may seem formidable because you think, "I won't be able to eat my favorite foods! I won't be able to go out to restaurants any more!"

Not so. Going gluten-free definitely means making changes in your nutritional sources and probably (but not necessarily) doing more cooking in your home. But it does not mean living the life of a gourmet hermit.

You will find that by eliminating gluten from your life, you will actually be setting yourself free. You will no longer suffer from the inexplicable symptoms that failed to respond to medication. You *will* feel better.

## LABEL READING

Probably the most arduous task confronting you is learning to read food labels.

In Europe, where gluten-free foods have been available for years, label reading is easy. Foods that meet Codex gluten-free standards can be labeled "gluten-free."

Codex is the abbreviated term for Codex Alimentarius, the food code of the World Health Organization. This food code is a collection of international food standards that cover all foods—raw or processed. Codex's goal is to protect the health of consumers and facilitate fair practices in the food trade.[1]

Codex standards state that a gluten-free food is:

- One consisting of or containing as ingredients such cereals as wheat, triticale (a hybrid form of wheat), rye, barley, or oats or their constituents, which have been rendered gluten-free

- One in which any ingredients normally present containing gluten have been substituted by other ingredients not containing gluten

The standard further defines gluten-free to mean "that the total nitrogen content of the gluten-containing cereal grains used in the product does not exceed 0.05 grams per 100 grams of these grains on a dry-matter basis."[2] The standard also dictates how manufacturers should test for gluten.

The world community recognized grain danger long ago. Codex adopted its original gluten-free standard in 1976.

Unfortunately, as of 2006, the United States still does not have a gluten-free standard, probably because until recently, the medical community did not believe that celiac disease (the worst type of gluten sensitivity) was prevalent in the United States. So, labeling foods gluten-free was not a priority.

That, however, is about to change. The Food Allergen Labeling and Consumer Protection Act of 2004 required the U.S. Food and Drug Administration to develop a proposed rule to define and permit the voluntary use of "gluten-free" labeling by August 2006, with a final rule due no later than August 2008.

In the meantime, all food manufacturers are required to list food allergens on food packaging as of January 1, 2006. Among the eight food allergens that must be listed is wheat. (The eight food allergens— milk, eggs, fish, crustacean shellfish, tree nuts, peanuts, wheat, and soybeans—account for 90 percent of known food allergies.)

Wheat is the primary gluten-containing grain used in food processing. But it is not the only one. Barley and, to a much lesser degree, rye (both gluten-containing grains) are also used in the manufacturing of some food products. Gluten is also used in the coatings of some pharmaceutical products.

So, until the FDA adopts gluten-free standards (and depending upon what those standards are), I recommend that you carefully read food labels, beginning with the food in your pantry, refrigerator, and freezer. Talk to your druggist about your prescriptions to make sure their coatings are gluten-free. Then move on to your cosmetics.

Yes, cosmetics. Cosmetic products—including lipsticks, lotions, and shampoo—may also contain gluten. For most people who are gluten sensitive, the gluten content of cosmetics should not pose a problem. But if you have a skin disorder, such as dermatitis herpetiformis, psoriasis, eczema, acne, or other type of dermatitis, it may be especially important to read labels, since it may be possible to absorb gluten through open lesions. (Note: No medical research has been done on the effect of gluten absorbed through the skin. But if you have dermatitis herpetiformis, using gluten-free cosmetics and shampoos may be advisable.)

## Unsafe Ingredients

Here are some of the obvious (and less than obvious) ingredient terms to look for on food and cosmetic labels:[3, 4]

- Amino peptide complex (from barley)
- Amp-isostearoyl hydrolyzed wheat protein
- Barley (including malted barley)
- Barley extract
- Brewer's yeast (unless prepared with a sugar molasses base)
- Disodium wheatgermamido peg2 sulfosuccinate
- Filler flour (this generally means wheat flour)
- Graham flour
- Hordeum vulgare (barley) extract
- Hydrolyzed vegetable protein or hydrolyzed wheat protein
- Hydrolyzed wheat gluten
- Hydrolyzed wheat starch
- Modified food starch (if the product is manufactured outside of the United States)
- Rye

- Triticum vulgare (wheat)
- Vegetable starch (it could be a mixture of starches, including wheat starch)
- Wheat (all types of wheat, including durum, semolina, spelt, kamut, bulgur, and triticale)
- Wheat amino acid
- Wheat bran extract
- Wheat dextrimaltose
- Wheat germ (extracts, glycerides, and oil)
- Wheat protein

In addition to these wheat-, rye- and barley-based gluten ingredients, I also recommend eliminating products that use oat-derived ingredients (usually found in cosmetics or shampoos) at least initially, especially if you have skin lesions. It's been my clinical experience that many people who are gluten sensitive do not tolerate oats well, even though oats do not contain gluten.

Oat-derived ingredients include:[5]

- Avena sativa (oat) flour
- Oat (avena sativa) extract
- Oat beta glucan
- Oat extract
- Oat flour
- Sodium lauroyl oat amino acids

## PANTRY PURGING

Now that you know which ingredients to look for (anything with wheat, barley, rye, and oats initially), it's time for you to raid the pantry.

When my coauthor's husband discovered he was gluten sensitive (*because of the research she did for this book!*), they made a meticulous foray into the foodstuffs stored in the refrigerator, freezer, and kitchen cupboards. While some things (such as flour and pancake mix) were "no-brainers," other items containing gluten surprised them. The lesson they learned: Read labels carefully; don't take *anything* for granted.

## Forbidden Foods

Here are *some* food items you want to purge from your pantry:

- Barbecue sauce (check the label for wheat or soy sauce)
- Beer and ale
- Bread, including hamburger and hot dog rolls
- Bread and cracker crumbs
- Breaded products (such as breaded chicken and fish)
- Cakes and cookies
- Canned and boxed soups (wheat is used as a thickener in most soups)
- Canned luncheon meat
- Cereal (even corn- and rice-based cereals; many use malt for flour, and malt is made from barley)
- Chocolate bars (check the label carefully)
- Chicken and beef broth (check to see if they contain wheat; some do not)
- Couscous
- Crackers
- Croutons
- Farina
- Flour
- Frozen vegetables with sauce packets
- Frozen prepared entrées
- Gravy (packaged and bottled)
- Ice cream cones
- Ice cream (if it contains gluten as a binder or in added ingredients, such as cookie dough; check the label carefully)
- Imitation bacon bits

- Imitation crab meat (surimi)
- Macaroni and spaghetti (and all other types of wheat-based pasta)
- Malt vinegar
- Meat marinades (with soy sauce)
- Noodles and noodle products
- Pie shells
- Pretzels
- Rice dinner mixes
- Salad dressings and meat marinades (if they contain wheat or soy sauce)
- Sausage products (check the label)
- Seitan (imitation meat made from wheat gluten)
- Soba noodles (unless they are 100 percent buckwheat)
- Soy sauce (unless it is specifically wheat-free or is labeled gluten-free)
- Stuffing mix
- Teriyaki sauce
- Vegetable side dishes that contain sauces or noodles

The list of "forbidden foods" is admittedly extensive. But if you examine it carefully, you'll see that its focus is *processed* foods—that is, foods that have been prepared for convenience.

## Safe Foods

Although the list of forbidden foods is extensive, you won't go hungry. Here are the things that are safe for you to eat or use in food preparation:

**Vegetables.** All vegetables are safe to eat (unless you have an allergy to them) and are an excellent source of needed vitamins and minerals. None contain gluten.

Best for you are fresh vegetables (preferably organically grown, so that they are not contaminated by pesticides and chemical fertilizers). Organic produce can provide up to six times (that's 600 percent!) more vitamins, minerals, and antioxidants when compared with conventionally grown produce. But, if fresh vegetables are not available, include frozen and even canned vegetables in your diet. (Always check the label to make sure frozen and canned vegetables do not have any gluten added to the processing.)

Be sure to include a variety of leafy green vegetables (such as broccoli, cabbage, collard greens, endive, escarole, kale, mustard greens, romaine lettuce, spinach, turnip greens, and watercress); yellow vegetables (such as carrots, pumpkin, sweet potatoes, and squash); legumes (peas, green beans, and lima beans); root vegetables (such as potatoes, turnips, and rutabaga); and other vegetables (such as asparagus, brussels sprouts, cabbage, cucumbers, eggplant, green and red peppers, mushrooms, okra, onions, radishes, tomatoes, and zucchini).

**Beverages.** All types of beverages make it to the "safe list," including coffee, tea, soda, and alcoholic products (wine and distilled spirits, but not beer).

*My recommendation:* Drink water (not tap unless it's run through a filter) and/or sparkling mineral water. It's the best no-calorie, thirst-quenching beverage. Unfiltered tap water can be loaded with pesticides, chemicals, prescription drugs, sewage waste, and parasites.

Stay away from sugar-sweetened drinks, especially in the initial stages of going gluten-free. Sugar-sweetened drinks can cause gas, and they are a major culprit in causing obesity and diabetes. I also recommend that you stay away from noncaloric beverages, especially those that contain aspartame. More adverse effects are associated with this artificial sweetener than any other on the market.

Additionally, the use of *any* sweetened beverage will keep you addicted to the taste of sweeteners. And—you may find this surprising—no noncaloric beverage has *ever* been shown to promote weight loss. In fact, numerous studies show that they may cause weight gain.

**Dairy products.** Provided you are not intolerant of dairy products, milk, yogurt, and hard and soft cheeses are okay to eat. I recommend, however, that you stop using dairy products when you first start your gluten-free diet, until your symptoms go away. (For more information on milk intolerance, see Chapter 13, What If Going Gluten-Free Doesn't Work?)

**Fruits.** Fruits provide needed nutrients and fiber. Fortunately, you can safely eat all fruits. Fresh is best, of course.

**Nuts.** Unless you have allergies to tree nuts and peanuts (which are actually a legume, not a nut), nuts are not only safe to eat, but they are also good for you, since they may help reduce cholesterol. They have a high fat content (unsaturated), however, so eat them in moderation.

**Meats, poultry, eggs, and fish.** No gluten, but lots of needed protein in these foods. Grilled and broiled are the best ways to preserve nutritional content.

**Grains.** You can eat all grains, *except* wheat, barley, and rye, since they contain gluten.

I also advise against consuming oats, at least until your symptoms subside. Although oats do not have known gluten content, they can become contaminated, since they may be grown in former wheat fields. Or contamination may occur during the processing stage of milling.

**Snacks.** Going on a gluten-free diet does not mean you have to give up snacks. As a nutritionist, I recommend snacking on nuts and fruit. But, realistically, I know how tempting other snack foods can be, especially salty snacks.

Potato chips and corn chips are okay, but be sure to check ingredients on the bag or container for gluten. Some flavored chips (such as barbecue flavor) contain gluten. Pressed potato chips that come in a paper may also contain gluten, which is used as a binder. Read the label carefully.

*My recommendation:* Choose baked snack products over those that are fried. If you eat popcorn, air-popped is a healthy source of fiber; microwave-popped is loaded with fat.

**Desserts.** Gelatin and boxed pudding mixes are on your "safe" list, as well as most ice creams and gelatos. (Avoid ice creams that have added ingredients, such as "cookie dough" or "cheesecake.") Although "regular" bakery items are taboo, you can eat baked goods prepared with wheat-flour substitutes. But all desserts other than fruit should be used only occasionally.

**Oils.** A well-balanced diet includes some unsaturated fats. A gluten-free diet can contain vegetable oils (preferably extra-virgin olive oil or coconut oil), butter, and margarine (nonhydrogenated, with no trans fats).

**Condiments.** Ketchup, salsa, herbs, pure spices, mustard, vinegars (except for malt vinegar), salad dressings, and marinades are gluten-free. *Exception:* Avoid any salad dressing or marinade that contains soy sauce.

**Sweeteners.** Sugar, honey, jellies and jams (preferably no-sugar-added and organic), and corn syrup are all safe to consume. Use in moderation, however.

When choosing sweeteners, look for those that have a naturally low glycemic index (GI), such as agave cactus and stevia. (The glycemic index is a numeric value given to the rate at which a particular food raises your blood sugar.[6] Refined sugars have a high GI.) You should know, however, that stevia is not approved as a sweetener by the FDA, despite its approval in many other countries. (The non-approval appears to be the result of politics, rather than of scientific disagreement.) Consequently, in the United States, stevia is sold as a dietary supplement.

Other low-GI sweeteners include sugar alcohols, such as xylitol and maltitol (which are also natural but may cause gas if you have inflammatory bowel disease [IBD]), and fructose. Remember, however, that any sugar can cause gas and loose stools in individuals with IBD.

Sucralose is another alternative. It is derived from sugar through a patented, multistep process that selectively substitutes three chlorine atoms for three hydrogen-oxygen groups on the sugar molecule. It appears to be well tolerated by most people and has a well-documented safety profile.

Do not use artificial sweeteners! As I indicated earlier, aspartame has more documented and proven adverse effects than any other artificial sweetener and should not be used by anyone.

**Miscellaneous foodstuffs.** Although you may not think of them as part of your diet, a number of ingredients are used in food preparation, either in baking or as thickeners. Arrowroot, baking soda and powder, cornstarch, cream of tartar, and yeast can be safely used.

## SUBSTITUTES

It should be clear by now that the only foods that do not belong on your well-balanced, gluten-free diet are those containing wheat, barley, and rye. Unfortunately, those three grains (especially wheat) are used as breakfast cereals, in side dishes, and in baked goods.

### Breakfast Cereals

You will be able to purchase online, in health food stores, and even in some mainstream grocery stores, hot and cold breakfast cereals that are similar in taste and texture to the many cereals you currently enjoy. Among the cereals you'll find are:

- Puffed millet
- Puffed rice
- Quinoa flakes
- Real corn flakes (without wheat added)

## Side Dishes

Although you can still eat many of the traditional side dishes you have always enjoyed, some will no longer be available to you, such as couscous and spaghetti.

Again, health food stores and online gluten-free shops can provide you with safe alternatives:

- Bean vermicelli
- Buckwheat
- Quinoa noodles
- Rice noodles (various sizes and shapes, many available in Asian markets)
- Spaghetti squash (an excellent pasta substitute)

## Flour Substitutes

If you are like most people who have grown up on the soft, gooey texture of white bread, or you have learned to savor the goodness of fresh-baked specialty breads and bagels, the one food item you will miss most on your new diet is bread.

Gluten—the protein that causes us so many problems—is the same protein that causes bread to rise and reach its chewy, savory consistency. You will be able to eat bread made from substitute grains, but regrettably it will not have the texture or consistency of the bread you have come to enjoy.

Nevertheless, you will be able to enjoy bread, buns, cakes, brownies, and other goodies. You will also be able to have crunchy or hot breakfast cereals. And you will be able to prepare side dishes similar to couscous (a forbidden food).

Here is a list of grain substitutes. I've indicated in which forms they are available (such as flour, grain, or flakes). Even if you do not bake, you will want to have some of these flour substitutes on hand, to use as thickeners or coatings.[7]

- **Almond meal or flour.** This flour is made from blanched, ground almonds and is used in sweet breads, cakes, and desserts.

- **Amaranth flour.** This is a flavorful flour that should be used in combination with other flours for added nutrition. In granular form, it can be added to soups or stews or be cooked for a hot cereal.

- **Besan (chickpea or garbanzo bean) flour.** This flour is popular in Middle Eastern cooking. It is often combined with fava beans for a blended flour. You may be able to find besan in Indian markets, as well as health food stores. You can even make your own by lightly roasting dried chickpeas, then grinding them in a blender or food processor until the mixture reaches the consistency of flour.

- **Buckwheat (soba) flour.** This grain has a unique taste that is especially good in quick and yeast breads. It can be substituted for other types of flours.

- **Buckwheat groats.** Groats are hulled buckwheat seeds that can be steamed, cooked like rice or as a hot cereal, or even milled at home into flour.

- **Buckwheat kernels (kasha).** Roasted buckwheat kernels can be used as a cereal or a side dish.

- **Corn (masa) flour.** Corn flour is used in many tortilla recipes. You can buy processed corn flour, but you can also make it from cornmeal in your blender.

- **Cornmeal.** Use this for corn bread. It is usually available in large grocery stores.

- **Fava bean flour.** This is often mixed with garbanzo bean flour to make garfava flour.

- **Flaxseed flour.** This flour is high in fiber and fat, as well as nutrients. Add a small amount for a nutty flavor and fiber.

- **Millet.** Hulled millet seed can be cooked as a hot cereal or as a side dish or can be added to bread recipes for a crunchy taste. It can be purchased as a seed, as a dry puffed cereal (similar to puffed rice), or as flour. You may be able to find millet in Indian markets, as well as health food stores.

- **Potato flour.** Use this flour in bread, pancake, and waffle recipes or as a thickener for smooth sauces, gravies, and soups.

- **Quinoa.** This is one of the oldest cultivated grains. It is high in protein, calcium, and iron. You can substitute quinoa flour for half of the all-purpose flour in many recipes or completely replace wheat flour in cakes and cookie recipes—even some breads. You can also purchase quinoa as cereal flakes (similar to wheat flakes) or as a grain, which can be cooked as a hot cereal or as a side dish.

- **Rice.** This is probably already in your pantry, either as white or whole-grain rice. Rice is also available as a flour (white and brown), which is a primary ingredient in many gluten-free bread recipes. Gluten-free puffed rice, ready-to-eat cereal is also available.

- **Sorghum (milo) flour.** This flour provides excellent flavor (similar to that of wheat) and nutrition. You can substitute sorghum for wheat flour in bread, cake, and quick-bread recipes, although because it tends to crumble easily, it is better to use it in combination with other flours, such as rice flour. It is generally available in Indian markets.

- **Soy flour.** This flour is made from ground soybeans. It has a slightly nutty flavor and can be used in combination with other wheat-flour substitutes. Soy flour is also used to condition bread dough. Try adding 1 tablespoon for each cup of flour for a lighter loaf.

- **Tapioca flour.** This flour is not made from grain but rather from cassava (yucca) root. It is a starchy, slightly sweet, white flour. Use up to ½ cup per recipe to sweeten breads made with rice and millet flour. You may be able to find this flour in Hispanic food markets, as well as health food stores.

- **Teff.** This is a very fine Ethiopian grain. Cooked, it makes a farina-like cereal. Ground into a very fine flour, it is used to make a traditional spongy flat bread, called injera.

- **Yam flour.** This flour can be used in cookies, piecrusts, and other baked goods.

# GROCERY SHOPPING

Picture, for a moment, your favorite grocery store. Walk around the exterior aisle. Except for the bakery/deli section (which is usually one of the first areas you come to), the food items you find on the outside aisle of your grocery store are fresh foods—meats, dairy, fruits, and vegetables. Processed foods are shelved on the inside aisles and freezers. (Exception: Canned and frozen vegetables and fruits without extra sauces or processing are generally gluten-free.)

You must carefully read the labels of anything that is packaged, but you have an abundance of delicious fresh food from which to select your menu.

Prepare your grocery list, take a list of forbidden ingredients and foods with you (until you have it burnt into your memory), and read every label before you put an item in your grocery cart. Grocery shopping will take longer than usual, but you don't want to take any packaged food for granted.

Unfortunately, you won't be able to find everything you want or need at your local grocery. Just as the medical community has been slow in accepting the prevalence of gluten sensitivity, so has the U.S. food industry been slow in recognizing the huge market for gluten-free foods, especially flours, breads, confections, and convenience foods.

That will change in time. But for now, you will have to use other resources:

**Health food stores.** Health food stores have the foods that you need (especially prepared foods). And their employees are generally knowledgeable and are customer-service oriented. These people know about gluten-free diets! You don't have to explain anything to them. Just tell them you are starting a gluten-free diet and need some help getting started.

**Health food departments.** Some mainstream groceries are entering the gluten-free market, albeit very slowly, with an aisle or two of health foods, some of which are gluten-free. A few chain groceries have sections devoted to gluten-free foods and make it a point to carry products that are labeled gluten-free by food manufacturers. (See Chapter 16, Gluten-Free Cooking 101, for shopping resources.)

**Online shopping.** Once you get "over the hump" in buying your first gluten-free foods in person, you may choose to venture into online shopping. Many resources are available to you—some are direct from food processors, others in virtual stores.

Online shopping has several advantages: You can do it 24/7; you are unlimited in the variety of goods you can purchase; and you may save money, especially if you deal directly with food manufacturers. (See page 279 for some excellent resources.)

**Specialty markets.** Some of the grains and flours you may want to try are used extensively by people of other cultures. If you live in an area rich in diversity, you may be able to find specialty markets in which to purchase these grains and flours.

## EATING OUT

Going gluten-free does *not* mean you are doomed to eating your own home-cooked foods day after day. Gluten sensitivity is not a handicap! It is a condition. And just as people who have diabetes and food allergies learn to deal with their conditions, so can you.

Asking questions and speaking up about your dietary needs are important. Restaurateurs are accommodating of people with special needs—especially food allergies. Because of the possible legal ramifications involved in serving customers with allergies the wrong food, they take extra caution to meet customer needs. The customer just has to make those needs known.

Yes—I know. Gluten sensitivity is *not* an allergy. But when you go to a restaurant for a meal, your goal is to eat a good, healthy meal. Meeting that goal is contingent on communicating your needs. Your server and the chef may not understand the term "gluten sensitivity." But they will understand "wheat allergy."

You will find that you can eat in any type of restaurant of any ethnic origin—even in restaurants you typically associate with gluten-containing foods, such as Italian restaurants. You simply have to choose your foods wisely, ask questions, let your special needs be known, and enjoy the food.

### Basic Restaurant Rules

Eating in a restaurant calls for "gluten common sense." Here are some tips:

**Have a snack before you go.** Especially if you are eating late, have a light snack before going to the restaurant. That way, you won't be tempted to reach for the hot bread.

**Tell your server you have a "wheat allergy."** As I indicated earlier, it's a small fib that will communicate efficiently your need to avoid wheat, barley, and rye.

Even better than telling your server about your "allergy"—use a restaurant card.

Many gluten-sensitive people carry a "calling card" to give to the server when ordering. The card indicates that you have a wheat allergy and need to refrain from eating foods prepared with wheat flour, including any sauces or gravies prepared with flour, croutons, bread, or soy sauce.

Ask the waiter to give the card to the chef. Restaurant kitchens are hectic areas. Verbal instructions are lost in the confusion. The restaurant card helps to minimize this confusion.

You can write and print your own restaurant card, or download free cards, available online. You can also purchase cards written in English and in other languages, especially helpful if you are traveling abroad or if you patronize restaurants owned and operated by native speakers. (Resources for these restaurant cards are given on page 278.)

**Bypass fried food.** It isn't good for you anyway! But aside from the dubious nutritional value of fried foods, these items are battered. And the batter is almost always wheat-based. Consequently, the oil in which foods are fried may be contaminated with gluten.

**Stick to plain protein, potatoes or rice, and vegetables.** Avoid sauces and gravies. Grilled or broiled meat, fish, or poultry basted with olive oil and lemon juice is a good choice. If you order rice, ask if it is cooked in chicken broth. Many broths contain gluten.

**Order naked salads.** No croutons, please. You don't want gluten crumbs in your greens.

**Use only oil and vinegar salad dressing.** And do it yourself. Although most bottled salad dressings do not contain gluten, you do not know the composition of commercial dressings. And some do have gluten, especially Asian-style dressings, which contain soy sauce. Better to limit your choice to mix-it-yourself oil and vinegar than to suffer gluten consequences later.

**Substitute rice, beans, lentils, or potatoes for pasta.** In Italian restaurants, ask for risotto instead of pasta.

## Restaurant Choices

Some gluten-sensitive people find that eating in family-owned or independent restaurants gives them more freedom. The owners or chefs are more accommodating of special needs because they prepare food from scratch, rather than purchase semiprepared goods in bulk from a central supply.

Although in any community, you will find many more independently owned restaurants than chain dining establishments, chains have spread throughout the country. Whether these restaurants sacrifice quality for quantity is a matter of taste. One good thing about chains, however, is that when they respond to the needs of the gluten-free community, the response is throughout the country, not just in one establishment.

Today, you are able to eat gluten-free in more than 70 chain restaurants.[8] And yes, fast-food and casual restaurants are among them. I don't recommend a steady diet of fast food because of its high fat content and imbalance of nutrients. But if you occasionally take a meal in one of these restaurants, order your sandwiches without a bun, don't order breaded foods (such as chicken, fish, or onion rings), and make sure that the french fries are cooked in a dedicated fryer.

Here are some of the chain restaurants that offer gluten-free items on their menus.[9] I suggest checking out their Web sites; many have gluten-free nutrition information available online, and some have gluten-free menus posted.

Even if you patronize a restaurant with a gluten-free menu, always tell your server that you are "allergic" to wheat, barley, and rye.

- Arby's, www.arbys.com[10]
- Bennigan's, www.bennigans.com[11]
- Blimpie, www.blimpie.com[9]
- Bob Evans Farms, www.bobevans.com[9]
- Bonefish Grill, www.bonefishgrill.com[12]
- Boston Market, www.bostonmarket.com[10]
- Burger King, www.bk.com[9]
- California Pizza Kitchen, www.cpk.com[10]
- Carrabba's Italian Grill, www.carrabbas.com[11]
- Chevys Fresh Mex, www.chevys.com[10]

- Chick-fil-A, www.chick-fil-a.com[11]
- Chili's, www.chilis.com[10]
- Chipotle, www.chipotle.com[10]
- Dairy Queen, www.dairyqueen.com[10]
- Denny's, www.dennys.com[9]
- Don Pablo's, www.donpablos.com[9]
- Fuddruckers, www.fuddruckers.com[10]
- Hard Rock Cafe, www.hardrock.com[10]
- Legal Sea Foods, www.legalseafoods.com[11]
- Lone Star Steakhouse and Saloon, www.lonestarsteakhouse.com[10]
- McDonald's, www.mcdonalds.com[9]
- Romano's Macaroni Grill, www.macaronigrill.com[10]
- Olive Garden, www.olivegarden.com[10]
- Outback Steakhouse, www.outback.com[11]
- Panera Bread, www.panerabread.com[9]
- P.F. Chang's, www.pfchangs.com[11]
- Ryan's Grill Buffet and Bakery, www.ryans.com[9]
- Smokey Bones Barbeque and Grill, www.smokeybones.com[10]
- Steak n Shake, www.steaknshake.com[9]
- Subway, www.subway.com[10]
- Taco Bell, www.tacobell.com[9]
- TCBY, www.tcby.com[10]
- Ted's Montana Grill, www.tedsmontanagrill.com[11]
- Wendy's, www.wendys.com[9]
- Whataburger, www.whataburger.com[9]

## PARTYING

Holidays and special gatherings with friends and family can be another trying time to people on a gluten-free diet. All of those delightful cookies, cakes, and treats! And meals! What to do?

Here are some tips:

**Talk to your host.** Before the party, tell your host about your special dietary concerns and find out what will be on the menu. It's not that you expect your host or hostess to cook special items for you. But you want to know what you should avoid.

**Volunteer to bring a food item.** The salad, side dish, or entrée you make will be gluten-free. You will have at least one item you can eat with gusto. And if you take a dessert, you can have a worry-free after-dinner sweet.

**Snack ahead of time.** Or have dinner before you go to the party. Then, if you find nothing (or few items) gluten-free on the buffet table, you won't be tempted to partake of a toxic item.

**Eat salad and vegetables.** Unless the salad is loaded with croutons, it is a safe alternative for you. Just make sure the salad dressing is gluten-free, too. Plain vegetables are another good option.

**Keep in mind what you can eat.** Not all party food is forbidden. You can't have beer, but you can have wine, soft drinks, and distilled alcoholic beverages.

You can't have crackers, but you can have cheese, plain corn chips (not flavored, unless you know they're gluten-free), and potato chips (but not processed canned chips, which contain gluten).

You can't have sandwiches, but you can have the lunchmeats (ham, turkey, or chicken, for example).

You can't have cakes or cookies, but you can have gelatin, pudding, most ice creams, and sorbet.

You can't have pasta salad, but you can have potato salad.

## FIRST STEPS

The only thing that is left for you to do is to start. Don't delay a second longer. I have a few more words of advice to help you on your way to a good life:

**Find a friend.** That friend may be a nutritionist who can guide you in your choice of foods and supplements. But if you cannot afford to go to a nutritionist, seek support through groups, either in person or at least online. Going gluten-free is an emotional decision that does affect your lifestyle to some extent. Having a gluten-free friend will help you maintain perspective.

**Go easy on raw veggies.** If you have severe gastrointestinal symptoms, your doctor has probably eliminated raw vegetables from your diet. Go easy on yourself during the initial stages of your healing. You may not be able to tolerate salads or raw or al dente vegetables initially. The goal is to eliminate gastrointestinal inflammation. So, to do this, reintroduce vegetables slowly and judiciously.

Prepare soups, and cook the vegetables until they are soft. Or steam them, and then puree them. These cooking methods help break down the fiber and make the vegetables more digestible.

When you start eating salads, chop the greens into fine pieces. Again, the chopping helps to break down the fiber and assist your digestion.

Don't worry. You won't have to do this forever—just until your symptoms go away. Then you will be able to introduce more-palatable vegetables to your diet.

**Make water your beverage of choice.** As I indicated earlier, sugary drinks may cause gas, especially if you have severe gastrointestinal symptoms. Drink lots of water, even bottled or sparking mineral water.

**Remember: You *always* have a choice.** Going gluten-free is a choice—your choice to improve your quality of life and to live symptom-free. Make the right choice for life.

# CHAPTER 12

## SUPPLEMENTING YOUR HEALTH

Once you have taken control over gluten by eliminating it from your diet—and you have given a gluten-free diet an adequate trial (from 2 weeks up to 3 months if you have severe symptoms)—you will be on your road to recovery.

You can—and should—give your recovery a boost, however, with dietary supplementation. Supplementation is important for improving immune function and detoxification, for decreasing oxidative stress and inflammation, and for healing and restoring mucosal integrity and the functioning of the gastrointestinal tract.

Immediately upon beginning your new dietary regimen, start taking the supplements listed under Stage 1.

After about 3 weeks, add the supplements in Stage 2. *A word of caution:* If you have inflammatory bowel disease (IBD), irritable bowel syndrome (IBS), or any other gastrointestinal problem as the key manifestation of gluten sensitivity, before you start Stage 2 supplementation, give the gluten-free (and casein-free) diet a fair chance to work their magic. My experience with patients is that when gluten and casein peptides are the culprits of intestinal disorders, and they are totally removed from the diet, the healing process that occurs just from this restriction is nothing short of amazing.

Finally, when you are feeling substantially better, add the supplements in Stage 3.

## STAGE 1 SUPPLEMENTATION

The supplements listed under Stage 1 will provide you with all the multinutrients and the major antioxidants your body requires. Begin taking them when you start your gluten-free diet.

## Multivitamins and Minerals

I recommend using a full-spectrum multivitamin/mineral supplement that provides the approximate amounts of nutrients described below. These nutrients are usually available in a multinutrient formulation that recommends a daily dose of four to six tablets or capsules. Split the dose in half, and take the tablets or capsules twice daily with meals—one half-dose with breakfast and one half-dose with dinner.

These types of multinutrients are available as tablets, capsules, and even as powders. Experiment with various delivery systems, because you may find that you have a personal preference for digesting capsules, tablets, or powders.

I have listed *optimal* amounts of nutrients, based on my revolutionary ODIs—Optimal Daily Intakes—which are generally more than a 1-per-day multinutrient formula provides.

Remember: These are *guidelines* to make choosing a supplement easier. Since various brands use different formulas, if a brand you choose does not have the amount of a nutrient listed below, consider supplementing with an additional amount of that nutrient.[1]

Below, you will find general recommendations based on a multivitamin formula that recommends four to six tablets or capsules per day. Several multinutrient powders provide these amounts as well.

*Note:* For a more in-depth look at detailed dietary supplements for specific disorders, consider consulting *The Real Vitamin & Mineral Book*.

- **Vitamin A:** 5,000 IU

- **Beta-carotene** (natural only): 11,000 IU

- **Vitamin $D_3$:** 400 IU

- **Vitamin E** (d-alpha-tocopheryl succinate): 400 IU

- **B complex:** A good-quality B-complex or multivitamin supplement generally will supply at least 25 milligrams each of thiamin ($B_1$), riboflavin ($B_2$), niacin ($B_3$), pyridoxine ($B_6$), pantothenic acid, PABA, choline, and inositol. It also may contain about 12 to 25 micrograms of vitamin $B_{12}$, 400 micrograms of folic acid, and 300 micrograms of biotin.

- **Folic acid:** 400 micrograms

- **Cyano- or methylcobalamin** ($B_{12}$): 25 micrograms

- **Boron:** 3 milligrams
- **Calcium:** 500 milligrams
- **Chromium:** 200 micrograms
- **Copper:** 0.5 milligrams (This is in many foods, so it is not critical to take as a supplement.)
- **Iodine:** 150 micrograms (unless you have a known reactivity to iodine)
- **Iron:** Take this only if you have a known iron deficiency and no active IBD. Supplementation can exacerbate inflammation and should be used only under professional guidance.
- **Magnesium:** 250 milligrams
- **Manganese:** 15 milligrams
- **Selenium:** 100 micrograms
- **Phosphorus and potassium:** You can get these easily through food, so supplementation is generally not necessary (though most multivitamins contain them).
- **Calcium and magnesium:** Your aim is an intake of 1,000 to 1,500 milligrams of calcium and 500 to 750 milligrams of magnesium daily *from a combination of supplements and diet.* If your diet does not provide this amount, you may need to add calcium and magnesium supplementation *in addition to your multivitamin/mineral formula.*
- **Vitamin D:** Additional vitamin D supplementation may also be necessary to prevent/treat bone loss. Recent research has shown that if you have very little sun exposure and wear sunscreen, you may be at risk for vitamin D deficiency! Your licensed health-care provider can have a simple blood analysis done for you to see if your levels of vitamin D are too low. If that is the case, you may require 2,000 to 4,000 IU of additional vitamin D. You can always seek the advice of an experienced clinician for a more individualized program.

### Fish Oil

Your body needs a number of different types of fatty acids to maintain good health. Among these are omega-3 and omega-6 fatty acids. These fatty acids, however, must be in balance.

Omega-3 essential fatty acids—eicosapentaenoic acid (EPA) and docosahexanoic acid (DHA)—are "good fats" that your body cannot produce on its own. EPA and DHA are used to create hormonal-like compounds known as prostaglandins, which (among other things) induce inflammation.

A good source for omega-3 fatty acids is fish oil.

Fish oil has been shown in numerous studies to be therapeutic for IBD and autoimmune disease. Fish oil also protects against heart disease and sudden death. It is important for bone health, and it is protective and potentially therapeutic for cancer, since it may halt the spread of metastasis. It is also essential for healthy skin and hair.

Although you can get omega-3 fatty acids from flax and walnuts, I recommend fish oil over them. The reason: Flax and walnuts first break down into another omega-3 fatty acid—alpha-linolenic acid—before undergoing several more enzymatic steps to become the more active EPA and DHA.

The more work your body has to go through to get to the EPA and DHA, the longer it takes. Fish oil gets faster results. And fish oil has also been studied more extensively than flaxseed oil. Its benefits are well documented.

Omega-6 fatty acids are commonly found in most vegetable oils as linoleic acid and are used by the body to form inflammatory prostaglandins. Arachidonic acid is another omega-6 fatty acid that is found in most meats, especially commercial beef and chicken, which comes from animals that are fed corn products and other foods that are deficient in omega-3 fatty acids but are rich sources of omega-6.

You need to be aware that inflammation is not all bad. We need an inflammatory response to activate our immune system and to heal. Chronic inflammation, of course, is another matter. When inflammation reaches that stage, it becomes an issue.

Chronic inflammation stimulates an overactive immune system and creates the potential for tissue and organ damage. It is a culprit in almost every disease.

We need both omega-3 and omega-6 fatty acids. But we need them in proper balance. Our ancestors consumed a diet with a balance of omega-6 and omega-3 fatty acids of approximately 1:1 to 2:1.

Today, because of the limited sources of omega-3 in our diets, we consume a diet of omega-6 to omega-3 of approximately 30:1! So most of us are walking around in state of chronic inflammation. No wonder there is so much research on EPA and DHA (omega-3 fatty acids) showing their therapeutic benefit on so many illnesses!

With respect to inflammatory bowel disease, EPA- and DHA-rich fish oil works like "natural" cortisone. It can dramatically reduce inflammation without the negative side effects associated with steroids.

Fish oil is safe and natural. You can find fish oil capsules, as well as liquid supplements, that taste quite good. Fish oil supplements should not have an offensive smell when you open the bottle. (A slight smell is okay.) If they do, the capsules may contain impurities that are causing rancidity.

Fish oil supplements also last longer if you store them in the refrigerator, where the low temperature also decreases the odor. Pharmaceutical-grade fish oil (which I take) has virtually no smell at all.

Many of the research studies conducted on fish oil required subjects to take as many as 9 to 12 capsules per day to overcome the inflammatory influence of omega-6 fatty acids in the diet.

*My recommendation:* Take a daily dose of four to six capsules (approximately 2 to 3 grams) of fish oil or the equivalent as a liquid. This amount will allow you to maintain a lower-fat diet (not more than 20 percent) yet reap the benefits of fish oil in controlling inflammation.[1]

If you find that fish oil "repeats" on you, check to make sure the capsules are not rancid. This is a primary cause. Also:

- Buy pharmaceutical-grade fish oil. This grade will be noted on the bottle.

- Look for enteric-coated fish oil. The coating stops the supplement from dissolving until it gets to the stomach.

## Coenzyme $Q_{10}$

Coenzyme $Q_{10}$ ($CoQ_{10}$) is known as ubiquinone because it is ubiquitous: It exists everywhere in the body.

Although $CoQ_{10}$ is not an essential nutrient because we make it in our bodies, chronically ill people do not make enough $CoQ_{10}$ to supply their needs. It is a powerful antioxidant, and a great amount of research has shown that it is important for both the prevention and treatment of many degenerative diseases, including heart disease and cancer.

The most important reason to supplement your diet with $CoQ_{10}$ is that it is crucial to supplying energy to every cell in your body. One of the reasons sick people feel so tired and achy is that illness and certain drugs such as statins deplete $CoQ_{10}$.

*My recommendation:* Take at least 100 to 200 milligrams per day of $CoQ_{10}$.[1]

## STAGE 2 SUPPLEMENTATION

Begin taking the two supplements listed here after you have been on your gluten-free diet for 2 to 3 weeks. By that time, you should begin feeling much better, although you won't be completely healed.

The supplements I recommend adding at this stage are additional antioxidants, which are important in regulating the immune function and decreasing inflammation. They are essential in the defense against oxidative stress, which occurs when toxic free radicals are formed at a rate greater than the amount we can handle with our body's antioxidant defense mechanisms.

Imagine rust forming around metal—a great visual for oxidative stress. Antioxidants stop the rust from forming.

Oxidation can occur anywhere in your body and in any cell. The multinutrient formula you started taking at Stage 1 should provide enough of the *major* antioxidants you need. Additional vitamin C and quercetin will further reduce inflammation and improve antioxidant defense.

*My recommendation:* Take 1,000 to 4,000 milligrams of vitamin C (buffered, nonacidic) per day, and 500 to 2,000 milligrams of quercetin per day.

## STAGE 3 SUPPLEMENTATION

As you continue on your gluten-free diet and the supplements in Stages 1 and 2, your body will continue to get better. Symptoms will go away. And finally, you will be substantially healed.

It is at this time—at least 1 month into your gluten-free diet—that I recommend taking Stage 3 supplements, which aid in the restoration of the intestine.

Intestinal restoration is an important part of therapy, especially in those with celiac disease (CD) or IBD caused by gluten and/or casein sensitivity.

Stage 3 supplements can dramatically improve the immune function in the gastrointestinal (GI) tract, heal the intestinal villi, increase protective mucin synthesis, and decrease intestinal permeability so that large peptides (such as a gluten) do not enter the bloodstream from the GI tract.

But—you may get a lot of gas from these supplements if your intestine is not completely healed. So, be patient before starting on these supplements.

Here are the additional dietary supplements to consider:

## Acidophilus and Other Beneficial Microorganisms

A number of "friendly," or "good," floras inhabit our gastrointestinal tract. These floras keep unfriendly (bad) microorganisms at bay.

Our GI tract is never sterile, nor would we want it to be. But the body struggles to maintain a balance between good and bad microorganisms. We want the beneficial floras to win, but constant inflammation and immune disruption cause the bad microorganisms to flourish.

Many food products contain beneficial microorganisms, such as:[2]

- *Lactobacillus acidophilus*

- *Lactobacillus bifidus*

- *Lactobacillus brevis*

- *Lactobacillus casei* GG

- *Lactobacillus cellobiosus*

- *Lactobacillus fermenti*

- *Lactobacillus leichmannii*

- *Lactobacillus plantarum*

- *Lactobacillus salivarius*

- *Lactobacillus sporogenes*

- *Saccharomyces boulardii* (This is available only by itself and is discussed below.)

- *Bifidobacterium* spp.

- *Enterococcus faecium*

- *Streptococcus thermophilus*

These beneficial bacteria can be purchased as supplements, either alone, such as *L. acidophilus* or *L. bifidus,* or in combination with the other beneficial flora that are listed.

*Saccharomyces boulardii* is a beneficial yeast that is sold by itself as a supplement. Research demonstrates that *S. boulardii* is rather specific for those who have been treated heavily with antibiotics and have developed antibiotic-resistant bacteria such as *Clostridium difficile.*

To reestablish the gut's beneficial flora after treatment with antibiotics, I recommend taking a *Lactobacillus* supplement, as well as the *S. boulardii.* A minimum therapeutic dose of *S. boulardii* is 500 milligrams per day. However, if you have developed antibiotic-resistant bacteria (such as *C. difficile*), you may have to take up to 3 grams per day to eradicate the bacteria.

Take *S. boulardii* (sold as Florastor) by itself to minimize gas. Always follow label directions for the best times to take the supplements and whether you should take them with meals or between meals.

The other friendly floras on the list are generally taken as anywhere from 1 billion to 10 billion viable organisms, rather than as milligrams.[2, 3, 4, 5]

A number of companies manufacture excellent dietary supplements containing one or more of these floras. In my clinical experience, I have found that *L. casei GG* (sold as Culturelle) is an excellent supplement to promote healthy flora. The company supports the product with excellent research.

Supplements such as *L. casei GG* also have the ability to improve immune function in the GI tract and may protect against bacteria and viral infection by improving mucosal integrity. Since different supplements provide different doses of the beneficial flora, it is best to follow label directions.[2, 3, 4, 5]

*My recommendations:*

- *L. casei GG*—Take 1 or 2 capsules each day.
- *S. boulardii*—Take 500 milligrams each day for antibiotic-resistant bacteria such as *C. difficile.* Consider taking 3 grams daily for an active *C. difficile* infection.

## Glutamine

Glutamine is an important amino acid in the GI tract because it modulates inflammation and promotes repair mechanisms. While it is not considered essential, because the body can actually produce it, we synthesize large quantities of it to produce from 30 to 35 percent of our total amino acid pool.

Glutamine is necessary for the synthesis of glucosamine, which, in turn, is necessary for the synthesis of mucin, the protective layer in the gut. (Research has shown that patients with Crohn's disease and ulcerative colitis have diminished amounts of the enzyme responsible for the biosynthesis of mucin.)

Glutamine is important for nourishing and restoring the intestinal villi that have been affected by immune reactivity and inflammation. It also helps prevent bacteria from attaching to the intestinal wall and growing and spreading.

Glutamine is indispensable for the formation of glutathione, a major antioxidant. Glutathione helps the liver detoxify the many toxins that we are exposed to in our environment, as well as those that form internally.

We form more toxins when we are sick and inflamed and when our immune systems are impaired. We are less able to clear these toxins when we do not have enough vitamins, minerals, antioxidants, and other nutrients such as glutamine, which support our body's detoxification mechanisms.

Supplemental doses of glutamine range from 1 gram to 8 grams per day. Some practitioners use higher doses if necessary.[4, 5, 6]

*My recommendation:* Take 500 to 3,000 milligrams of L-glutamine. Higher doses should be taken only under professional advice.

## Phosphatidylcholine

Phosphatidylcholine (PC) may prevent collagen deposition and stricture formation that can occur when colonic tissue is inflamed. In animal studies, it was shown to reduce colitis, decrease permeability, and heal the intestinal mucosa.

PC is available in capsule and granule forms. Follow label directions for capsules, since it comes in different strengths. If you are using the granules (which are generally less expensive), take from 1 to 3 tablespoons each day, mixed in juice (or half juice, half water) or just about any cold or room-temperature beverage.[5, 6]

*My recommendation:* A daily dose of 100 to 300 milligrams. However, PC is generally derived from either soy or chicken yolks, so if you have sensitivity to either of these, try a lower dose first.

## Fiber

Fiber is great for keeping the intestines and bowels healthy and regular and for detoxification. Soluble fiber, such as psyllium and ground flax-seeds, is fermented by colonic bacteria and forms the short-chain fatty acids butyrate, acetate, and proprionate, which are the primary fuel sources for the colon. Fiber decreases the pH of the intestines, which encourages the growth of beneficial flora and suppresses the growth of the bad bacteria.[5]

If you add fiber to your diet, start with 1 tablespoon per day, added to food or beverages. You can increase the amount as needed, up to 3 tablespoons per day, or as tolerated.

I would not recommend taking a fiber supplement initially unless you are constipated or do *not* have IBD. The reason: Fiber can cause excessive gas if the digestive tract is inflamed.

Fiber is available in various forms. I am a fan of flaxseeds, which are a tasty and better alternative than flaxseed oil. Ground flaxseeds give you the beneficial fiber, omega-3 fatty acids, and lignans that are superb for promoting hormonal health.

Common sources of supplemental fiber that you should not use are wheat and barley bran, which may contain gluten, or oat bran, which may be contaminated with gluten.

*My recommendation:* 1 to 2 tablespoons of fiber supplement. Follow the label directions.

## Other Anti-Inflammatories

A number of other specific dietary supplements, such as *Boswellia serrata,* bromelain, turmeric,[6] and SierraSil, may also help decrease inflammation and can be taken if needed.[7]

## Additional Dietary Supplements

Many of my colleagues and I often recommend more-active forms of specific dietary supplements, depending upon the needs of our patients. A practitioner who specializes in nutritional biochemistry can determine if you should take these types of supplements, which may include:[1]

- **Pyridoxal-5-phosphate** (the active form of vitamin $B_6$)
- **Methylcobalamin** (the active form of $B_{12}$, often given sublingually or by injection)

- **Folinic acid** (the active form of folic acid)

Additionally, practitioners sometimes recommend additional supplements to help the body rid itself of toxins. Many of these recommendations are based on laboratory evaluation of toxic metals, detoxification pathways, and even genetic issues that can affect our ability to detoxify.

Based on the results of these evaluations, practitioners well versed in detoxification may recommend:

- N-acetylcysteine

- Glutathione

- Milk thistle (silymarin)

- Garlic

- Artichoke

- Turmeric

- Infrared saunas to assist the body in eliminating toxins

If you have been sick for some time, I would recommend that a more intensive detoxification be done under professional advice.

| The Best Ways to Take Your Supplements |
|---|
| 1. Always take your supplements with food—unless otherwise instructed on the label of the bottle. For example: It is recommended that some acidophilus supplements be taken between meals. |
| 2. Start slowly—especially with gastrointestinal disorders. If you have IBS, IBD, CD, or any other gastrointestinal disorder, you may want to add the supplements slowly, starting with the lower dose. For example: If you are going to take a six-per-day multivitamin, instead of immediately starting with two at each meal, try one with each meal for a few days. |
| 3. Start with a lower dose. If you have IBS, IBD, CD, or any other GI disorder, you may want to start with the lower dose of a particular supplement. For example: You may want to try 500 milligrams of vitamin C for several days before going up to a dose of 1 gram or more each day. |
| 4. Store your supplements in a cool, dry place. You can store fish oil in the refrigerator if you prefer. |
| 5. Always check expiration dates of your supplements. If they are expired, throw them away and buy new ones. The potency of most supplements will last 6 to 12 months after the container is opened. |
| 6. Find your preference. Experiment with taking tablets, capsules, and powders. See which works best for you. |

## ENZYMES TO THE RESCUE

Supplementation will help heal you and will help keep you healthy. But "gluten slips" happen.

What happens if you are eating out or are on the road and you inadvertently eat some gluten? Are you doomed to suffer the full consequences?

Fortunately, you have a remedy—digestive enzymes.

A study was conducted with 21 CD patients who were in remission.[8] The study involved challenging them with a modest amount of gluten every day over a period of 2 weeks and giving the experimental group an enzyme extract three times a day. (The control group was given a placebo.)

The enzyme therapy significantly reduced symptoms in the experiment group compared with those taking the placebo. The most common symptom reported in these individuals was abdominal pain and bloating, rather than diarrhea.

This study demonstrates that enzyme therapy can substantially minimize symptoms in people with CD who are exposed to gluten. It would also be effective for gluten-sensitive individuals who experience gastrointestinal symptoms when exposed to gluten.

Unfortunately, the study looked *only* at serum levels of antibodies and intestinal biopsies. It is unlikely that a recovered CD patient would have full-blown villous atrophy in a matter of 2 weeks when exposed to a modest amount of gluten. Therefore, the symptom scores were a better indicator of the benefit of the enzyme therapy.

The enzyme used was a proprietary, patented animal enzyme formula called Glutenon (Glutagen Pty. Ltd., Melbourne, Australia). At the time of publication, this enzyme was not yet available in the United States. But it may be soon; search for it on the Internet.

Although the tested enzyme is currently unavailable, a number of other enteric-coated enzyme preparations are available to you. One of the most studied enteric-coated enzyme preparations is Wobenzym N (Mucos Pharma, GmbH & Co., Berlin, Germany). It is available in the United States and is backed by more than 25 years of extensive research.

Wobenzym N is a patented multi-enzyme product with a proprietary blend of proteolytic (protein-digesting) enzymes. Enteric coating ensures that the tablet will not be digested by stomach acid and will instead move into your lower intestines before the active enzymes are released to do their job.

This is why an enteric-coated enzyme can help alleviate some of the gas and bloating: It works where the gluten causes the inflammation—in the intestines. Also, protein is digested in the intestines, not in the stomach. Since gluten is a protein, this type of enzyme can help digest it and render it less irritating.

While the enzyme won't completely eliminate the problem, it may help alleviate at least some of the gas and bloating that many gluten-sensitive and CD patients experience when they eat gluten but may not know it until after the fact.

*My recommendation:* Always carry this type of enzyme with you. Make sure that whichever enteric-coated enzyme preparation you use provides proteolytic enzymes. They are the *only* enzymes that digest protein.

I can also say from clinical experience that some people feel better and digest their food better when they use enteric-coated enzymes. Follow the label directions, since formulation strength varies among brands.

As a preventive measure—when you don't have perfect control over what you're eating—it is best to take enteric-coated enzymes on an empty stomach—at least 30 minutes before a meal. If you miss that opportunity, take them as soon as possible after you eat. Always carry the enzyme with you, so you have it when you need it. But don't take enzymes and think that you can continue eating gluten if it is causing you health problems. *This is not a cure.* Research has shown that the enzymes may simply help the symptoms of gas and bloating.

# CHAPTER 13

## WHAT IF GOING GLUTEN-FREE DOESN'T WORK?

I learned a long time ago that every problem has *at least* one solution—but sometimes, the solution is not easy or simple. If you experience symptoms that suggest gluten sensitivity, a strict gluten-free diet often brings results in as little as 2 weeks. But sometimes, it doesn't. Be patient. Give it a try (no cheating!) for up to 3 months. Remember that problems a long time in the making take a long time in solving.

### CROSS-REACTIVITY

A gluten-free diet is the single, easy solution to one problem—gluten sensitivity. But the human body is a complex mechanism, a sum of our environment, the food we eat—and genetics. Often, all these conditions predispose us to concurrent problems that are similar in nature. This is especially true about autoimmune diseases. If you have an immune reaction to one type of food, you may experience cross-reactivity to other foods.

Cross-reactivity is a condition in which the autoimmune antibodies your body generates (such as antigliadin IgA antibodies, which cause a reaction when you eat gluten) mistake other food proteins for the ones you cannot tolerate. When you experience a cross-reaction to other foods, the effect on your body is the same as if you had ingested gluten.

If going on a gluten-free diet fails to bring the results you anticipate, I recommend eliminating the following foods (one at a time, in the order given), because you may be experiencing cross-reactivity:

**Dairy products.** As you have already read throughout this book, my colleagues and I advocate eliminating *all* dairy products (from cows) from your diet—and I advise doing this concurrent with going on a gluten-free diet if you have severe digestive problems.

Drs. Fine and Vojdani, researchers who have developed methods of testing for gluten (See Chapter 10, Are You Gluten Sensitive?), have found that patients with gluten sensitivity have a high frequency of cross-reactivity to milk—most notably the milk protein casein (sodium caseinate and calcium caseinate) and whey.

Do not confuse immunoreactivity to milk with lactose intolerance. They are completely different! Lactose intolerance is an inability to digest lactose (milk sugar) because of limited production of the lactase enzyme in the intestines. Virtually all babies are born with lactase, but around the age of 2, a lactase deficiency develops in most people. It is estimated that between 30 million and 50 million Americans are lactose intolerant.[1]

Diet is the only way to control the symptoms of lactose intolerance. Individuals who react to small amounts of lactose can take lactase enzymes, which are available without a prescription. The tablets must be taken with the first bite of dairy food.

But I want to reiterate: Lactose intolerance in *not* the same as immunoreactivity to milk.

Immunoreactivity to casein and whey is similar to the immune response your body has to gluten if you are gluten sensitive. The only treatment for this condition is a diet free of casein and whey—eliminating not only milk but also cheese, yogurt, and ice cream—*anything* that has milk in it, even soups and soy burgers that have cheese added to them—and protein drinks that have casein added.

(Some people who cannot tolerate milk products turn to soy as an alternative. However, if you think that soy products are safe, think again! Read labels carefully. Some of these products have casein added to them.)

*Suggestion:* Remain on a dual gluten-free/casein-free diet for 3 weeks after all symptoms have gone away. Then try reintroducing goat, sheep, or rice milk products in a limited amount to see if you can tolerate them. If not, remain casein-free.

**Nightshades.** Nightshades—tomatoes, white potatoes, eggplant, peppers, and tobacco—are a class of plants that have a protein called lectin, which is similar to gluten and which has been associated with celiac disease.[2] When you eat these foods, antibodies you have formed against gluten react to the nightshade lectin, resulting in the same type of immune reaction you have to gluten.

Dr. Norman Childers, professor emeritus at the University of Florida and retired professor of horticulture from Rutgers University, discovered a significant link between nightshades and autoimmunity. When Dr. Childers, who is now in his late nineties, was 50 years old, he was diagnosed with diverticulitis—a condition involving inflammation of the microscopic pockets that line the intestine.

When he stopped eating foods in the nightshade family, all of his colon problems, as well as his arthritic problems, disappeared. His personal experience spurred him to study the relationships between nightshades and autoimmune disorders, especially arthritis. In surveys of patients with arthritis, he found that 94 percent had complete or substantial relief from symptoms when they adhered to a rigid nightshade-free diet.[3]

Dr. Childers admits that it is difficult to adhere to a nightshade-free regimen because of the prevalence of these foods in our diet. However, he writes that allowing even some nightshades in your diet can jeopardize recovery.

The recommendation, therefore, is to eliminate all nightshades if you continue to have symptoms despite being on a strict gluten-free diet.

**Peanuts and soy.** Not only are these legumes known to cause allergic reactions, they may also cause autoimmune reactions because of their high lectin content. Avoiding these two foods has become easier with the advent of the new food-labeling law in the United States, which took effect January 1, 2006. Peanuts and soy are among the eight allergens that food processors are required to list on labels.

However, when you eliminate these foods, take care when you eat out. Soy is one of those hidden ingredients in foods and is included in such benign-looking foods as margarine.

## OTHER DIETARY CHANGES

Although cross-reactivity is the most common reason that some people fail to respond to a strict gluten-free diet, there are others that you should consider.

I spoke with a colleague, Dr. Melvyn Grovit, who is an appointed member of the New York State Board for Dietetics/Nutrition, as well as the Governing Board for the Certification Board for Nutrition Specialists. Dr. Grovit is also professor emeritus in the department of medical sciences, New York College of Podiatric Medicine, the former chairman of the department of medical sciences at the New York College of Podiatric Medicine, and former chief of the department of primary podiatric medicine at the Foot Clinics of New York.

Although Dr. Grovit was a successful podiatrist, his passion has always been nutrition. That passion was sparked when he had Crohn's disease as a teenager and had 18 feet of his intestine surgically removed in order to save his life. (Living with short bowel syndrome is the ultimate nutrition challenge!)

He left his position at the New York College of Podiatric Medicine in 2004 to pursue the practice of nutritional medicine, which specializes in helping people who have severe forms of inflammatory bowel disease (IBD). Many of his patients are children whose parents have been told that they have exhausted every type of medical means to improve the quality of their children's lives.

Dr. Grovit says that in the food chain, a number of specific foods and additives may cause inflammation and severe immune reactions. In addition to the recommendations we've already discussed, he advises:

**Avoid foods that contain carrageenan.** Carrageenan is a food additive and thickening agent derived from red algae that gained prominence during the low-fat craze that hit America several years ago. Food processors use this additive in many different foods because it adds softness and smoothness to products.

Among the different types of products that contain carrageenan are some brands of chocolate pudding, soy milk, chewable vitamins and minerals, turkey roll and other processed meats, cottage cheese, and soy products that are made to look and taste like deli items.

Although it is generally not found in powdered baby formulas, carrageenan is an overlooked ingredient in liquid infant formulas. Because carrageenan is in so many liquid infant formulas, Dr. Grovit speculates that this additive may influence the statistics that show that breast-fed babies have a lower incidence of IBD.

The extensive use of carrageenan means that you may be eating a significant amount of it. Like gluten, it is something that has been introduced into our food chain at levels that were never before available in whole, unprocessed food.

**Limit consumption of *all* high-fiber grains.** Dr. Grovit also suggests limiting the consumption of *all* high-fiber grains (and legumes) while the intestinal tract is inflamed and in trouble.

Eating a high-fiber diet is healthy and good for most people. But in his experience, and mine, most people with IBD have some degree of carbohydrate intolerance and fare better on a lower-fiber diet.

After the intestinal tract is substantially healed, you may again be able to tolerate high-fiber foods.

**Eliminate suspect foods.** Dr. Grovit is a firm believer, as I am, in paying attention to anything you eat that you believe makes you sick. You should eliminate any food you suspect causes you to feel ill and see if you feel better after omitting it. If you do feel better, stay away from that food.

**Avoid corn.** While corn products are generally used as a substitute grain for those with celiac disease and gluten sensitivity, Dr. Grovit has found that corn in the setting of inflammatory bowel disease is a food best not eaten. It is too difficult to digest.

Another reason why Dr. Grovit has his patients avoid corn is because more than 50 percent of all corn (and 50 percent of conventional soybeans and 100 percent of conventional canola) grown in the United States has genetically modified DNA.[4] Much of the alteration has come about through cross-pollination from fields of genetically modified strains to nonmodified crops.[5]

Food engineers have theoretically modified grains to improve specific qualities and to improve their resistance to insects and disease. However, the effect these genetically modified plants have on human beings (or animals, for that matter) is largely unknown for the long term.

**Use an enzyme-based antigas food supplement.** Consider taking an antigas food enzyme such as Beano when you eat nutrient-dense foods, such as broccoli, cabbage, cauliflower, legumes, grains, cereals, nuts, seeds, and many other foods, if you have IBD. The supplement helps break down the natural sugars in these foods and makes digestion easier.

## TO A BETTER LIFE

Gluten sensitivity is a cunning and powerful condition affecting a significant portion of Americans. It is cunning because it masquerades itself as symptoms of other diseases. It is powerful because it alters the lifestyle and health of anyone who has it.

*But it is easily treatable.*

If this book has raised your level of awareness, and you now suspect you may be gluten sensitive, take the next step: Go gluten-free.

It's really not that difficult:

1. **Eliminate all gluten from your diet.** Read labels, ask questions of food manufacturers and restaurants when eating out, and be careful. In other words: Be diligent about what you eat.

2. **Supplement.** Take appropriate supplements (as identified in Chapter 12, Supplementing Your Health) to speed your recovery and ensure wellness.

3. **Remove other offending foods.** If your gluten-free diet has not given you the results you seek, don't give up. Eliminate dairy products, then (if necessary) nightshades, peanuts, and soy.

4. **Be patient!** Chances are excellent that you will feel better within 2 weeks. But if you don't, give yourself 3 months. Your symptoms didn't become severe overnight nor will recovery happen overnight.

Gluten is not an essential protein for your good health. You do not need wheat, barley, rye, or oats to live a happy, healthy life.

In fact, if you *don't* eat them, you will have a *better* life. What do you have to lose?

# CHAPTER 14

## WHY DIDN'T MY DOCTOR TELL ME ABOUT THIS?

A little knowledge about a health condition can be a wonderful—yet dreadful—thing. Wonderful because knowledge sets you free. Putting a label on a symptom gives you tremendous liberty. You know what you are dealing with, and that removes feelings of powerlessness.

But dreadful because it can stir up feelings of anger and frustration. You become angry with yourself, sometimes blaming yourself for not seeing the "obvious." Or—probably more often—you become angry with those in whom you had placed your trust and well-being—your medical providers. Why didn't they *do* something about the condition long ago? *Why didn't they tell you about this?*

When my coauthor began researching Part 2 of this book, one of the areas she looked into was scientific studies concerning gluten sensitivity and gastric problems. (See Chapter 6, Digestive Disorders.) She discovered that researchers had found a strong relationship between colitis and gluten sensitivity. Specifically, they found that 15 percent of patients suffering from one type of colitis—lymphocytic colitis—had celiac disease (CD).[1]

This study was particularly intriguing to her because for 3 years, her husband, JC, had been suffering from that specific type of colitis.

To treat the problem, JC's gastroenterologist had prescribed an expensive medication called mesalamine, which was supposed to mitigate the diarrhea. But, the doctor warned, it would not cure the colitis, which would be a lifelong condition. The doctor said it was something JC would have to live with for the rest of his life.

My coauthor's husband didn't want to "live with" the condition. He didn't want to have to take up to 12 tablets a day—at $1 a tablet!

143

Besides, the mesalamine did not work. Some days, his diarrhea seemed to be under control; other days, it was as bad as ever.

So, when my coauthor found the research that linked gluten sensitivity with this particular type of colitis, she gave JC the studies, and his first stop was with his internist. He asked the internist to order a blood test. She ordered a celiac panel, which (not surprisingly) came back negative. *Blood tests show only full-blown celiac disease; they do not show gluten sensitivity.*

Because of my research on testing, I encouraged JC to have a stool test for gluten sensitivity. (See Chapter 10, Are You Gluten Sensitive?) This test is very sensitive.

He took the stool-sample test; *it came back positive.*

He then went on a strict gluten-free diet. And within 2 weeks, he was completely symptom-free and medication-free!

But wait! There is more to this story: On the road to full recovery and elated that he had found the cause of his prolonged illness, JC went back to his gastroenterologist to report the good news. *The gastroenterologist refused to accept the test results. He refused to review the studies. He refused to accept that gluten could be the culprit in this malady.*

According to him, because there was no diagnosis of celiac disease (remember, the blood test came back negative; likewise, the biopsy the doctor had *insisted* on doing had come back negative for CD), gluten could *not* be the cause of the problem!

Despite the doctor's denial of reality, JC remains symptom-free, thanks to a gluten-free diet. But improvement in his quality of life did not alleviate the anger he and my coauthor felt.

I wish this were an isolated instance, but it is not. I'd like to share another case that is illustrative of medical ignorance:

In 2002, I met GC while we were working on a television project together. Although she was never my patient, she shared with me that she had been diagnosed with Crohn's disease when she was 17 years old. Her doctors had tried virtually every medication to control the disease: cortisone, prednisone, tetracycline, donnatel, and azulfadine. Nothing helped.

At age 21, she had 7 feet of intestines and part of her colon removed to treat the condition. Despite the surgery, she continued to have bloating, intestinal blockage, gas, cramps, and bloody stools. And, of course, the surgery did not cure the Crohn's; it only removed necrotic tissue.

When I met GC, her condition was essentially the same at her current age (45) as it had been for 18 years.

I told GC about gluten and its cross-reactivity to dairy products. She was intrigued with the information I shared, especially the success stories of patients I had worked with. But she didn't think she could go gluten-free (GF). Her excuse? *She was Italian.* How could she give up all that wonderful pasta and bread?

Shortly after our conversation, though, she had dinner in an Italian restaurant and feasted on bread, pasta, and cheese—enjoying it all, until severe diarrhea and nausea rushed her to the bathroom. As the evening ended in the emergency room, GC resolved to give a gluten- and casein-free diet a try. She was sick and tired of being sick and tired.

Three weeks later, her bloating and diarrhea had disappeared. Within 6 weeks, she felt like a new person. She went off all medications and has since remained true to a gluten-free and dairy-free diet.

As in the case of my coauthor's husband, however, there is more to GC's story.

Because of her advanced condition, GC has to manage stress carefully, otherwise, it can trigger a relapse of the Crohn's.

Last year, GC was involved in a particularly stressful project, which resulted in gastrointestinal symptoms severe enough to send her to the hospital. She experienced an intestinal blockage caused by adhesions from previous surgeries.

When her gastroenterologist updated her history, she told him that she had been completely symptom-free for years since she went off gluten and dairy products and that she took no medications for Crohn's.

Her doctor replied, "I tested you for celiac disease, and you are not *allergic.* You don't have it. You can eat flour and dairy."

When GC left the hospital, she decided to give both milk and wheat a try...after all, her doctor said it was all right!

She was "in heaven" for a brief moment. The French bread, apple pie, cheese...they tasted so good! But then it hit her: A night-long episode of diarrhea and vomiting. That was enough to convince GC that the doctor was wrong. Gluten and casein were the culprits in her misery.

Her doctor *still* contends that she does not have an "allergy" to gluten or dairy. But now GC knows better than to believe him. She is again gluten- and casein-free—*and* free of all her symptoms.

Why didn't these learned gastroenterologists know about gluten sensitivity? And why wouldn't they accept the facts as presented to them—by tests and by a lack of symptoms?

Why, indeed, especially since the problem of gluten sensitivity has been accepted all around the world—*except* in the United States.

## AWARENESS AND ACCEPTANCE ABROAD

Gluten sensitivity in the form of celiac disease has been known to mankind as far back as AD 250, when Aretaeus of Cappadocia included a detailed description of the symptoms in his writings.

In 1888, Dr. Samuel Gee of the Great Ormond Street Hospital for Children in the United Kingdom set out clinical accounts of the disease, noting that the cure was to regulate diet. He said, "If the patient can be cured at all, it must be by means of diet."[2]

It wasn't until 1952, however, that a Dutch pediatrician, Dr. Willem Karel Dicke, identified wheat as the primary culprit of the symptoms. By the mid-1950s, Dicke, Professor Charlotte Anderson, and others, working in Birmingham, England, identified gluten as the specific offending protein, and from that point, the recognized treatment for this condition was a gluten-free diet.[3]

Classic cases of celiac disease were first diagnosed by clinical observation of symptoms and (after the endoscope was invented and perfected in the 1950s) biopsy. Biopsy became the gold standard for diagnosing and confirming CD—and, unfortunately, remains the standard for the majority of medical doctors in the United States. (I say unfortunately because—as we discussed in Chapter 10—by the time gluten sensitivity progresses to the stage of flattening the intestine's villi, you've got a serious problem—one that could easily have been prevented by going gluten-free earlier.)

In the 1960s, testing procedures improved with the development of serological screening for antigliadin IgA antibodies. These tests seemed to indicate an escalation in the incidence of CD (which counts the number of new cases that are *reported*). What really occurred is that doctors were finally able to put a label on symptoms and therefore were able to report a specific cause—hence, the increased incidence. The increased incidence rate, however, served a purpose: It stirred up considerable interest in *celiac disease* within the medical research community—*in Europe*.

*Incidence* points out that there is a problem. *Prevalence* tells how widespread the problem is. Researchers began studying the prevalence of celiac disease—among healthy populations, as well as among populations of people with various types of diseases, such as osteoporosis, diabetes, and thyroid disease.

In 2004, researcher William R. Treem wrote, "There has been an explosion in knowledge about celiac disease in the last decade, based on the availability of serologic screening tests and the elucidation of some of the important disease susceptibility genes. What has been discovered is that CD is among the most common inherited diseases with a worldwide prevalence of almost 1 percent of the population."[4]

Celiac disease has been well studied in countries around the world. Today, it is accepted that CD is a common disorder not only in Europe (where it is most prevalent), but also in populations of European ancestry, including North and South America and Australia, North Africa, the Middle East, and South Asia, where until a few years ago, it was considered rare.[5]

The medical community abroad is aware of the problem of celiac disease and, to a lesser degree, of its lesser but more prevalent cousin, gluten sensitivity. Even though doctors may not fully accept the extent of this condition, they at least are aware of its symptoms and that it can masquerade as symptoms of other diseases. They perform tests for it and think of "gluten-free" as a possible treatment.

From the time that celiac disease was recognized for what it was, it did not take long for the enormity and importance of this problem to be quickly accepted in Europe.

Because the only treatment for celiac disease is a gluten-free diet, a demand for ready-made gluten-free foods was created. The European food-processing community began to oblige the demand.

But a problem still existed: How would the public know that a processed food product was truly gluten-free?

The solution was the development of a universal standard that defined "gluten-free." By 1976, the Codex Alimentarius Commission, a joint effort between the World Health Organization and the Food and Agricultural Organization of the United Nations, adopted the Codex Standard for gluten-free foods.

The Codex Standard was amended in 1983 to define "gluten-free" as a food whose "total nitrogen content of the gluten-containing cereal grains used in the product does not exceed 0.05 g per 100 grammes [0.05 percent] of these grains on a dry matter basis."[6] According to the current Codex standard, gluten-free foods are also those "that contain the cereal ingredients wheat, triticale, rye, barley, or oats or their constituents, which have been rendered gluten-free." Thus, the standard allowed for science to develop safe forms of wheat, rye, barley, and oats.

The revised standard is now in committee, awaiting additional revision to a more restricted definition of gluten allowances, with specific tolerances of gluten dictated.

Following Codex standards is voluntary by the 192 members of the World Health Organization. (The United States is a member but does not follow this standard.) However, in the European community, the Codex gluten-free standard is widely accepted and followed.

In other parts of the world, some countries have chosen to adopt more-stringent standards. For example, Canada's Food and Drug Regulations (Section B.24.018) state:

"No person shall label, package, sell, or advertise a food in a manner likely to create an impression that it is a gluten-free food unless the food does not contain wheat, including spelt and kamut, or oats, barley, rye, triticale, or any part thereof."[7]

The Canadian standard was developed in conjunction with the Canadian Celiac Association. The government also considered public comment on the proposed standard. In the end, the government felt that there was insufficient scientific evidence to establish a safe level of gluten intake for people with celiac disease, so its standard is an absence of any gluten.

Another example of a strict standard for gluten-free food labeling is the Australia New Zealand Food Standards Code 1.2.8, clauses 1 and 16, which state that foods claiming to be gluten-free must not have detectable gluten and no oats or cereals containing gluten that have been malted. Additionally, a claim that "a food has a low gluten content must not be made in relation to a food unless the food contains no more than 20 mg gluten per 100 g of the food."[8]

These standards have made it easy to travel abroad. GC, the friend I described earlier, travels frequently in Europe. Shortly after she went gluten-free, she visited Finland, Sweden, and France, and in every country, she found gluten-free selections on menus! She has also discovered that if a restaurant does not offer a gluten-free selection, and she brings her GF pasta, the chef is happy to prepare it for her!

That doesn't happen here in the United States. Some restaurants are beginning to prepare gluten-free menus, but it is rare. And it is exceptional to pick up a box or can of processed food and see the label "gluten-free" imprinted on it.

## U.S. RELUCTANCE

Why has the problem of gluten sensitivity—even in its most commonly accepted form, celiac disease—been hidden from the American public? Isn't a problem that potentially affects up to 30 percent of the population worthy of study, diagnosis, and treatment?

You would think so. But I can think of several reasons that gluten sensitivity remains obscure knowledge with the medical community.

### Limited Educational Exposure

I speak at medical conferences throughout the world, and I have found that physicians are very open-minded: They want to learn, and they want to do what's right for their patients.

*But they can't give what they do not have.* And what they do not have is information—in this case, information and knowledge about gluten sensitivity.

Medical education in the United States is demanding. Generally, it requires:

- An undergraduate degree, with an emphasis on the sciences (physics, biology, mathematics, and inorganic and organic chemistry)

- Completion of 4 years of medical school, which includes 2 years of classroom and laboratory study in anatomy, biochemistry, physiology, pharmacology, psychology, microbiology, pathology, medical ethics, and laws governing medicine, and 2 years of working with patients under supervision

- From 3 to 8 years of internship and residency, working in a specialized area of medicine

The study is intense, the hours are long, and the training is the best in the world. However, despite its excellence, students are *not* sufficiently exposed to academic and clinical areas affected by gluten sensitivity. What they are taught is what I also learned in my formal studies: *The only patients who are gluten sensitive are those who have celiac disease.*

We now know that this is not true, but unfortunately, that knowledge has not made its way into the medical community.

Perhaps the most important of studies that could affect the future diagnosis of gluten sensitivity is nutrition—a study that crosses over the spectrum of human physiology and function.

Medical science recognizes that good nutrition is essential in controlling chronic disease. Yet, despite this knowledge, medical colleges have been slow to adopt an effective nutrition component into their curricula.

In 2004, *Today's Dietitian* published the results of a survey[9] that assessed the teaching of nutrition in medical schools. Among the survey's findings:

- Only approximately 40 percent of all medical and osteopathic schools provide a separate, required course in nutrition.

- At schools that require the study of nutrition, the mean number of credit hours was 2.5, with a range of 1 to 10 credits.

- Only 13 percent of schools offer nutrition as an elective course.

- Nutrition is integrated into other courses at 24 percent of the colleges.

- Elective courses of 2 credit hours attract less than 25 percent of the medical school enrollment.

- About 23 percent of schools do *not* offer nutrition instruction at all.

Aside from the lack of a nutrition component in medical education, medical students are exposed to only a periphery of information about gluten sensitivity (in terms of celiac disease), mostly through a rotation in gastrointestinal medicine. Is it no wonder, then, that symptoms are not recognized or linked to the cause—gluten intolerance?

## Too Much Information in Too Many Places

An obvious solution for a lack of formal education about gluten sensitivity is to keep up by reading medical journals.

But "keeping up" is hard to do. It's the curse of the information age: We have so much information available that it is too much to know. And often, the information is not linked together. The result is missed diagnoses.

In 2002, the American Academy of Family Physicians admonished its members:

"Recent population studies indicate that celiac disease is more common than was previously thought. Some patients with gluten-sensitive enteropathy have minimal or no symptoms and are unlikely to be referred to a gastroenterologist unless the disease is considered. Hence, family physicians need to be familiar with the diagnosis and management of gluten-sensitive enteropathy."[10]

It *is* the family physician—the general practitioner or internist—who is the first point of contact for patients. So it is the family physician who *should* be most "on top" of research and most familiar with the signs of gluten sensitivity. Yet as recently as 2005 in patient surveys, only 11 percent of celiac-disease patients were diagnosed by their primary-care physicians. And in physician surveys, only 35 percent of primary-care doctors had ever diagnosed celiac disease![11]

Just how hard is it for a family physician or an internist (or any other doctor) to keep up? In this book alone, we have cited references from *53 different journals,* specializing in allergies, neurology, pediatrics, gastroenterology, psychiatry—and more! These are journals in which academic studies on gluten sensitivity have been published.

Could any one doctor keep up with all that information?

### (Mis)Managed Care

If doctors had more time, keeping up would be easier to do. Time is a problem. And much of the time problem centers around managed care.

Managed care is the health-care insurance system that was put into place in the 1980s, a period when health-care costs were escalating. Managed care is *still* in place, and costs *still* continue to increase (at double-digit rates), despite the fact that the system was supposed to put checks and balances into health-care delivery, so that doctors could order only procedures that were medically necessary.

When managed care was introduced, provider network systems were created. Doctors and hospitals joined these networks to gain access to patients whose group insurance policies gave coverage only if patients went to doctors, hospitals, and laboratories in the network.

In return for gaining access to patients, doctors accepted a reduced fee and agreed to be reimbursed at "reasonable and customary" rates (which were established by the insurance company) for specific procedures.

The managed-care system is fraught with problems that affect you and the probability that you will succeed in getting adequate medical care for your gluten sensitivity:

**Low reimbursements.** Managed-care organizations (including Medicare) establish rates for medical procedures and office visits. With some exceptions, doctors are reimbursed a relative value for any specific procedure—no matter if they spend 10 minutes with the patient or 30.

A 2006 report[12] published by the American College of Physicians states:

"Medicare payment policies discourage primary-care physicians from organizing care processes to achieve optimal results for patients because they are paid little or nothing for the work performed outside of the visit or procedure code; low fees for [evaluation and management] services discourage spending time with patients; prevention is under-reimbursed or not covered at all; low reimbursement coupled with high practice overhead makes it impossible for many primary-care physicians to invest in health-information technology and other practice innovations…"

Medicare does not dictate usual and customary charges, but the codes by which it reimburses doctors are used by insurers and serve as a model for their reimbursement practices.

**Diagnosis.** Managed care also demands documentation of medical necessity—not a bad thing, of course. But "medical necessity" is often determined by insurance companies, who frequently deny payment for diagnostics and treatments that are not mainstream and do not conform to clinical guidelines.

A case in point—blood tests. Blood tests are not definitive (as we have seen) in diagnosing gluten sensitivity. But many insurance companies will not reimburse for stool and saliva tests that are given at only a few laboratories, because these labs are not part of their network and because the tests are not "mainstream."

Yet, without established medical necessity, further *reimbursable* treatment through nutritional counseling is doubtful.

And (sadly), without a definitive diagnosis that can be provided through stool or saliva testing, some patients will not accept that they have gluten sensitivity, especially if they have learned to "live with" their symptoms.

**Time.** Gluten sensitivity is not a condition that can be explained in 15 minutes; it takes up to an hour or more to explain the condition and to teach patients about a gluten-free diet. And it takes time for follow-up visits.

Under the current health-care system, doctors do not have the time to spend with patients to teach them, to encourage them, and to monitor their diets. As previously indicated, managed care may not pay for that time.

Managed care has made consumer-patients dependent on insurance coverage: If a procedure is not covered, they will not pay for it out of pocket—often because of the high expense attached to it.

## Few Diagnostic Laboratories

Let's take managed care out of the equation for now and assume that doctors could order and respond to any diagnostic test they deemed necessary. Clinical laboratories are slow to accept new testing procedures. Currently, only two laboratories offer saliva and stool sampling that detect gluten intolerance with a high level of sensitivity.

In my presentations to medical groups, doctors are quick to take note of these laboratories, because they did not know that such tests or laboratories existed. Although insurance companies may not reimburse for the tests, doctors are eager to have a valuable testing resource available to them and their patients.

The two laboratories discussed in Chapter 10 (Enterolab and Immunosciences Laboratory) are both CLIA-certified, which means that they are registered with the U.S. Department of Health and Human Services as part of the Clinical Laboratory Improvement Amendments (CLIA). The agency oversees clinical laboratory standards and quality and can perform tests for people in all states—except one.

The state of New York requires out-of-state laboratories that run diagnostics for its citizens to acquire an expensive New York State laboratory permit.[13] New York State does not recognize the U.S. government's certification of quality standards.

At the current time, neither Enterolab nor Immunosciences Laboratory has separate New York State permits to do the special gluten-sensitivity testing. (Immunosciences is licensed to do blood work in New York State but not saliva testing.)

## Lack of Incentives

For researchers to invest time and money in the study of a medical problem, two conditions generally have to be met:

- The problem has to be widespread.

- It cannot be mitigated by any current solutions.

Unless these two requirements are met, pharmaceutical and biotechnology companies, which are the primary benefactors of medical investigations in the United States, are not motivated to invest in research. These companies funnel their monies into projects that have the potential to yield large returns—most often on drugs that halt symptoms and require lifelong use. (A good example is cholesterol-lowering drugs.)

Until recently, gluten sensitivity—in its worst-case form, celiac disease—was thought to be rare in the United States, affecting only one in several thousand people. Thus, it failed the first requirement to be considered for research.

Now, of course, the medical community is waking up to the fact that gluten sensitivity is far more prevalent. Doctors who are up-to-date on digestive disorders accept that 1 in 133 people in the United States have celiac disease, whether or not they show symptoms. (Doctors, however, have not yet accepted—or are just unaware of—the fact that up to 30 percent of the population may be gluten sensitive.)

So, on the basis of the prevalence requirement, gluten sensitivity qualifies as a research topic. But it fails the second requirement: *It has a cure.* If you are gluten-sensitive, eliminate gluten from your diet. You will get well.

The cure may not be ideal for people who have the condition and perceive that their quality of life is changed because of it. But it kills the incentive to research—at least from the perspective (and pockets) of pharmaceutical and biotechnology companies.

Perhaps you believe that research could and should be done in the public sector—such as at publicly funded medical schools or the National

Institutes of Health (NIH). Think again. Even these institutions receive support from the pharmaceutical industry.

The NIH is one of the world's most prestigious medical research centers, as well as the federal center of research in the United States. Comprised of 27 separate institutes, its mission is to:

"Acquire new knowledge to help prevent, detect, diagnose, and treat disease and disability, from the rarest genetic disorder to the common cold. The NIH mission is to uncover new knowledge that will lead to better health for everyone. NIH works toward that mission by: conducting research in its own laboratories; supporting the research of non-Federal scientists in universities, medical schools, hospitals, and research institutions throughout the country and abroad; helping in the training of research investigators; and fostering communication of medical and health sciences information."[14]

Despite these lofty goals, the NIH came under fire in 2005 with the discovery that some of its employees were consulting (for large paychecks) with pharmaceutical and biotechnology firms. As a consequence, the NIH "came clean" with the American public and refined its ethics policies.

The final ethics rules went into effect in August 2005, banning outside consulting with "pharmaceutical, biotechnology, or medical device manufacturing companies, health-care providers or insurers, and supported research institutions."[15] Nevertheless, the NIH receives grants amounting to millions of dollars from pharmaceutical companies.

Educational institutions are also at risk of being influenced by pharmaceutical companies, which foot a large part of their bills. An article published in *The Chronicle of Higher Education*[16] stated:

"Every day, in teaching hospitals across the country, doctors and medical residents can enjoy lunches paid for by pharmaceutical companies. Drug-company representatives can roam the halls...Meanwhile, researchers plug away in their laboratories, working on new therapies and procedures, trying not to let the fact that a company is paying for the research influence their findings."

The effect of this influence is that increasingly, researchers have less liberty to choose their projects. Their funding dictates where they spend their intellectual capital.

To be sure, a few (very few) researchers are searching for a better understanding of gluten intolerance. However, U.S. scientists contributed to only 10 percent of research papers on celiac disease published from 1985 to 1990, while researchers in the United Kingdom and Italy contributed to 38 percent of the papers.[17]

In 2000, at the 9th International Symposium on Celiac Disease, dedicated scientists prioritized the areas they would like to study:[18]

- A search for celiac disease genes
- Development of a vaccine against CD
- Criteria for screening for CD
- Engineering gluten-free grains
- Development of noninvasive, fast, and reliable tests for the diagnosis and follow-up of CD

Progress has been made in *some* of these areas, as we have already discussed in this book. But notice: All the priorities focus on celiac disease—not gluten sensitivity.

In Part 2 of this book, we looked at the research some scientists have done to identify the link between gluten sensitivity and other devastating diseases. Other scientists are experimenting with various novel solutions that would allow people with gluten sensitivity to eat "normally." In 2002, for example, a team composed of researchers from Stanford University and the University of Oslo in Norway isolated a specific type of bacterial enzyme that might, in the future, be used to break down offending peptides in gluten.[19]

If these researchers harness that enzyme, they might be able to develop a "glutaid" pill—a pill that individuals who are gluten sensitive could take before eating wheat, barley, or rye, similar to the one that people who are lactose intolerant take before eating ice cream or drinking milk.

And as recently as 2005, Dutch researchers (not researchers in the United States) were exploring the possibility of producing varieties of wheat that are safe for people with gluten sensitivity.[20] They found that the level of toxicity of the different types of wheat varies greatly: More-modern varieties of wheat—which have been crossbred and modified to produce considerably more gluten—are more toxic to people with gluten sensitivity than ancient varieties were.

A "glutaid pill"? A nontoxic wheat? Perhaps. As the American public becomes aware of its problem, it will demand alternative cures.

Who knows what is possible in the future? And who knows if future "solutions" will be better for us or even if they will ultimately be safe?

One thing is certain: Until the financial markets see the possibility of gain from researching gluten sensitivity, the future for gluten-sensitive people is a gluten-free diet.

## WHAT CAN YOU DO?

So—you accept that you are gluten sensitive. And you are angry that your doctor didn't tell you about it. What can you do?

Vent your anger.

*Then move on.* The important thing is that you now know about your condition and can do something about it! And you can help others, too.

GC has made it her personal mission to let everyone know about the miracle of going gluten-free. She has convinced her 85-year-old Italian father (who also has Crohn's) to give up gluten. And now he has been symptom-free for almost 2 years.

She told her neighbor, who was experiencing stomach problems, about her success. The neighbor learned to cook gluten-free and no longer feels sick. GC tells anyone who will listen about her personal "miracle."

Whether you tell others or not, if you see and accept the gluten-free solution, then this book has achieved its purpose: It has empowered you—and your doctor, your chiropractor, your nurse practitioner, or any other health-care provider—to do something about your gluten sensitivity.

I wish you good health. And now you know that good health is within your reach.

# PART 4

# COPING WITH COOKING

Some people love to cook. Others hate it. Most people are somewhere in between but opt for easy-to-prepare foods because cooking takes time. And time (at least discretionary time) is in short supply for most of us. That, of course, is why the food-processing industry has prospered.

Cooking is a skill. And although you can master a skill, that doesn't mean you *like* to use it. So, we have written this section to accommodate different levels of skills and interests. You'll find ideas, tips, menus, and recipes in several chapters.

CHAPTER 15: A SUBSTITUTE FOR ALL REASONS. This chapter provides you with the substitutes you'll need for gluten-free cooking, including common dairy-free substitutes.

CHAPTER 16: GLUTEN-FREE COOKING 101. In this chapter, you'll find a lot of prepared foods by product name. If cooking is involved, it is minimal.

CHAPTER 17: GLUTEN-FREE COOKING 201. You know the acronym KISS—Keep It Simple, Sam! In this chapter, we apply the KISS principle to cooking. We'll keep the number of ingredients and skill level required to a minimum.

CHAPTER 18: GLUTEN-FREE COOKING 301. Here you will find some more-involved recipes, including some comfort foods. Nothing really gourmet, but definitely good.

CHAPTER 19: GIVE ME BREAD! Bread is the one food type that almost everyone on a gluten-free diet misses—even if you weren't a big bread eater before going on the diet. So, we'll give you some proven bread options.

CHAPTER 20: *MMM, MMM* GOOD GF DESSERTS. I'm a nutritionist, but I'm a realist, too. So, I know that you probably have a sweet tooth or a craving for junk food once in a while and would like to indulge it—in moderation, of course. In this section, you'll find some recipes for things that you can't buy on the street because of their gluten content but you *can* make at home—if you are willing to take the time and experiment a bit.

CHAPTER 21: A 14-DAY GF DIET. The previous chapters gave you recipes. In this chapter, you'll put a healthy 14-day menu together. Plus, you'll get ideas on how to stay on your GF diet while eating out.

Before you turn to the next chapter, a caveat: *"Tryer beware!"*

Being a nutritionist does not make me a cook or a baker. I've spent time in the kitchen, but I do not intend to pass myself off as an expert in the recipe department. On the scale of "I hate to cook" to "I'm an expert cook," I fall somewhere in between.

So does my coauthor. She is a writer and a researcher. Like me, she knows her way around the kitchen quite well, but she is not a cook or a baker. Like most people, she tries to keep things simple in the kitchen.

So, mind the caveat. We have tried many of these recipes but not all. So we have relied on the veracity and enthusiasm of those who have shared them with us.

With that, as Alton Brown of Food TV fame says, "Good eats!"

# CHAPTER 15

## A SUBSTITUTE FOR ALL REASONS

One of our goals in writing this section of the book is to prove to you that cooking—and living—gluten-free is not hard. You will find that you can take almost any recipe you enjoyed in your "gluten-eating" days and adapt it to gluten-free cooking.

But some of these recipes will require making key substitutions. So, listen up! Here are some basics to take to heart.

## FLOUR SUBSTITUTES

We have adapted many of the following recipes to accommodate the special needs of a GF diet. You'll see that some call for flour.

Most of us, in our pre-GF days, never thought much about flour. Recipes most often called for general-purpose flour or self-rising flour. Once in a while, perhaps, we purchased a specialty flour—but not often. Wheat was our friend.

Not anymore.

Since wheat is off-limits, you have a wide variety of flours from which to choose. We told you about many of these flours in Chapter 11, such as almond, amaranth, buckwheat, corn, fava, millet, quinoa, potato, rice, sorghum, soy, tapioca, and teff. Most of these flours are not used by themselves; they are mixed in various proportions and with rising agents, such as xanthan or guar gum, to make them taste and act more like wheat.

When you bake (especially bread), you will find that experimenting with a variety of flours will be fun (if not sometimes disastrous!). In general cooking, however, I recommend keeping things simple. Try either of these two choices:

**A premixed all-purpose flour.** Bob's Red Mill All Purpose Baking Flour is a good substitute. This flour is made of a combination of assorted wheat-flour substitutes: garbanzo flour, potato starch, tapioca flour, sorghum flour, and fava. You can order it online (www. bobsredmill.com), or you can purchase it in most health food stores.

**Bette Hagman's featherlight rice flour mix.**[1] Bette Hagman has become known in celiac circles as the bread goddess. Her bread flour mixture (minus the rising agents) makes the perfect all-purpose flour to keep on your pantry shelf.

Here's how to mix it:

# Bette's Featherlight Rice Flour Mix

### INGREDIENTS

3   cups rice flour

3   cups tapioca flour

3   cups cornstarch

3   tablespoons potato flour (This is potato flour, not potato starch!)

### DIRECTIONS

Thoroughly mix or sift all these ingredients and keep in a dry place. This recipe makes 9 cups of flour.

*Tip: You can adjust the recipe up or down; just keep the proportions the same. (For the potato flour, use 1 teaspoon per cup of flour mix.)*

## DAIRY SUBSTITUTES

Throughout this book, I have recommended that when you begin a gluten-free lifestyle, you also go dairy-free, at least for 2 to 3 weeks, because of the possibility of cross-reactivity. This is especially true if your gluten sensitivity has exhibited itself in gastric problems. Until your body heals, it may fool itself into thinking that casein is gluten. Obviously, that would mean a continuation of the same problems you had while eating gluten.

That's why I recommend going dairy-free.

Patients who accept GF often balk at going dairy-free. How, they wonder, can they do that? So much of cooking and baking calls for milk or cheese.

Do not despair. Going dairy-free is possible. And a good resource for guidance is just a mouse click away: Go Dairy Free, www.godairyfree.org.

This Web site tells you about substitutes—and even guides you into preparing many of them. I've listed a few of the recipes from the Web site if you wish to prepare some of the milk substitutes at home.

I encourage you to explore the Web site, which provides a substitute for every type of milk product. Here are some of the more common substitutes, based on ingredients used in many cooking recipes.

I also suggest that you experiment with the different milk substitutes. They all have different tastes that subtly lend themselves to recipes. When you go dairy-free milk shopping, please read labels closely. Some milk substitutes use sugar to sweeten them. Instead of buying a presweetened (with sugar) milk substitute, buy the product unsweetened and add vanilla extract or the sweetener of your choice if you would like a little extra sweet taste.

You will find many dairy substitutes for milk, including almond milk, cashew milk, rice milk, coconut milk, and soy milk. Oat milk may work well for some people as well—but be sure that it is certified GF to avoid possible reactivity problems from contamination.

### Goat's Milk and Sheep's Milk

Many people who are sensitive to the casein in cow's milk find that they can tolerate goat's milk and sheep's milk—and milk products made from these animals. Goat's milk is available in health food stores and many supermarkets. Sheep's milk may be more difficult to find; look in health food stores.

### Soy Milk

I'm sure you have seen soy milk in the dairy case at the grocery. It has become a very popular drink, in "regular," as well as vanilla and even chocolate.

Soy has a distinctive taste. It is made from ground soybeans, filtered water, and a small amount of brown rice sweetener. Usually it is fortified with calcium to match that of milk. Note: If you are reactive to soy (and many people are—it is one of the eight top food allergens), use another milk substitute!

You can prepare soy milk from scratch at home, although you may find it easier to buy it, since it is readily available at the supermarket.

# Soy Milk[2]

## INGREDIENTS

1 *cup dried soybeans*
  *Your choice of sweetener, as desired*
1½ *teaspoons vanilla or almond extract (optional)*

## DIRECTIONS

1. Soak the soybeans in 5 cups water for 12 to 14 hours.
2. Heat another 5 cups water in a large saucepan over medium heat.
3. Drain the beans.
4. Add the beans and 1½ cups lukewarm water to a blender and blend on high for 1 minute.
5. Immediately transfer the soybean blend to your heated water in the saucepan.
6. Repeat this process with the remaining soybeans, 1 cup at a time.
7. As soon as you have added all the beans to the saucepan, bring it slowly to a boil, stirring constantly.
8. Reduce the heat and simmer, stirring constantly, for 15 minutes. Be careful not to scorch the milk while cooking.
9. Remove from the heat. Strain the milk through a cheesecloth or tea towel.
10. Press any remaining milk through with a large spoon.
11. You may pour another ½ cup water through, in order to get it all.
12. Your soy milk is now complete and can be sweetened and flavored if it is intended for drinking purposes.

## Rice Milk

This "milk" is made from brown rice, water, and brown rice sweetener. You can find it on the grocer's shelf in most supermarkets.

You will find it a little pricier than soy milk, though. So, if it better suits your budget, you might want to try making it at home—it's quick and cheap to do.

## Rice Milk

### INGREDIENTS

1    *cup warm/hot rice (cooked)*

4    *cups hot water*

1    *teaspoon vanilla extract (omit the vanilla if using the rice milk for savory dishes)*
     *Your sweetener of choice (optional)*

### DIRECTIONS

1. Put the rice, water, vanilla extract, and sweetener, if using, in a blender, and puree for 3 to 5 minutes, until smooth.
2. Let it stand for 30 minutes or more, up to several hours.
3. Then, without shaking, pour the rice milk into another container, being careful not to let the sediments at the bottom pour into the new container.
4. Alternatively, if you are in a hurry, strain the rice milk through a cheesecloth.
5. This makes 4 to 4½ cups.

### Almond Milk

Almond milk, prepared from ground almonds, is a wonderful substitute for dairy milk, especially if you do not like the taste of rice or soy milk. It is my personal favorite. My favorite is an unsweetened brand flavored with natural vanilla for my cappuccino. Go Dairy Free says that you can make almond milk at home, but it may be more expensive than just buying it ready-made. Almond milk is also a little more expensive than rice or soy milk.

However, almond milk can be substituted for cow's milk in any recipe.

### Potato Milk

This was new to me, too! But potatoes can be made into a milk substitute just as easily as you can make rice milk. And if you want to try potato milk, you actually may have to prepare it yourself, since it is so new that it is difficult to find.

Go Dairy Free says it is still in the "conceptual stages," which means that it hasn't been tested in all types of cooking. But if you want to experiment, you may find this to be a cooking substitute that works for you.

# Potato Milk

## INGREDIENTS

1    large potato (equal to 1 cup chopped), peeled
3    cups hot/warm water
     Salt
1    teaspoon vanilla extract
¼    cup sliced almonds (for calcium)
2    tablespoons honey or maple syrup, to sweeten

## DIRECTIONS

1. Boil the potato in the water with a little salt.
2. Reserve the cooking water and add enough warm water to make 4 cups.
3. In a blender, add the water, potato, vanilla extract, almond slices, and honey and blend for approximately 5 minutes.
4. Strain through a tea towel or cheesecloth.

### Coconut Milk

Have you ever used coconut milk in a cake recipe or perhaps in a Thai dish? That same milk can be thinned and used as a dairy substitute. And, like other milk substitutes, you can prepare this one at home, if you desire. Coconut milk is one of the healthiest and most delicious dairy substitutes you can use.

# Coconut Milk

## INGREDIENTS

1    cup water
1    cup dried coconut

## DIRECTIONS

1. Bring the water to a boil. Remove from the heat.
2. Add the coconut and cool.

3. Mix in a blender at high speed.
4. Strain to desired consistency.

## Buttermilk Substitute

When a recipe calls for buttermilk, you can create an excellent substitute, much the same as you would with cow's milk, by adding a souring agent.

# "Buttermilk"

### INGREDIENTS

2–3   *teaspoons lemon juice, apple cider vinegar, or cream of tartar*
      *Plain or unsweetened milk alternative (soy, rice, almond, etc.)*

### DIRECTIONS

1. Mix the lemon juice with the milk alternative, adding enough of the milk alternative to make 1 cup.
2. Let the solution stand for 10 minutes before adding to your recipe.

## Cheese

Try goat or sheep cheese as a cheese substitute. Tofu makes a good soft-cheese substitute. And you will find some hard and soft soy "cheeses" in the health food store.

Here are recipes from Go Dairy Free for preparing noncheese substitutes for two popular cheeses: Parmesan and cream cheese.

# Parmesan Substitute

Go Dairy Free adapted this Parmesan substitute from *The Uncheese Cookbook*, by Joanne Stepaniak.

### INGREDIENTS

1   *cup raw almonds, blanched and peeled*
1   *cup nutritional yeast flakes (available in health food stores)*
½   *teaspoon sea salt*

### DIRECTIONS

1. To blanch and peel the almonds yourself, soak them in boiling water for 5 minutes. The skins should pop off easily.

2. Pat the almonds dry to remove excess moisture.
3. Place the almonds, yeast flakes, and sea salt in a food processor or blender and reduce to a fine powder.
4. Store in the refrigerator for a fairly long shelf life.

# Cream Cheese Alternative

## INGREDIENTS

1   *cup firm silken tofu*

2   *tablespoons olive oil*

3   *tablespoons lemon juice or 2 tablespoons vinegar*

1   *tablespoon sugar*

½   *teaspoon sea salt*

## DIRECTIONS

1. Combine the tofu, oil, lemon juice, sugar, and salt in a blender and process until smooth.
2. Pour into a bowl and chill.

## Butter

Butter is a dairy product. If you cannot tolerate dairy, I do *not* recommend using margarine because of trans fats. One alternative is to use coconut oil, which is an excellent fat to replace butter in recipes. It has the same characteristics of butter, margarine, or shortening.

You can also use extra-virgin olive oil (which is extremely healthy), a lighter tasting olive oil (which has a milder taste), or a soy-based substitute (available in health food stores). (Did you know that you can even bake with olive oil instead of solid shortenings? You will have to use less oil than you would shortening, however; otherwise the baked goods may be too oily.)

My top recommendation for a butter substitute, however, is coconut oil.

Coconut oil is solid at room temperature. It can be exchanged 1:1 for butter or shortening. But that is only one of its attributes. Others include:[3]

• It doesn't spoil at room temperature.

• It contains no trans fat.

- It is a healthy saturated fat.
- It lowers cholesterol levels.
- It is good for your skin.

Try coconut oil in all your cooking and baking. I think you'll like the taste, and your body will enjoy its health benefits.

## Sour Cream

If you want a dairy-free substitute for sour cream, blend silken tofu until it is smooth. For an even more sour cream–like taste, try this:[4]

# Sour Tofu Cream

### INGREDIENTS

| | |
|---|---|
| 1 | *package (8 ounces) silken tofu* |
| 3 | *tablespoons lemon juice or 1½ tablespoons vinegar* |
| 2 | *tablespoons olive oil* |
| 1½ | *teaspoons maple syrup, honey, or sugar* |
| ⅛ | *teaspoon sea salt* |
| 1 | *tablespoon unsweetened or plain soy milk, plus additional for consistency* |

### DIRECTIONS

1. Combine the tofu, lemon juice, oil, maple syrup, salt, and soy milk in a blender and puree until smooth.
2. You may add the soy milk 1 tablespoon at a time, until your desired consistency is reached.

## Sugar Substitutes

In Chapter 11, Setting Yourself Free, I told you about a number of sugar substitutes that are on the market. These include:

- Agave cactus
- Fructose
- Honey
- Maltitol
- Maple syrup

- Stevia (sold as a supplement in the United States, not as a sugar sub-stitute)
- Xylitol

Sucralose is another alternative, along with some newer products that incorporate sucralose as part of their formulas. It appears to be well tolerated by most people.

# CHAPTER 16

## GLUTEN-FREE COOKING 101

Do you wake up in the morning too rushed to prepare and eat a proper breakfast? And when you come home at night, are you too tired and have too little interest in the kitchen to cook anything that requires more than a quick warming?

Perhaps your kitchen is in pristine condition because you almost never have to wash a pot, let alone a dish or a glass!

If this describes you, then you'll be glad to know that you *can* survive on a gluten-free diet without doing much cooking at all.

However, this will come at a price. But it's a price that you are probably already paying: quality of food. Not that processed gluten-free food is bad, but home-cooked meals are so much better!

Another price you will pay is the cost of processed gluten-free foodstuffs. Prepared gluten-free food costs considerably more than its non-gluten-free equivalents.

However, I know that *nothing* I can say will convince you to dust off (literally) your dishes and pans and learn the fine art of cooking. So, if you are intent on staying out of the kitchen—or just want to take a break from preparing entire meals from scratch—here are some resources, as well as recipes, in this chapter that we've entitled "Gluten-Free Cooking 101."

*A word of caution:* Always, *always* check labels! And read them carefully. The food-allergens labeling law that went into effect on January 1, 2006, specifies that eight common allergens, including wheat (but not rye or barley), must be clearly stated in plain English on the label. Many manufacturers note these allergens in bold letters in a separate statement from the rest of the ingredients.

Others, however, do not make a separate statement and merely list the allergens (such as wheat) within the list of ingredients, which may be printed in very fine print. So, take your time and read carefully.

Keep in mind, too, that manufacturers may change processing methods and ingredients. A product you purchased last month that did not contain gluten could have changed formulation! So, it's always wise to read first, eat later.

Although some food processors reveal, on their Web sites or by request, which of their foods are gluten-free, others will not commit to saying their products do not contain gluten, probably because of liability issues. And others print a disclaimer on their labels, stating that the product "may be manufactured in a plant that processes wheat" or other allergens.

In other words: Be prudent in all your purchases but especially in those that involve any type of processed foods.

## GF FOODS IN YOUR LOCAL GROCERY STORE

In an earlier chapter, we discussed things that you should avoid eating and how to spot gluten-containing foods. Not all prepared foods contain gluten, however—even foods that you find in your local grocery store.

I hope you are fortunate enough to have a well-stocked health food store, such as a Whole Foods Market, in your neighborhood. Whole Foods (and other) grocery stores carry organic, dairy-free, and gluten-free products in every category. In a single visit, you are able to fill your grocery cart with every type of gluten-free product you could imagine—freshly baked goods, main courses, snacks, breads, crackers, condiments, and desserts.

But if you don't have such a grocery close by, you can still enjoy gluten-free eating with minimal preparation.

Many "regular" chain grocery stores are beginning to stock gluten-free items. For example:

**Super Wal-Mart.** Although you may not find a special GF aisle in your local Super Wal-Mart, look at private-label goods to check GF status. In 2005, Wal-Mart began to require manufacturers to identify gluten in its private-label products.

**Albertson's.** This national grocery-store chain includes the Albertson's, Jewel-Osco, Shaw's, and Sav-on names. It carries house brands that are gluten-free.

**Publix.** This large chain operates in the Southeast. It offers consumers a list of products that are gluten-free. It is slowly installing natural and organic sections in its stores, with some limited gluten-free-labeled products available.

**Winn–Dixie.** This is another large grocery chain that operates in the Southeast. It offers some house brands that are gluten-free. And it provides, in some stores, both frozen goods and packaged goods in its "natural" aisle.

**Safeway.** This chain includes Safeway, Vons, Dominick's, Randall's, Tom Thumb, and Genuardi's stores throughout the United States. It carries house brands that are gluten-free but does not require suppliers to label the foods as such.

**Wegmans.** This chain operates in New York, Pennsylvania, New Jersey, Virginia, and Maryland. It provides consumers with an extensive list of gluten-free house brands. The list is available online and is updated weekly. (Wegman's Web site, www.wegmans.com, also offers a searchable recipe database, which can be defined by gluten-free.)

**Hannaford.** This chain has 140 supermarkets and combination food stores and drugstores in Maine, New Hampshire, Massachusetts, New York, and Vermont. Gluten-sensitive individuals who are lucky enough to live near one of its stores can find a wide variety of GF foods. The company provides a list of GF products in a downloadable brochure on its Web site, www.hannaford.com.

## Finding GF at Your Local Grocery

Let's take a "walk" through your local grocery and see the different gluten-free foods that are "ripe" for picking. Just be careful with your choices. Just because something is gluten-free doesn't mean it's healthy!

**Fresh fruits.** All fresh fruits are gluten-free. Buy whatever is in season, and enjoy the nutrients and refreshment they offer. Fresh fruits make a perfect dessert or a light snack.

**Canned, jarred, and frozen fruits.** Peaches, pears, oranges, applesauce—all canned fruits—are gluten-free, although they are not as nutritious as fresh fruits. Select no-sugar-added varieties for healthier eating. Frozen fruits are more nutritious and better tasting than canned.

**Juices.** Do you enjoy a glass of orange juice in the morning? Apple juice? Or how about mango-peach? Juices are gluten-free. Enjoy. (But stay away from "super juices" or "green" juices, which contain many nutrients but include wheat and barley grass.)

**Fresh vegetables.** Like fruits, all vegetables are gluten-free. All can be prepared easily—even if you don't like to cook!

**Canned, jarred, and frozen vegetables.** What's your preference? Peas, carrots, beans, asparagus, mushrooms, artichokes, spinach—canned, jarred, and frozen vegetables are all gluten-free. The only thing you have to be careful about is the packets of sauces in frozen vegetables. It's a sure bet that those little packets of flavorings contain gluten. The best alternative, of course, is to choose fresh—preferably organic—vegetables. They are far more nutritious.

**Salads.** Leafy salads sold in bags are gluten-free. *Tip:* For the most nutrients, avoid salads made primarily of iceberg lettuce, which has the fewest nutrients of all types of lettuce. As a rule of thumb, lettuce that is a darker green is more nutritious. For example, romaine or watercress have seven to eight times as much beta-carotene, two to four times the calcium, and twice the amount of potassium as iceberg lettuce.[1]

**Deli counter.** If you are not on a dairy-free diet, cheese is a good choice. It is naturally gluten-free. I recommend selecting brands that have lower fat and lower salt contents, prepared without nitrates and nitrites. A number of Boar's Head deli meats, for example, do not contain additives and are certified by the Feingold Association. (The Feingold diet eliminates additives that may trigger behavioral problems.) I also highly recommend organic cheeses, which you can find at some health food stores and some supermarkets.

Many of the meats are also GF, such as roasted turkey, chicken, and ham. So are many of the salads in the deli case, such as gelatin, potato salad (but obviously not macaroni salad!), three-bean salad, and carrot salad. *But*—before you take a bite, ask to read the ingredient labels of these foods. You'll be pleasantly surprised to find that most do not contain gluten, but always be safe rather than sorry.

**Prepared deli entrées.** Large grocery stores often sell main courses, as well as side dishes, for heat-and-eat meals. Fried chicken is forbidden (because of its coating), but roasted or rotisserie chicken is okay unless its label says it has been prepared with a flavoring containing gluten. Avoid gravies and anything breaded. Ask how the entrée was cooked to make sure it is devoid of gluten.

**Dairy products.** Milk, sour cream, soft and hard cheeses (such as cream cheese, ricotta, mozzarella, Cheddar, Edam, provolone, and Swiss, to name a few), and yogurt are all naturally gluten-free. The healthiest products are low-fat and low-salt, as well as low-fat and fat-free unsweetened yogurts. (*Caution:* If you are considering a processed cheese or a low-fat yogurt or one that has flavoring added to it, check the label carefully. These products may have gluten added to them.)

Are you dairy-free, too? The dairy case still contains products that you can buy ready-to-eat, such as milk substitutes (soy or rice milk) and tofu.

Keep in mind: Soy is one of the foods that many food-sensitive folks react to. If you are one of those individuals, you still have alternatives, although you may have to find them in a health food store instead of your grocer's dairy case.

Consider almond milk, available in some groceries (and definitely at the health food store). It comes in vanilla (no sugar added). More options include other types of nut milks.

For cheeses (which can be found at the local grocer), look for goat and sheep cheese, as well as other substitute products.

Always, always read the product labels to make sure they do not contain casein if you are dairy-sensitive.

**Eggs.** Eggs are a great source of protein. They are naturally gluten-free. Egg substitutes (such as Egg Beaters) are also gluten-free. I personally love organic eggs, which are high in omega-3 fatty acids—great for your heart!

**Shelf-stable foods.** These are foods that can be stored and transported without refrigeration and are easy to take with you when you are on the go. They are heated in a microwave or by placing the pouch in boiling water.

One source of shelf-stable gluten-free foods is Market America (www.marketamerica.com). This online company is one of the first to offer shelf-stable GF entrées to its customers. A number of its entrées, bars, and shakes are made without wheat, barley, or rye.

**Meats, fish, and poultry.** Excellent choices! I recommend selecting organic when these meats, fish, and poultry are available and affordable. These can be easily transformed into nutritious main courses that provide you with necessary protein.

What to be leery of? Meatless meats, fish, and poultry. Vegetarian counterfeits are not appropriate substitutes for gluten-sensitive individuals. Gluten is a primary ingredient in these protein alternatives.

What about lunchmeats and sausages? Always check the label, but most varieties are gluten-free. Not all sausages or hot dogs are, however. Read labels carefully!

*On a good note:* Prior to the allergen food-labeling law, which went into effect January 1, 2006, in the United States, the gluten in these meatless meats was largely hidden. Now, however, if you read the label, you will see "wheat" clearly mentioned.

**Canned meats, fish, and poultry.** Already cooked, canned meats (such as some brands of ham, corned beef, stews, and similar foods), fish (such as tuna, salmon, kippers, and sardines), and poultry (such as chicken and turkey) are convenience items that can be easily used as an ingredient or prepared as a protein source. These foods often have a high sodium content, however, so use them in moderation. And be careful not to select processed meat spreads (such as potted meats); they may have gluten added.

**Side dishes.** Pasta, rice, and potatoes are probably the most common starchy side dishes to American meals.

Wheat-based pasta in any form—spaghetti, elbow macaroni, spirals, linguini, lasagna—is, of course, off-limits. But a number of grocery stores are beginning to carry gluten-free varieties of pasta, made from corn, rice, buckwheat, or quinoa. Rice noodles, usually found in the Asian-cooking section, are also a good substitute for wheat pasta; so are soba noodles, which are made from buckwheat. (Check the label carefully, though. Some soba noodles are prepared with a combination of buckwheat and wheat flours.)

All varieties of rice are gluten-free (though brown rice is healthier than white). But many brands of boxed rice-based side dishes are *not* gluten-free, such as New Orleans' style "dirty" rice and red beans and rice. Always check the labels carefully to see what types of additives rice dishes contain.

Couscous, a fine pasta used in Mediterranean cooking, is wheat-based. A good substitute is kasha, a gluten-free buckwheat product, or wild rice.

You already know that raw potatoes (including sweet potatoes and yams) are gluten-free. How about instant potatoes and instant potato side dishes, such as scalloped potatoes? Unless the label says otherwise, these should be okay—and they are easy to prepare. (Take a close look at any box of instant potatoes that has extra flavoring packets. The flavoring may contain gluten.)

Some frozen hash browns, french fries, and potato nuggets that do not have extra coatings (and gluten) are okay. Since these are pre-fried, I recommend using them sparingly. Better: Substitute yams or wild rice for your starch.

**Condiments.** Spices add zest and taste to prepared foods. Always check labels, but spices and herbs are naturally gluten-free. Mustard, ketchup, and salsa are also gluten-free. I've checked the labels on many different brands of mayonnaise and have not yet found one that contains gluten.

Some meat marinades contain soy sauce that uses wheat as an ingredient. Also, some steak sauces include wheat in their ingredients. Hot sauces are gluten-free.

Vinegars, except for malt vinegar, are gluten-free and should not cause you a problem.

Pancake syrups are also gluten-free; likewise, most jams and jellies. But always read labels.

**Cereals.** With the exception of oatmeal—which is technically gluten-free—the cereals you find in the cereal aisle of most groceries contain a hidden source of gluten—malt, which is made from barley.

I do not recommend eating oats (even steel-ground oatmeal) because of the risk of cross-contamination. The exception is a gluten-free oatmeal, which can be purchased online. (See Helpful Resources for Gluten-Free Living, on page 275, for more information.) Although the company cannot guarantee that its oatmeal is GF, the oats are processed in a dedicated mill, and the company "reckons that the level of non-oat grains [is] less than 0.05 percent."[2] This brand of oatmeal is available in supermarkets, as well as online.

Some grocery stores are beginning to carry a few varieties of gluten-free cereals, which may be found in an "organic" or "natural" section of the grocery. I have purchased corn flakes, quinoa flakes, rice crispies, puffed rice, puffed millet, and puffed corn in the local grocery.

**Snack foods.** Popcorn is okay; check the label for gluten on popcorn that contains flavorings. Plain corn chips have no gluten. Nor do unflavored potato chips. Before you reach for flavored chips, such as barbecue or Cheddar cheese, look at the ingredients. As a nutritionist, I urge you to eat these snacks sparingly and to select baked chip varieties over fried. (Fresh fruit, nuts, and baby carrots make great GF snacks!)

Your neighborhood grocery store probably does *not* carry gluten-free pretzels.

*A word of caution:* Although many brands of snacks are gluten-free, the ingredients may note that they are made in facilities that process wheat. Cross-contamination may be an issue, especially if you are extremely sensitive to gluten.

**Desserts.** If you are not dairy-intolerant, ice cream, sorbets, and sherbets are almost always gluten-free, unless they include ingredients such as "cookie dough," "cheesecake," or "brownies." Virtually all brands, even premium brands, of ice cream use carrageenan to improve texture. If you want to reduce your intake of this additive, stick to making your own ice cream at home.

Cakes, pies, and cookies found at the local grocer are all wheat-based and must be on your not-to-buy list.

**Beverages.** Coffee, tea, natural fruit juices, and soda are all gluten-free. Check the label on hot chocolate mixes.

**Alcohol.** You won't find gluten-free beer sold in your local grocery (yet), unless you are fortunate enough to live near one of the three breweries in North America (two in the United States, one in Canada) that brew GF beer. But you can indulge in wine and other distilled spirits, including rum, whiskey, gin, and vodka.

## GF IN SPECIALTY STORES

As you can see from the list of gluten-free foods available in your local grocery, even if you do not cook, your gluten-sensitivity will not be an excuse to go hungry! You have plenty to choose from.

Although the corner grocery is beginning to offer a variety of gluten-free products to satisfy the tastebuds of those of you who prefer not to cook, three national chain stores (and I am certain many, many local ones) offer extensive gluten-free products to their customers. These chains are:

**Whole Foods Market** (www.wholefoodsmarket.com) is quite possibly the largest retailer of natural and organic foods, with 181 stores in North America and the United Kingdom.

**Wild Oats Markets** (www.wildoats.com) is an organic and natural food market that has 110 stores in 25 states and Canada. It offers its own brand of gluten-free foods and has a product guide available for down-loading.

**Trader Joe's** (www.traderjoes.com). This chain of more than 200 specialty stores operates throughout the United States. It carries more than 2,000 items under its own label, including a wide variety of gluten-free products.

If you are fortunate enough to have one of these markets in your community, I recommend visiting it at least to supplement your gluten-free purchases. These groceries feature many gluten-free products, including fresh and frozen meals, which are unavailable (as yet) in most supermarkets. You can also purchase prepared mixes of all sorts—for breads, quick breads, pancakes, brownies, or cookies, for example.

Even if you do not have access to one of these large specialty stores, your community most likely has at least one health food store. There you can also supplement your gluten-free purchases with items such as:

**Frozen waffles.** Yes, you can buy GF frozen waffles that taste just like the "real" things. (Van's Gluten-Free Waffles are available in many supermarkets, as well as health food stores.)

**Bread.** Try the millet bread; it toasts well and tastes good. But don't limit your selection to one kind. (You ate different kinds of wheat bread, didn't you? Variety makes eating fun!) You'll find several different types of rice breads—even 100% corn tortillas (which you can use as a sandwich bread)—available in health food stores, usually in the cooler section, where they are kept refrigerated or frozen. (Unless you eat a lot of bread, I recommend storing your bread in the freezer. GF bread tends to dry out quickly. Freezing prolongs its life.)

**Snack items.** Want a cookie or snack cake? You can find these more easily at health food stores.

## GF ONLINE

Health food stores can provide you with basic food items (see above) to supplement what you buy at your regular corner grocery. Individuals who want the convenience of prepared foods along with a wide variety of products will find it easy to shop online.

In Helpful Resources for Gluten-Free Living, on page 275, we provide a list of online stores. However, to prove to you that you can enjoy a wide variety of prepared foods and to help you plan your meals,

I collected product information and have sorted it into meal categories. I've also indicated if the product is in the "I Hate to Cook" category (1); "Keep It Simple, Sam" category (2); or "Cooking? No problem!" category (3). You'll find this list at the end of this chapter.

Keep in mind as you browse through the list that I did not include every item! I selected only representative products in each category. I think you will be quite impressed with how far food processors have gone to meet the needs of a rapidly growing gluten-free society.

Now on to cooking!

## GF COOKING 101: BREAKFASTS

On the run? Don't skimp on breakfast. It's the most important meal of the day.

Breakfast helps regulate your metabolism, so it's important to eat the right foods—foods that are not too high in sugar—so the fact that a gluten-free diet excludes Krispy Kremes is a good thing!

Although you can't stop at the corner doughnut shop, you can still have breakfast on the go. Simply select from a wide variety of take-and-eat GF foods, such as:

- Bagels
- Breakfast bars (available in fruit flavors)
- Muffins (available in several flavors)

If you have time to sit down, enjoy a bowl of cereal (but not "regular" cereal, which is flavored with malt, a derivative of barley). You will find gluten-free cereals in a number of varieties, including:

- Buckwheat flakes
- Corn flakes
- Corn puffs
- Peanut butter puffs
- Puffed millet (very similar to old-fashioned puffed oats)
- Puffed rice
- Rice crispies

Before you rush out the door, however, ensure good nutrition by supplementing your on-the-go breakfast item with a glass of juice—or better—a piece of fresh fruit or milk or dairy-free milk. You can, of course, have a cup of coffee or tea; I recommend decaffeinated.

Breakfast bars, muffins, and cereal can become boring—and although they are gluten-free, many are still high in carbohydrates and simple sugars. A more nutritious beginning to your day would come from a breakfast high in protein.

Try the following GF breakfasts. You'll enjoy variety and will kick-start your day in a healthy way.

## Tropical Breakfast Shake[3]

Here's a quick and easy GF and dairy-free on-the-go breakfast. It will take about 5 minutes to prepare and will serve two. (Or, if you prefer—drink one and save one for tomorrow!)

The hardest part of this recipe is cutting up the fruit for the drink.

### INGREDIENTS

| | |
|---|---|
| 3 | ounces (about ¼ cup) GF soft tofu, silken style |
| 2 | tablespoons honey |
| ½ | cup orange juice |
| 2 | teaspoons lemon juice |
| 1 | cup pineapple, chopped |
| 1 | small banana, sliced |
| 6 | ice cubes |

### DIRECTIONS

1. Combine the tofu, honey, orange juice, lemon juice, pineapple, banana, and ice cubes in a blender.
2. Puree for about 30 seconds, or until well blended and frothy.

*Optional: Garnish with cubed fruits such as mango, kiwifruit, and raspberries on skewers.*

## Peanut Butter Waffles

Who doesn't enjoy a good waffle every once in a while? Waffles are high in carbohydrates, but you can "offset" those carbs by avoiding syrups to top them off. Instead, try this:

## INGREDIENTS

2   *GF frozen waffles*

2   *tablespoons peanut butter or raw or toasted almond butter*

## DIRECTIONS

1. Set the waffles out for a few minutes to warm. (This will help them toast faster.)
2. Pop them into a toaster or toaster oven, toasting both sides until crisp.
3. Spread your favorite peanut butter on them for a flavorful boost of protein and energy.
4. For an even tastier treat, add some all-fruit jam over the nut butter.

# Turkey on Toast

Turkey on toast? Whoever heard of eating turkey for breakfast? Well, why not? Turkey is lean and is all protein. It takes your body longer to digest protein, so a breakfast of turkey on toast will keep you satisfied longer into the day.

## INGREDIENTS

1   *slice GF bread*

    *Mustard or mayonnaise, to taste*

1   *slice turkey*

1   *slice tomato*

## DIRECTIONS

1. Toast the bread and spread with the mustard
2. Place the turkey and tomato on the bread.
3. Enjoy your lunch-for-breakfast treat.

# Toasted Bagel and Cream Cheese

No, these aren't New York bagels with their overload of gluten. But if you are craving a bagel and cream cheese, try toasting one of these.

**INGREDIENTS**

1   GF bagel, thawed

1   tablespoon butter, all-fruit jam, or cream cheese or cheese substitute

**DIRECTIONS**

1. Toast the bagel.
2. Top with the butter, all-fruit jam, or cream cheese.

*Tip: For a really good treat that is more nutritious, top the bagel and cream cheese with slices of smoked salmon (lox) or kippers (available in the canned fish section of the grocery).*

# Orange Pink-Grapefruit Smoothie[4]

This is a sweet-and-sour breakfast treat that is ready in minutes.

**INGREDIENTS**

2   oranges

1   pink grapefruit

8   ice cubes

    Honey, to taste

**DIRECTIONS**

1. Cut the oranges and grapefruit into pieces, carefully removing all the membranes and seeds.
2. Chill the fruits in the freezer for a while for smoother consistency.
3. Combine the fruits in a blender with the ice and as much honey as you like—at least 1 teaspoon. Adjust to taste.
4. Enjoy.

# Peanut Butter and Banana Toast[5]

Store-bought gluten-free bread tends to be crumbly, dries out easily, and does not toast as well as wheat bread. This toast hides the texture and provides nutrition from the peanut butter.

**INGREDIENTS**

2–3   *slices GF bread*

¼   *cup chunky peanut butter or raw or toasted almond butter*

1   *banana*

**DIRECTIONS**

1. Toast the bread (both sides). (*Note:* GF bread does not usually turn to a toasted color, like wheat bread does.)
2. Spread the peanut butter on each slice of toast.
3. Slice the banana crosswise, and add a layer of banana slices on top of the peanut butter.
4. Eat as is—or for a treat, put the toast under a grill in a toaster oven for a minute to warm the peanut butter.

*Optional: Add honey on top of the banana and pop under the grill until it starts to sizzle.*

# Hot Honey Spread[6]

As long as you have bread, bagels, muffins, or other GF bread stuffed in your refrigerator or freezer, spice them up with different types of spreads for an easy breakfast. Sure, it will take you a few minutes to prepare this spread—but once done, it's *done* and ready to use.

This hot honey spread is hot to the taste—peppers make it that way.

**INGREDIENTS**

1   *cup honey*

1   *teaspoon crushed red pepper flakes*

**DIRECTIONS**

1. Combine the honey and pepper flakes in a heavy saucepan.
2. Warm over low heat for 10 minutes.
3. Cover and turn off the heat.
4. Let the mixture stand for 1 to 2 hours. Don't rush this step! This is when the heat and flavor of the red peppers permeates the honey.

5. Strain the mixture through a fine sieve, and pour into steril-
ized jars with tightly fitting lids.
6. Store at room temperature.

*Tip: You can easily adjust this recipe (up or down). Just keep the ratio of 1 teaspoon of red pepper flakes for each cup of honey.*

# Breakfast Burrito

Breakfast burritos are usually made with wheat flour tortillas. Instead of flour tortillas, buy a package of corn tortillas, and keep them in your refrigerator.

## INGREDIENTS

1   *large egg*
    *Shredded Cheddar cheese or cheese substitute*
1   *corn tortilla*
    *Salsa, hot sauce, or taco sauce, to taste*

## DIRECTIONS

1. Scramble the egg.
2. As the egg begins to set in the pan, sprinkle on the cheese.
3. While the egg is cooking, warm the tortilla in a toaster oven.
4. Fill the center of the tortilla with the egg mixture. Add salsa or sauce, to taste. Fold in the ends and overlap the sides.
5. Enjoy!

*Variations: If your culinary creativity becomes stimulated (and you have time), sauté green bell peppers and onion in the skillet before adding the egg. Brown hash brown potatoes. Build the burrito beginning with the hash browns, and then add the egg mixture. Top with salsa. Wrap in foil. You can make several of these and keep them in your refrigerator until you are ready to eat them.*

## GF COOKING 101: LUNCHES

What do you like to eat for lunch? Sandwiches? Salads? Soup? You can have all of these items on a gluten-free diet.

*Tip:* For some satisfying "crunch," add a few corn tortilla chips (baked is better for you than fried), along with salsa, to your lunch bag. With some fruit and perhaps some raw vegetables (broccoli, cauliflower, mushrooms, or carrots, for example), you will have a satisfying lunch.

For quick lunches, choose from a variety of prepared GF foods, such as:

- GF macaroni and cheese
- Soup. You have many varieties to choose from, such as split pea, cream of tomato, miso, French onion, and potato leek. You can order these online or purchase them in a natural food grocery. But don't overlook "regular" soups that are gluten-free, which come in a number of varieties, such as roasted chicken and rice, lentil, and chowder.
- Asian noodles (many different varieties of Thai noodles are available on the grocer's shelf)
- Mexican "pot" meal
- Instant stroganoff with beef and rice

When you get tired of grab-and-go lunches, try the following gluten-free foods.

## Turkey-Bacon Lettuce Wrap

Instead of a traditional BLT sandwich, try this bread-free bacon lettuce wrap.

### INGREDIENTS

| | |
|---|---|
| 3 | leaves romaine lettuce |
| 3–6 | strips turkey bacon |
| | Mayonnaise to taste |
| | Tomatoes, sliced lengthwise |

### DIRECTIONS

1. Wash the lettuce and pat dry.
2. Cook the bacon, until crisp.
3. Spread the mayonnaise, to taste, on each lettuce leaf.

4. Place 1 or 2 slices of bacon and as many slices of tomato as desired in the center of each lettuce leaf.
5. Wrap lengthwise. Enjoy!

## Chef Salad to Go

Some fast-food restaurants and many deli counters at grocery stores offer fresh salads. But, if they are prepared ahead of time, you will probably find them covered in croutons. Picking croutons off the salad is not an option for anyone who is gluten-sensitive, because crumbs may contaminate the salad.

Instead, prepare your own salad, and store it in an insulated bag or in the "community" refrigerator at work.

### INGREDIENTS

*Bagged salad (Italian blend or garden blend with a variety of lettuces)*
1   *hard-cooked egg*
*Leftover ham, chicken, or turkey*
*GF salad dressing*
*Tortilla chips*

### DIRECTIONS

1. Place a luncheon-size serving of the salad in a plastic container.
2. Slice the egg and place on top of the salad greens.
3. Slice the ham, chicken, or turkey and place on top of the greens and egg.
4. When you are ready for lunch, add the salad dressing. The tortilla chips? They make a nice "side" in place of crackers.

*Tip: If you do not have leftover ham, chicken, or turkey (and you probably don't, since you hate to cook!), you can use canned or deli meats.*

## Open-Faced Toasted Tuna Salad with Cheese

Do you have a toaster oven available at home or at work? This is an easy recipe. One can of tuna will make at least two, possibly three, open-faced sandwiches.

## INGREDIENTS

1   *can chunk-style tuna (preferably packed in water)*

1   *rib celery, finely chopped*

¼   *medium onion, finely chopped*

¼   *cup white or purple seedless grapes (optional)*

¼   *cup finely chopped walnuts or pecans (optional)*

2   *tablespoons mayonnaise*

3   *slices GF bread*

3   *slices Swiss or Cheddar cheese or cheese made from goat, sheep, rice, or soy milk*

*Salt and pepper, to taste*

## DIRECTIONS

1. Drain the tuna and place in a medium-size bowl.
2. Add the celery, onion, grapes (if using), nuts (if using), and mayonnaise. Mix thoroughly.
3. Spread mixture on the bread.
4. Place a slice of cheese on top of the sandwich.
5. Place the sandwich in a toaster oven set to Broil.
6. Toast until the cheese melts. Add salt and pepper, to taste.
7. Remove and eat!

*Tip: If you don't have celery, substitute chopped water chestnuts.*

# Tuna-Salad Lettuce Wrap[7]

Tuna is an excellent source of protein. It is low in fat and high in energy. And it mixes into great salads that can be used in a number of ways. Here is another tuna salad for lunch at home or on the go.

## INGREDIENTS

4   *baby carrots*

6   *olives*

1   *plum tomato*

1   *can tuna, drained*

1   *teaspoon garlic powder*

1     *teaspoon salt*

1     *teaspoon ground black pepper*

2     *tablespoons GF Caesar salad dressing*

4     *lettuce leaves*

## DIRECTIONS

1. Finely chop the carrots and olives. (*Tip:* Use a food processor. It's quick and easy.)
2. By hand, dice the tomato into small chunks.
3. Combine the tuna, carrots, olives, and tomato in a small mixing bowl.
4. Add the garlic powder, salt, pepper, and salad dressing. Mix thoroughly to combine all ingredients.
5. Place ¼ of the mixture in the center of a large lettuce leaf. Fold the bottom up, and then fold in the sides to wrap the mixture.
6. For lunch on the go, wrap in foil.

# Egg Salad[8]

Eggs are versatile and the "perfect" food. Hard-cooked eggs are easy to prepare, can be eaten "as is," or used in many different recipes, including egg salad. Serve on GF bread as a sandwich or over crisp lettuce as a salad. Here is a simple egg salad that will make 4 servings.

## INGREDIENTS

8     *eggs*

1     *tablespoon mayonnaise*

2     *tablespoons prepared Dijon-style mustard*

1     *teaspoon dried dillweed*

1     *teaspoon ground paprika*

½     *medium red onion, chopped*

      *Salt and pepper, to taste*

## DIRECTIONS

1. Place the eggs in a saucepan and cover with cold water.
2. Bring the water to a boil. Cover, remove from the heat, and let the eggs stand in the water for 10 to 12 minutes.

3. Remove the eggs from the water. Cool under cold water, peel, and chop.

4. In a large bowl, combine the eggs, mayonnaise, mustard, dill-weed, paprika, onion, and salt and pepper, to taste. Blend well with a fork or wooden spoon.

# Busy-Day Lunch

Want something really easy? This will take minutes to prepare. It's light, healthy, and flavorful.

## INGREDIENTS

1   *can sliced carrots*

    *Cheese (Monterey Jack, Cheddar, pepper jack, Edam, or other varieties)*

1   *onion, chopped*

1   *apple, chopped*

1   *individual serving box raisins*

    *Green bell pepper pieces*

    *Italian dressing*

## DIRECTIONS

1. Drain the carrots well.
2. Cut the cheese into ½" cubes. (For variety, include several types of cheese.)
3. Mix together the carrots, cheese, onion, apple, raisins, and bell pepper.
4. Pour the dressing on the ingredients, to taste, and toss.
5. Store in a spill-proof plastic container.
6. This lunch travels well in an unrefrigerated lunch bag. The hardest part of the recipe is opening the can.

# Spinach Salad

Spinach is a good source of vitamins and minerals. This spinach salad takes a little preparation but does not require making a dressing from scratch—just make sure your dressing (poppyseed is recommended) is gluten-free.

## INGREDIENTS

2   *cups fresh spinach*

¼   *medium purple onion or sweet onion*

1   *hard-cooked egg, shelled and sliced*

¼   *cup sliced fresh mushrooms*

1   *slice bacon, fried crisp and crumbled (You can purchase real bacon crumbs without gluten in your grocery store.)*

    *Poppyseed dressing, to taste*

## DIRECTIONS

1. Wash and tear the spinach leaves into bite-size pieces.
2. Place the spinach in a large bowl.
3. Slice the onion into rings, adding to the salad as you slice.
4. Add the egg, mushrooms, and bacon to the salad.
5. Pour on the dressing and toss—or use it on the side.

*Tip: If you take this salad to work or school in a plastic container, do not add the dressing until you are ready to eat.*

## GF COOKING 101: DINNERS

What's for dinner? You want it quick, and you want it easy. Check out the "instant" gluten-free dinners you can get online or through a large health food store. For example, you can purchase:

- Frozen pizza
- Instant pizza dough
- Chili
- Mexican dinners
- Chicken dinners
- Thai noodle dinners (in a variety of flavors)
- Beef stew (You can even buy a gluten-free variety of "regular" beef stew at your grocery.)

Add a small salad, some fruit, a serving of vegetables, and possibly a piece of GF bread (or roll), and you have a complete dinner with virtually no work.

For tastier dinners, be a little daring! The following recipes require a little work, but not much. And you'll really enjoy the homemade taste of your labor.

## Pad Thai with Vegetables

A number of prepared Thai noodle dinners are gluten-free and are available at your local grocery store. They are quick to prepare (about 15 minutes) and are tasty alternatives to eating out. You will be surprised at how good this dinner for two is!

### INGREDIENTS

| | |
|---|---|
| 1 | box Thai Kitchen original pad thai dinner |
| 3 | tablespoons vegetable oil |
| 1 | egg |
| 4 | ounces cut-up chicken, shrimp, or tofu |
| 4 | ounces vegetables (Try flash-frozen mixed vegetables. Use what you want and store the rest in the freezer.) |
| ½ | cup fresh bean sprouts (found in the produce department) |
| ¼ | cup crushed peanuts |
| | Lime wedges, fresh chiles, and cilantro (optional) |

### DIRECTIONS

1. In a medium saucepan, boil 3 cups of water.
2. Turn off the heat and soak the noodles in the water for 3 to 5 minutes, or until they are soft but still firm.
3. Drain the noodles well.
4. Rinse the noodles under cold water for 30 seconds. Set aside.
5. In a wok or large skillet, heat 1 tablespoon of the oil.
6. Add the egg and scramble.
7. Remove the egg and set aside.
8. In the wok or skillet, heat the remaining 2 tablespoons of oil.
9. Add the chicken, shrimp, or tofu and vegetables and cook until done. The chicken or shrimp will turn white in color, and the vegetables should be crisp-tender.
10. Add the noodles and sauce from the package.
11. Cook for 3 to 4 minutes, or until the sauce is absorbed into the noodles.

12. Add the bean sprouts and egg.

13. Mix well to combine.

14. Sprinkle with the peanuts and garnish with the lime wedges, chiles, and cilantro, if using.

*Variation: Serve with white rice. Season to taste with GF soy sauce and chili sauce.*

# Red Beans and Rice with Sausage

It is said that red beans and rice are traditionally prepared and served on Mondays in New Orleans. That was wash day, and because washing was labor-intensive, it was necessary to prepare a meal that could be put on the stove to simmer and forget.

Today, you can eat red beans and rice any day of the week. But be careful when you shop for them in the grocery. Almost all brands have gluten added to them!

I found one brand, however, that has no gluten—Louisiana Fish Fry Products, New Orleans Style Red Beans & Rice Mix.

The following recipe will fill your house with a savory smell, and within about 20 minutes, you will have a delicious one-pot meal.

## INGREDIENTS

1     *tablespoon butter or extra-virgin olive oil*

8–12  *ounces turkey sausage*

1     *8-ounce package red beans and rice*

      *Louisiana hot sauce*

## DIRECTIONS

1. Bring 4 cups of water and the butter to a full boil.

2. While you are waiting for the water to boil, cut the sausage into thin slices.

3. Add the contents of the package to the boiling water and mix well.

4. Add the sausage.

5. Boil for 2 to 3 minutes.

6. Reduce heat to low.

7. Cook, covered, for 25 to 30 minutes, stirring often.
8. Remove from the heat and let stand for 5 minutes before serving.
9. Season with hot sauce, to taste.

# Easy Spaghetti Dinner

Before you went on a gluten-free diet, how did you prepare a spaghetti dinner? Did you open a jar of spaghetti sauce, heat it, and pour it over your pasta?

Homemade spaghetti sauce is better (you'll find a recipe for it later in this book). But when you are in a hurry, you can still enjoy an easy-to-prepare Italian meal.

## INGREDIENTS

1   box GF spaghetti pasta (I prefer quinoa. But you may find rice or corn pasta in your health food store or online.)
1   jar spaghetti sauce (Just check to make sure it does not contain gluten.)
    Garlic powder, basil, and thyme
    GF bread
    Trans-free margarine
    Dinner salad and salad dressing

## DIRECTIONS

1. Cook the pasta according to directions. Be careful not to overcook it! GF pasta can easily turn to mush if you overcook it.
2. Place the spaghetti sauce in a saucepan and heat. Season it with garlic powder, basil, thyme (or other herbs), to taste, to "doctor" its store-bought taste.
3. While the sauce is heating, slice the bread and spread with the margarine. Sprinkle with garlic powder, to taste.
4. Place the bread under a broiler until toasted. (Remember: GF bread does not get to a toasty color like its wheat counterparts.)
5. When all ingredients are ready, spoon the sauce over a helping of pasta, and serve with the dinner salad and garlic toast.

*Tip: For a heartier meal, brown lean ground beef or ground chicken or turkey, and add it to the sauce while it is warming. And for a savory change from garlic bread, slice and toast the GF bread and dip it into extra-virgin olive oil flavored with balsamic vinegar and a dash of Italian herbs. Mmmm!*

# Broiled Salmon with Mustard Sauce[9]

Salmon is an excellent choice in fish. It is high in omega-3, low in saturated fat, and low in calories. And it is easy to prepare, as this recipe demonstrates.

## INGREDIENTS

| | |
|---|---|
| 1 | *cup sour cream* |
| ½ | *cup finely chopped green onion* |
| 1½ | *tablespoons Dijon mustard* |
| 1 | *tablespoon chopped parsley* |
| ½ | *teaspoon salt* |
| ½ | *teaspoon thyme* |
| | *Dash of pepper* |
| 4 | *salmon steaks, cut 1" thick* |
| | *Salt and pepper to taste* |

## DIRECTIONS

1. Preheat the broiler.
2. Stir together the sour cream, onion, mustard, parsley, salt, thyme, and the dash of pepper. Set aside.
3. Sprinkle the salmon steaks lightly with salt and pepper.
4. To broil, line a shallow pan with foil, arrange the steaks on the foil, and broil 6 inches below the broiler for 7 minutes.
5. Remove the pan from the oven.
6. Spread the sour cream mix generously on top of each steak.
7. Return the salmon to the broiler and broil for about 5 minutes longer, or until the fish flakes easily with a fork.

# Roasted Chicken and Kasha Pilaf

Who doesn't like hot roasted chicken? Pick one up at the grocery; it's ready to eat. Keep it warm while you prepare this easy side dish, kasha pilaf.

Not familiar with kasha? Kasha is 100 percent roasted buckwheat, available at your local grocery. It's a great alternative to rice or couscous, even without added ingredients. Fine grained, it has a nutty flavor and can be cooked in a number of ways. This recipe makes about 4 cups.

## INGREDIENTS

| | |
|---|---|
| 2 | tablespoons butter |
| ½ | cup chopped onions |
| ½ | cup chopped celery |
| ½ | cup sliced mushrooms |
| ¼–½ | teaspoon salt |
| ⅛ | teaspoon pepper |
| 2 | cups GF chicken broth |
| 1 | egg or egg white |
| 1 | cup kasha |
| 1 | precooked roasted rotisserie chicken |

## DIRECTIONS

1. Melt the butter in a medium saucepan and heat until sizzling.
2. Add the onions, celery, and mushrooms and cook until tender. Remove to a bowl.
3. In a small saucepan, add the salt and pepper to the chicken broth and heat to boiling.
4. Lightly beat the egg in a bowl with a whisk or fork.
5. Add the kasha to the egg and stir to coat all kernels.
6. In the medium saucepan, add the egg-coated kasha. Cook over high heat for 2 to 3 minutes, stirring constantly until the egg dries on the kasha and the kernels separate. Reduce the heat to low.
7. Quickly stir in the boiling broth and add the sautéed vegetables. Cover tightly and simmer for 7 to 10 minutes, or until the kasha kernels are tender and the liquid is absorbed.

8. Slice the chicken and serve with the kasha pilaf.

*Tip: Look in your refrigerator and pantry to see what kinds of vegetables you have on hand. Experiment! You can add or substitute peas, chickpeas, lima beans—just about any type of vegetable that appeals to you.*

# Potatoes with Chorizo and Onions[10]

Rachael Ray, a Food TV personality, specializes in 30-minute meals. In 30 minutes, she proves that cooking is not difficult, and the results are excellent. She suggests this recipe as a side dish, but it makes a hearty skillet dinner, provided you accompany it with a salad and a vegetable.

Check the ingredients to make sure the chorizo—a spicy Spanish sausage—is gluten-free.

## INGREDIENTS

2    *tablespoons extra-virgin olive oil*

1    *¾-pound package chorizo sausage, very thinly sliced on an angle (Pull away any loose casings)*

6    *small Yukon gold potatoes, very thinly sliced*

1    *medium onion, very thinly sliced*

     *Salt and pepper to taste*

2    *teaspoons sweet ground paprika*

¼    *cup chopped flat-leaf parsley, a generous 1 or 2 handfuls*

## DIRECTIONS

1. Heat a medium skillet over medium-high heat.
2. Add enough of the oil to coat the pan in two turns. Add the sausage.
3. Cook for 2 minutes.
4. Flip the sausage and cook for 1 minute longer.
5. Add the potatoes and onion to the pan in an even layer, covering the sausage.
6. Season the potatoes and onion with the salt, pepper, and paprika.
7. With a spatula, turn sections of the potatoes so that the chorizo

is on top and the potatoes and onion are on the bottom.

8. Place a smaller skillet on top and press down. Weight the skillet down with a few heavy cans. This will help the potatoes cook more quickly and brown nicely.

9. Cook for 10 to 12 minutes.

10. Remove the weight and turn again to combine all ingredients.

11. Cook for 3 to 4 minutes longer, and add the parsley.

12. Remove from the heat and serve.

*Tip: If you can't find a GF chorizo—or if a spicy sausage is not to your liking—substitute smoked turkey sausage.*

## GLUTEN-FREE PREPARED FOODS AVAILABLE ONLINE

Reminder: If the product is in Category 1, it is GF Cooking 101; in Category 2, Cooking 201; and in Category 3, Cooking 301.

| Meal | Item | Brand | Store | Category |
|------|------|-------|-------|----------|
| Any meal | Bread | Cybro's Gluten-Free Rice Bread | Gluten-Free Mall | 1 |
| Any meal | Bread | Enjoy Life Foods Gluten-Free Rye-less "Rye" Sandwich Bread | Gluten-Free Mall | 1 |
| Any meal | Soda crackers | Glutano Crackers | Gluten-Free Mall | 1 |
| Any meal | Biscuits/ quick bread | GFP Quick Mix | Gluten-Free Pantry | 2 |
| Any meal | Bread | Buttermilk Brown Rice Pancake Mix | Gluten-Free Pantry | 2 |
| Any meal | Bread | Country French Bread Mix | Gluten-Free Pantry | 2 |
| Any meal | Bread | Dairy-Free Sandwich Bread Mix | Gluten-Free Pantry | 2 |
| Any meal | Bread | Multi Grain Bread Mix | Gluten-Free Pantry | 2 |
| Any meal | Bread | Orgran Apple/Cinnamon Pancake Mix | Gluten-Free Pantry | 2 |
| Any meal | Bread/ muffins | Yankee Cornbread, Muffin, Corncake Mix | Gluten-Free Pantry | 2 |

| Meal | Item | Brand | Store | Category |
|------|------|-------|-------|----------|
| Any meal | Soup/ bouillon | Celifibr Vegetarian Beef Bouillon Cubes | Gluten-Free Market | 2 |
| Any meal | Bread mix | Favorite GF Bread Mix | Gluten-Free Pantry | 3 |
| Breakfast | Bagels | Enjoy Life Foods Gluten-Free Cinnamon Raisin Bagels | Gluten-Free Mall | 1 |
| Breakfast | Bagels | Josef's Bagels | Josef's Gluten Free | 1 |
| Breakfast | Breakfast bars | Enjoy Life Foods Soft and Chewy Caramel Apple Snack Bars | Gluten-Free Mall | 1 |
| Breakfast | Breakfast bars | Glutino Breakfast Bars— Blueberry | Gluten-Free Pantry | 1 |
| Breakfast | Cereal | Enjoy Life Foods Cinnamon Crunch Granola | Gluten-Free Pantry | 1 |
| Breakfast | Cereal | Nature's Path Corn Flakes | Gluten-Free Pantry | 1 |
| Breakfast | Cereal | Quinoa Hot Cereal Variety Pack | Gluten-Free Pantry | 1 |
| Breakfast | English muffins | Foods By George Gluten-Free English Muffins | Gluten-Free Mall | 1 |
| Breakfast | Granola | Apple Raisin Walnut Granola | Gluten-Free Pantry | 1 |
| Breakfast | Muesli | Orgran Muesli with Fruit & Almonds | Gluten-Free Pantry | 1 |
| Breakfast | Muffins | Foods By George Gluten-Free Blueberry Muffins | Gluten-Free Mall | 1 |
| Breakfast | Cereal | Mesa Sunrise Cereal | Gluten-Free Pantry | 1 |
| Breakfast | Cereal | Panda Puffs Cereal | Gluten-Free Pantry | 1 |
| Breakfast | Bread | Muffin, Scone & Quick Bread Mix in Bulk | Gluten-Free Pantry | 2 |
| Breakfast | GF oats | Old-Fashioned Rolled Oats | Gluten Free Oats | 2 |
| Breakfast | Quick bread | Apple Spice Quick Bread Mix | Gluten-Free Pantry | 2 |
| Breakfast | Quick bread | Banana Quick Bread Mix | Gluten-Free Pantry | 2 |
| Breakfast | Quick bread | Harvest Pumpkin Quick Bread Mix | Gluten-Free Pantry | 2 |
| Breakfast | Hot cereal | Orgran Porridge | Gluten-Free Pantry | 1, 2 |
| Breakfast | Instant hot cereal | Quinoa Hot Cereal— Chocolate | Gluten-Free Pantry | 1, 2 |

| Meal | Item | Brand | Store | Category |
|------|------|-------|-------|----------|
| Breakfast | Biscuits | 1-2-3 Gluten Free— Southern Glory Biscuits | Shopbydiet.com | 2 |
| Dessert | Cake | Almondy Daim Caramel Crunch Almond Gluten-Free Torte | Gluten-Free Mall | 1 |
| Dessert | Cake | Foods By George Gluten-Free Pound Cake | Gluten-Free Mall | 1 |
| Dessert | Cake | Jer's Creamy Cheesecake | Gluten-Free Pantry | 1 |
| Dessert | Cookie bar | Glutano Break Bar | Gluten-Free Mall | 1 |
| Dessert | Cookies | Glutino Chocolate Dreams | Gluten-Free Pantry | 1 |
| Dessert | Cookies | Glutino Shortcake Dreams | Gluten-Free Pantry | 1 |
| Dessert | Cookies | Glutino Vanilla Dreams | Gluten-Free Pantry | 1 |
| Dessert | Cookies | Peanut Butter Cookies | Gluten-Free Pantry | 1 |
| Dessert | Ice cream cone | Waffle Cones | Gluten-Free Pantry | 1 |
| Dessert | Pie | Gillian's Foods Gluten-Free Pumpkin Pie | Gluten-Free Mall | 1 |
| Dessert | Pie | Natural Feast Gluten-Free Apple Streusel Pie | Gluten-Free Mall | 1 |
| Dessert | Brownie | 'Cause You're Special Chocolate Fudge Brownie Mix | Gluten-Free Mall | 2 |
| Dessert | Cake | Danielle's Chocolate Cake Mix | Gluten-Free Pantry | 2 |
| Dessert | Cookies | Chocolate Chip Cookie Mix | Gluten-Free Pantry | 2 |
| Dessert | Dessert | Chocolate Truffle Brownie Mix | Gluten-Free Pantry | 2 |
| Dessert | Piecrust | Perfect Pie Crust Mix | Gluten-Free Pantry | 2 |
| Dessert/ snack | Graham crackers | Graham Crackers (Egg Free) | Josef's Gluten Free | 1 |
| Dinner | Beef stew | My Own Meal: Beef Stew | Gluten-Free Pantry | 1 |
| Dinner | Bread | Chebe Gluten-Free Bread Sticks—Frozen Dough | Gluten-Free Mall | 1 |
| Dinner | Chicken | My Own Meal: Chicken & Black Beans | Gluten-Free Pantry | 1 |
| Dinner | Chicken | My Own Meal: Mediterranean Chicken Meal | Gluten-Free Pantry | 1 |

| Meal | Item | Brand | Store | Category |
|---|---|---|---|---|
| Dinner | Chicken dinner | My Own Meal: My Kind of Chicken | Gluten-Free Pantry | 1 |
| Dinner | Chili | Mimi's Gourmet Gluten-Free Black Bean & Corn Chili | Gluten-Free Mall | 1 |
| Dinner | Corn muffins | Foods By George Gluten-Free Corn Muffins | Gluten-Free Mall | 1 |
| Dinner | Dinner rolls | Chebe Gluten-Free Cheese Bread Rolls—Frozen Dough | Gluten-Free Mall | 1 |
| Dinner | Noodle dinner | Annie Chun's Original Pad Thai Noodles | Gluten-Free Market | 1 |
| Dinner | Noodle dinner | Thai Kitchen Noodle Cart, Roasted Garlic | Gluten-Free Market | 1 |
| Dinner | Noodle dinner | Thai Kitchen Noodle Cart, Thai Peanut | Gluten-Free Market | 1 |
| Dinner | Sauce | Amy's Premium Organic Pasta Sauce, Tomato Basil (Gluten-Free) | Shopbydiet.com | 1 |
| Dinner | Sauce | Amy's Family Marinara Pasta Sauce | Gluten-Free Market | 1 |
| Dinner | Sauce | Seeds of Change Pasta Sauce, Three Cheese Marinara | Gluten-Free Market | 1 |
| Dinner | Skillet dinner | Mayacamas Skillet Pasta Mix, Garden | Gluten-Free Market | 1 |
| Dinner | Soup | Glutino Beef Soup Base | Gluten-Free Market | 1 |
| Dinner | Beans | Amy's Traditional Refried Beans | Shopbydiet.com | 2 |
| Dinner | Bread | Dr. Schar Grissini Breadsticks | Gluten-Free Pantry | 2 |
| Dinner | Chinese meal | Singapore Sweet & Sour Noodles Skillet Meal | Gluten-Free Pantry | 2 |
| Dinner | Chinese meal | Szechwan Noodles Skillet Meal | Gluten-Free Pantry | 2 |
| Dinner | Egg noodles | Hoffner's Fine Noodles | Gluten-Free Mall | 2 |
| Dinner | Falafel | Orgran Falafel Mix | Gluten-Free Pantry | 2 |
| Dinner | Pasta | Glutano Brown Rice Fettuccini Pasta | Gluten-Free Mall | 2 |
| Dinner | Gravy | Glutino Brown Gravy Mix | Shopbydiet.com or Gluten-Free Market | 2 |

| Meal | Item | Brand | Store | Category |
|------|------|-------|-------|----------|
| Dinner | Macaroni | Ancient Harvest Quinoa Pasta Elbows | Gluten-Free Mall | 2 |
| Dinner | Pasta | Bi-Aglut Spaghetti | Gluten-Free Pantry | 2 |
| Dinner | Pasta | Bionaturae Elbows | Gluten-Free Pantry | 2 |
| Dinner | Pasta | Glutino Spaghetti 10 oz. | Gluten-Free Pantry | 2 |
| Dinner | Pasta | Hoffner's Elbow Pasta | Gluten-Free Gourmet | 2 |
| Dinner | Pasta | Pastariso Macaroni and Cheese (Macariz) | Gluten-Free Pantry | 2 |
| Dinner | Pasta skillet meal | Pasta Fagioli Skillet Meal | Gluten-Free Pantry | 2 |
| Dinner | Pasta, dairy-free | Road's End Penne & Chreese Alfredo | Gluten-Free Pantry | 2 |
| Dinner | Pizza | Gillian's Foods Gluten-Free Pizza Dough | Gluten-Free Mall | 2 |
| Dinner | Pizza | Gluten-Free Pantry's White Rice Pizza Crust | Gluten-Free Pantry | 2 |
| Dinner | Rotini | Heartland's Finest Rotini Pasta | Gluten-Free Mall | 2 |
| Dinner | Soup mix | Glutino Onion Soup Mix | Gluten-Free Market | 2 |
| Dinner | Pasta | Ancient Harvest Quinoa Spaghetti Pasta | Gluten-Free Mall | 2 |
| Dinner | Skillet meal | Stroganoff Skillet Meal | Gluten-Free Pantry | 2 |
| Dinner | Tex-Mex | Tex-Mex Skillet Meal | Gluten-Free Pantry | 2 |
| Dinner | Cheese sauce, dairy-free | Road's End Chreese Dip (Mild) | Gluten-Free Pantry | 1, 2 |
| Dinner | Pizza | Muir Glen Pizza Sauce, LF | Gluten-Free Market | 1, 2 |
| Dinner | Pizza crust | Gluten-Free Pantry's White Rice Pizza Crust | Gluten-Free Pantry | 1, 2 |
| Dinner | Bread crumbs | Hoffner's Bread Crumbs—Unflavored | Gluten-Free Gourmet | 2, 3 |
| Dinner | Pasta | Pastariso Vermicelli | Gluten-Free Pantry | 2, 3 |
| Dinner | Soup stock | Glutino—Beef-Flavored Soup Base | Shopbydiet.com | 2, 3 |
| Dinner | Spice | Taco Seasoning | Gluten-Free Pantry | 2, 3 |
| Lunch | Beef | Instant Gourmet Stroganoff with Beef and Rice | Gluten-Free Mall | 1 |

| Meal | Item | Brand | Store | Category |
|------|------|-------|-------|----------|
| Lunch | Chicken | Instant Gourmet Texas BBQ Chicken | Gluten-Free Mall | 1 |
| Lunch | Chili | Amy's Organic Chili, Black Bean | Shopbydiet.com | 1 |
| Lunch | Hot dogs | Buffalo Guys Gluten-Free Buffalo Hot Dogs | Gluten-Free Mall | 1 |
| Lunch | Meal bar | Think Thin—Peanut Butter Low Carb Diet Meal Alternative Nutrition Bar | Shopbydiet.com | 1 |
| Lunch | Meal cup | Glutano Mexican Rice Pot Meal | Gluten-Free Mall | 1 |
| Lunch | Meal cup | Instant Gourmet Bay Shrimp Bisque Soup | Gluten-Free Mall | 1 |
| Lunch | Noodles | Lemon Grass & Chili Instant Noodles | Gluten-Free Pantry | 1 |
| Lunch | Pita bread | Hoffner's Gluten-Free Pita Flats | Gluten-Free Mall | 1 |
| Lunch | Soup | Amy's Organic Soup, Cream of Tomato | Gluten-Free Market | 1 |
| Lunch | Soup | Amy's Organic Soup, Potato Leek | Gluten-Free Market | 1 |
| Lunch | Soup | Amy's Organic Soup, Split Pea | Gluten-Free Market | 1 |
| Lunch | Soup | Gluten-Free Pantry French Onion Soup Mix | Gluten-Free Market | 1 |
| Lunch | Soup | Miso Soup—Reduced Sodium | Gluten-Free Pantry | 1 |
| Lunch | Mac and cheese | Pastariso Dolphin Rice Macaroni Yellow Cheese | Gluten-Free Mall | 2 |
| Lunch | Hamburger buns | Ener-G Foods Tapioca Hamburger Buns | Gluten-Free Pantry | 1, 2 |
| Lunch | Hot dog buns | Ener-G Hot Dog Buns | Gluten-Free Pantry | 1, 2 |
| Lunch, dinner | Sandwich buns | Chebe Gluten-Free Sandwich Buns—Frozen Dough | Gluten-Free Mall | 1 |
| Lunch, dinner | Pizza | Foods By George Gluten Free Cheese Pizza | Gluten-Free Mall | 1 |
| Lunch, dinner | Croutons | Hoffner's Croutons | Gluten-Free Gourmet | 1 |

| Meal | Item | Brand | Store | Category |
|------|------|-------|-------|----------|
| Snack | Cookies | Glutano Lemon Cream Filled Wafers | Gluten-Free Pantry | 1 |
| Snack | Crackers | Garlic Cheese Crackers (Kitchen Table Bakers) | Gluten-Free Pantry | 1 |
| Snack | Pretzels | Glutano Hard Pretzels | Gluten-Free Pantry | 1 |
| Snack | Pretzels | Pretzels—1 oz. Family Bag | Gluten-Free Pantry | 1 |
| Snack | Snack bar | Boomi Bar Almond Protein Plus | Gluten-Free Mall | 1 |
| Snack | Snack crackers | Mary's Gone Crackers Herb Crackers | Gluten-Free Mall | 1 |
| Snack, dessert | Filled cookies | Glutano Custard Cream Cookies | Gluten-Free Pantry | 1 |
| Snack, dessert | Oreo-style cookies | Glutano Chocolate O's Sandwich Cookies | Gluten-Free Pantry | 1 |
| Snack, dinner | Melba toast | Glutino Rusks | Gluten-Free Pantry | 1 |
| Snack, dinner | Saltine crackers | Dr. Schar Crackers | Gluten-Free Pantry | 1 |
| Snack, lunch | Crackers | Glutano Crackers | Gluten-Free Pantry | 1 |

# CHAPTER 17

## GLUTEN-FREE COOKING 201

If you can read, you can cook. Cooking is just a matter of following directions.

Of course, cooking from scratch takes time—a commodity that's in short supply for most of us. So, in this chapter—GF Cooking 201—we'll focus on KISS cooking.

You know KISS—Keep It Simple, Sam! We'll apply that principle to the ingredients, prep, and cooking time. And although you'll need to spend some time in the kitchen, I think you'll be happy with the results.

I'd like to emphasize that I always encourage using *fresh* ingredients, preferably organic, whenever they are available and affordable. You may or may not taste the difference in organic ingredients, but your body will definitely feel the effect of not ingesting residual pesticides, herbicides, and chemical fertilizers that are used on mass-produced fruits and vegetables.

We have adapted many of the following recipes to accommodate the special needs of a GF diet. You can find recommended substitutions for dairy products and GF flour in Chapter 15.

## GF COOKING 201: BREAKFASTS

## Classic Omelet[1]

An omelet can be dressed up in many different ways. Start with this basic recipe, then use your imagination with additional ingredients—whatever you have on hand or whatever suits your breakfast whims.

## INGREDIENTS

¼–⅓   *cup filling, such as apples, potatoes, onions, bell peppers, leeks, meat, or cheese*

2   *eggs*

1   *tablespoon milk, milk substitute, or water*

   *Salt and ground pepper, to taste*

   *Herbs such as basil, dill, cilantro, rosemary, and parsley, finely chopped (optional)*

1   *teaspoon butter (or 2 teaspoons if cooking filling)*

## DIRECTIONS

1. Cook the filling ingredients as needed. Set aside.
2. If you are making a cheese omelet, thinly slice the cheese (so that it will melt easily) or shred it. Set aside.
3. Crack the eggs into a small mixing bowl, and whisk until well beaten.
4. Add the milk, salt, ground pepper, and herbs, if using. Stir to mix. Set aside.
5. Heat a 6" to 8" omelet pan or skillet over high heat until very hot (approximately 30 seconds).
6. Add the butter, making sure it coats the bottom of the pan. As soon as the butter stops bubbling and sizzling (and before it starts to brown), slowly pour in the egg mixture. Tilt the pan to spread the egg mixture evenly.
7. Let the eggs cook and firm up for about 10 seconds. Then shake the pan and use a spatula to gently direct the mixture away from the sides and into the middle. Allow the remaining liquid to flow into the space left at the sides of the pan. Cook for 1 minute longer, or until the egg mixture holds together.
8. Add the filling. Put in the vegetables or fruit or meat first, then any cheese. (The middle will still be runny.)
9. Tilt the pan and use the spatula to fold one-third of the omelet toward the middle.
10. Shake the pan to slide the omelet to the edge of the pan.
11. Hold the pan above the serving plate, then tip it so that the omelet rolls off and folds itself onto the plate. The two edges will be tucked underneath.

# Goat Cheese Omelet[2]

Most omelets are prepared with cheese made from cow's milk. If you cannot tolerate cow's milk but find goat's milk easily digestible (or just want a change of taste), try this omelet, which serves two.

## INGREDIENTS

3   *eggs*

2   *teaspoons water*

⅛   *teaspoon salt*

2   *ounces plain goat cheese*

## DIRECTIONS

1. Beat the eggs in a small mixing bowl.
2. Add the water and salt and beat well.
3. Coat a skillet with drizzled olive oil or coat with a GF nonstick cooking spray, such as Pam.
4. Add half the egg mixture, swirling over the pan evenly.
5. Cook for 30 seconds, or until the mixture starts to firm up.
6. With a spatula, push the sides of the omelet to the center and tip the pan for the uncooked egg to cover.
7. Sprinkle half of the goat cheese over half of the omelet.
8. Fold the omelet in half. Continue cooking until the bottom is lightly browned.
9. Turn over and cook for 30 seconds longer.
10. Slide onto a plate.
11. Repeat with the second half of the egg mixture.
12. Serve with GF toast and all-fruit jam or jelly.

# Baked Herb Cheese Omelet[3]

We usually think of omelets as being prepared on the stove top. Here is one that is easily whipped together and is baked in the oven. It will serve four.

## INGREDIENTS

| | |
|---|---|
| 4 | *eggs* |
| ¾ | *cup GF flour* |
| 2 | *cups milk or milk substitute, such as soy, rice, or almond milk* |
| ½ | *cup shredded cheese or cheese substitute* |
| 2–3 | *tablespoons fresh basil, chopped* |

## DIRECTIONS

1. Preheat the oven to 400°F.
2. Break the eggs into a medium mixing bowl.
3. Whisk the eggs and gradually add the flour until mixed well.
4. Add the milk and whisk until well combined.
5. Coat a 10" or 12" cast-iron skillet or heavy glass baking dish with a GF nonstick cooking spray (such as Pam).
6. Sprinkle the cheese and basil into the skillet.
7. Pour the egg mixture over the cheese.
8. Bake for 30 minutes, or until puffed and brown on top.
9. Cut into sections and serve warm.

*Tip: To make a heartier baked omelet, add ½ cup cubed ham.*

# Homemade Gluten-Free Waffles[4]

In the previous chapter, you learned that you can buy frozen gluten-free waffles, pop them into your toaster, and have a quick on-the-go breakfast.

For a less-expensive and fresher alternative (who can deny the wonderful fragrance of baking waffles?), try this recipe.

## INGREDIENTS

| | |
|---|---|
| 2 | *cups GF flour* |
| ½ | *teaspoon xantham gum* |
| ½ | *teaspoon salt* |
| 3 | *teaspoons baking powder* |
| 1½ | *cups milk or milk substitute, plus a little more if needed* |
| 2 | *eggs* |
| 4 | *tablespoons butter, melted and cooled* |

## DIRECTIONS

1. Combine the flour, xantham gum, salt, and baking powder. Set aside.
2. Mix together the milk and eggs, and stir in the butter.
3. Stir the egg mixture into the flour mixture.
4. Add more milk until the batter is a little thicker than pancake batter.
5. Spread a ladleful or so of batter onto the waffle iron and bake until the waffle is done, usually for 3 to 5 minutes, depending on your iron.

*Tip: Make an entire batch (or even double the batch) and freeze leftovers. You'll have a quick breakfast without the fuss.*

## Slow-Cooker GF Oatmeal

Oatmeal is gluten-free, but it may be contaminated with gluten—either in the field, if the oats are grown near a wheat field, or during processing, if it is not processed in a dedicated mill.

Oatmeal certified to be GF is available online (see Helpful Resources for Gluten-Free Living on page 275). Another possible alternative is John McCann's Steel Cut Irish Oatmeal, which is available in many supermarkets. Although the company does not certify that its product is gluten-free, it claims that any contamination would be less than 0.05 percent, which is the Codex standard accepted in Europe.

GF oatmeal is a great way to start the day. It not only tastes great, but it is also known to lower cholesterol. Here is an easy and delicious slow-cooker recipe. Prepare the ingredients before you go to bed, and in the morning, you will have a hearty and delicious breakfast. The hardest part about it is cleaning the slow cooker!

## INGREDIENTS

2   *cups milk or milk substitute*

3   *cups water*

1   cup steel-cut oats (also called pin oats). Do not use rolled oats or instant oatmeal!
Pinch of salt
½   cup (or more) dried fruit, cut into bite-size pieces (Raisins, cranberries, prunes, and apricots are all good choices.)

## DIRECTIONS

1. Pour the milk and water into the slow cooker.
2. Add the oats and salt.
3. Turn the slow cooker on low heat for 8 hours.
4. Go to bed and when you wake up, you'll have a great breakfast ready to help you start your day.

Tip: Leftovers? Keep them in the refrigerator. Although the consistency will not be the same when you warm them, the oats will still taste great.

# Hot Kasha Breakfast Cereal

If you can't get GF oatmeal and don't want to risk exposure to gluten from other oatmeal brands, try hot kasha cereal.

## INGREDIENTS

¼   teaspoon salt
2½   cups water, milk, or milk substitute
½   cup kasha (roasted buckwheat)
½   cup raisins, chopped dried apricots, or prunes (or a combination)

## DIRECTIONS

1. In a medium saucepan, stir the salt into the water, milk, or milk substitute.
2. Bring to a boil.
3. Stir in the kasha, as well as any dried fruit you would like to add.
4. Cook, uncovered, stirring frequently, while maintaining a gentle boil, for 8 to 11 minutes, or until it reaches the consistency you prefer.
5. Serve plain or with milk or milk substitute and a favorite sweetener, such as honey.

# Quinoa Flakes Hot Cereal

Do you miss cream of wheat cereal? Try hot quinoa flakes. The consistency is like cream of wheat; the taste is slightly nutty; and it takes only 90 seconds to prepare.

## INGREDIENTS

1    *cup water (for thicker cereal, use less water; for thinner, use more)*
⅓   *cup quinoa flakes*
     *Dash of salt (optional)*

## DIRECTIONS

1. In a small pot, bring the water to a rapid boil.
2. Add quinoa flakes and salt, if using, to the boiling water.
3. Bring the mixture back to a boil and cook for 90 seconds, stirring frequently.
4. Remove from the heat and allow to cool. (The cereal will thicken slightly as it cools.)
5. Sweeten to taste.

# Pancakes

This recipe has been adapted from a basic pancake recipe found in *Betty Crocker's New Cookbook*. As you experiment, you'll find that you can substitute GF flour with a little xantham gum to help the "gluing" process along.

Once you are comfortable with a recipe such as this, prepare a larger quantity of the dry ingredients, label the container, and store it in a dry cupboard. It'll be ready for you when you want to make a batch.

## INGREDIENTS

1    *large egg*
1    *cup GF flour*
¾   *cup milk or milk substitute*
1    *tablespoon sugar or packed brown sugar*
2    *tablespoons olive oil*

3    *teaspoons baking powder*

½    *teaspoon xanthan gum*

¼    *teaspoon salt*

*Butter or nonstick cooking spray*

## DIRECTIONS

1. Break the egg into a medium bowl and beat it or whisk it by hand until it is fluffy.
2. Beat in the flour, milk, brown sugar, oil, baking powder, xanthan gum, and salt until the batter is smooth. For thinner pancakes, add more milk.
3. Heat the griddle or skillet over medium heat or to 375°F. (An electric skillet is handy for this, since you can easily regulate the temperature. If you don't have an electric skillet or griddle with a heat gauge, test the griddle by sprinkling with a few drops of water. If bubbles jump around, the heat is just right.)
4. If necessary, grease the skillet with the butter.
5. For each pancake, pour slightly less than ¼ cup of batter.
6. Cook the pancakes until they are puffed and dry around the edges.
7. Turn over and cook the other side until golden brown.

*Tips: Make the pancakes extra special by stirring in fresh or frozen (but thawed and drained) blueberries or blackberries. Mmm!*

*Did you prepare too much batter? Finish cooking the pancakes and freeze them. Pop them into your toaster oven for a quick on-the-go breakfast.*

## GF COOKING 201: LUNCHES

### BLT and P (Bacon, Leek, Tomato, and Potato) Soup[5]

Sure, you can open a can of Progresso soup (many are gluten-free). But you won't find a soup like this on your grocer's shelf.

This is adapted from *Rachael Ray's 30-Minute Meals* on Food TV. Instead of bacon, use turkey bacon, a much healthier substitute.

Although the soup has a number of ingredients, none requires much prep work. And the cooking time for the soup is less than 15 minutes. Enjoy!

## INGREDIENTS

*Extra-virgin olive oil, for drizzling*

6 *slices lean, smoky good-quality turkey bacon, chopped into ½" pieces*

3 *small ribs celery from the heart of the stalk, finely chopped*

2 *small to medium carrots, peeled*

3 *leeks, trimmed of rough tops and roots*

1 *bay leaf*

*Salt and pepper, to taste*

3 *medium starchy potatoes, such as Idaho, peeled*

2 *quarts GF chicken stock or broth*

1 *can (15 ounces) petite diced tomatoes, drained*

*Handful of flat-leaf parsley, finely chopped*

*GF bread, for dunking and mopping*

## DIRECTIONS

1. Heat a medium soup pot or deep-sided skillet over medium-high heat.
2. Drizzle the oil in the pot and add the turkey bacon.
3. Cook the turkey bacon until brown and crisp. Remove from the pot and set aside.
4. Add the celery to the pot.
5. Lay the peeled carrots flat on a cutting board. Hold each carrot at the root end and use the vegetable peeler to make long, thin strips.
6. Chop the thin slices into small carrot bits or carrot chips, ½" wide.
7. Add the carrot chips to the celery in the pot and stir.
8. Cut the leeks lengthwise and then into ½" half moons.
9. Place the leeks into a colander and run under cold rushing water, separating the layers to wash away all the trapped grit.

10. When the leeks are separated and clean, shake off the water and add to the celery and carrots.

11. Stir the vegetables together, add the bay leaf, and season with the salt and pepper.

12. While the leeks cook to wilted (3 to 4 minutes), slice the potatoes.

13. Cut each potato across into thirds. Stand each piece of potato upright and thinly slice it. The pieces should look like raw potato chips.

14. Add the stock to the vegetables and bring to a boil.

15. Reduce the heat and add the potatoes and tomatoes. Cook for 8 to 10 minutes, or until the potatoes are tender and starting to break up a bit.

16. Add the turkey bacon and parsley and stir.

17. Adjust the seasonings, if necessary. Remove the bay leaf. Serve immediately with GF bread.

*Tip: Try substituting ham or leftover cooked pork roast for the bacon.*

# Brown-Bagged Halibut[6]

Fish is an excellent source of protein. It is quick to prepare and delicious to eat. Here is a recipe using halibut fillets, a fish that has a mild, sweet taste that we've adapted for GF eating. It can be prepared for either lunch or dinner.

## INGREDIENTS

4   *tablespoons olive oil*

4   *standard-issue lunch-size brown paper bags*

4   *(6-ounce) halibut fillets*

   *Salt and pepper, to taste*

2   *tablespoons GF soy sauce (La Choy brand is GF)*

2   *tablespoons freshly squeezed lime juice*

3   *tablespoons freshly grated ginger*

   *Papaya or Mango Salsa (page 216)*

## DIRECTIONS

1. Preheat the oven to 425°F.
2. Drizzle 1 tablespoon of the olive oil over the outside of each bag, and rub it with your hand until all surfaces of the bag have absorbed the oil.
3. Rinse the fillets and pat dry. Season both sides with salt and pepper.
4. In a small bowl, mix the soy sauce, lime juice, and ginger.
5. Set the bags on their broad side and place one fillet flat inside each bag.
6. Then, using a tablespoon, reach into the bag and spoon one-quarter of the soy-lime-ginger mixture over each of the fillets.
7. Force excess air from the bags, roll up the open ends, and tightly crimp to seal shut.
8. Bake on a cookie sheet for 10 minutes.
9. To serve, tear a slit in each bag, peel back the paper to expose the fish, then spoon the salsa over the top.

*Tip: You can use thawed halibut fillets. If fresh fish is available, you can substitute sea bass, snapper, or monkfish.*

## Papaya or Mango Salsa[7]

If you are fortunate enough to have access to fresh papayas or mangoes, whip up this easy salsa. It is a good accompaniment to the brown-bag halibut recipe and can be used to complement other fish, chicken, or pork recipes.

### INGREDIENTS

2    *ripe papayas, skinned, seeded, and chopped into ¼" cubes. (If papayas are unavailable, replace with one or two mangoes.)*

4    *scallions, trimmed, then minced*

½    *cup lightly packed cilantro leaves, chopped*

4    *tablespoons freshly squeezed lime juice*

4    *tablespoons red bell pepper or red cabbage, finely chopped*

2    *jalapeño chile peppers, seeds and membranes removed, chopped*

## DIRECTIONS

1. Combine the papayas, scallions, cilantro, lime juice, bell pepper, and chile peppers in a medium bowl.
2. Mix thoroughly.
3. Use immediately, or store, covered, in the refrigerator. Flavors will blend together.

# Buffalo-Chicken Lettuce Wrap Lunch

## INGREDIENTS

| | |
|---|---|
| 1 | *pound boneless chicken breast (organic is best)* |
| 1 | *teaspoon garlic powder* |
| 1 | *teaspoon chili powder* |
| ½ | *teaspoon ground paprika* |
| 2 | *tablespoons GF flour* |
| 1 | *tablespoon olive oil* |
| 2 | *tablespoons hot sauce* |
| ¾ | *cup red onion, sliced* |
| ¾ | *cup cucumber, sliced* |
| ½ | *cup GF ranch dressing* |
| | *Large lettuce leaves, washed* |
| 4 | *tablespoons blue cheese, crumbled* |

## DIRECTIONS

1. Cut chicken breast into bite-size chunks, approximately 1".
2. In a plastic bag, mix the garlic powder, chili powder, paprika, and flour.
3. Add the chicken and shake to coat.
4. Heat the oil in a skillet over medium-high heat.
5. Add the chicken. Turn it frequently to brown and cook on all sides. This will take about 7 minutes, or until a fork can be inserted easily.
6. Drizzle hot sauce over the chicken, toss to coat, and set aside.
7. In a medium bowl, mix the onion and cucumber with the dressing.

8. On each lettuce leaf, place one-quarter of the chicken mixture.
9. Top with the dressing, and sprinkle with the blue cheese.
10. This can be eaten either hot or cold.

# Chicken Salad Sandwich

The next time you roast a chicken or a turkey and have leftovers, mix up a batch of this salad. No leftovers? Buy a rotisserie chicken from the grocery. Chill and slice off white or dark meat to make the salad.

## INGREDIENTS

| | |
|---|---|
| 1½ | cups cooked chicken or turkey, finely chopped |
| ½ | cup celery |
| ½ | cup thinly chopped green onions |
| 1 | tablespoon lemon juice |
| ⅓ | cup GF mayonnaise |
| ½ | cup sliced seedless grapes |
| ¼ | cup chopped walnuts or pecans |
| | Salt and pepper, to taste |
| | GF bread |
| | Lettuce and tomato |

## DIRECTIONS

1. Mix the chicken, celery, onions, lemon juice, mayonnaise, grapes, and nuts in a mixing bowl.
2. Season with the salt and pepper, to taste.
3. Spread the chicken salad on the bread.
4. Garnish with the lettuce and tomato.

*Tip: Go bread-free! Serve the chicken salad in the center of a large lettuce leaf. Or scoop out a tomato and fill the center with the salad.*

# Asian Salad and Dressing

In my pre-GF days, one of the salad dressings I enjoyed most was an Asian dressing. I found, however, that the commercial brands all contain gluten, probably in the soy sauce used in the dressing. (Keep that in mind the next time you are tempted to order an Asian salad in a restaurant!)

Here is an Asian salad and dressing to complement your luncheon menus.

## INGREDIENTS

### ASIAN SALAD DRESSING

8   tablespoons rice vinegar (preferred) or white vinegar

6   tablespoons GF soy sauce

4   tablespoons sugar or sweetener substitute (such as xylitol or stevia)

2   tablespoons sesame oil

1½  teaspoons grated fresh ginger

2   tablespoons chopped cilantro

A few drops of hot chili oil (optional)

### SALAD

½   cup fresh snow peas (blanched)

Bagged lettuce greens

1   small can mandarin orange slices

1   large tomato, sliced in half and quartered

½   cucumber, thinly sliced

3   green onions, sliced

1   small can sliced water chestnuts

## DIRECTIONS

1. To make the dressing: Combine the vinegar, soy sauce, sugar, sesame oil, ginger, cilantro, and chili oil, if using, in a container that you can shake to thoroughly mix.

2. Refrigerate for at least 1 hour to blend the seasonings. This will keep in the refrigerator.

3. To make the salad: Snip the ends from the snow peas.

4. Bring a pot of water to a boil and blanch the snow peas for about 45 seconds. (Do not overcook.)

5. Remove from the boiling water and immediately transfer to an ice bath to stop the cooking.
6. Combine the snow peas, lettuce greens, orange slices, tomato, cucumber, onions, and water chestnuts and toss.
7. Just before serving, toss with the Asian salad dressing.

*Tip: For a more filling lunch, add leftover pork, chicken, or turkey, cut in strips.*

# Cream of Mushroom Soup

You can find many different types of canned GF soups in your local grocery store; Progresso has a number of them. But one type of soup you may not be able to find even in your health food store or online is cream of mushroom soup.

Here is a recipe for a quick cream of mushroom soup that you can make for a luncheon meal or use in other recipes.

## INGREDIENTS

| | |
|---|---|
| 1 | *pound mushrooms (any type; using a variety gives a nicer flavor)* |
| 2–3 | *tablespoons butter or coconut oil* |
| ½ | *teaspoon salt* |
| 3 | *tablespoons GF flour* |
| 1 | *cup milk, fat-free evaporated milk, or milk substitute* |
| 1 | *can (14½ ounces) GF chicken broth (Swanson brand is GF)* |
| ¼ | *cup sherry (optional)* |
| | *Freshly ground pepper* |

## DIRECTIONS

1. Wipe the mushrooms to clean them.
2. Slice enough mushrooms to measure 1 cup. Chop the remaining mushrooms.
3. Melt the butter or coconut oil in a 3-quart saucepan over medium heat.
4. Cook all of the mushrooms for about 10 minutes, or until they are nicely browned.
5. Mix the salt into the flour.

6. Sprinkle the browned mushrooms with the flour and salt mixture.
7. Cook, stirring constantly, until the mixture thickens.
8. Gradually stir in the milk and broth. Stir to thoroughly mix and avoid lumps.
9. Heat. Stir in the sherry, if using.
10. Sprinkle with the pepper, to taste, and serve.

## GF COOKING 201: DINNERS

Most people who work during the day don't have much time to prepare complicated dinners at night. That's where KISS dinners come in— simple, yet nutritious, and, of course, gluten-free.

Here are a number of not-too-complicated dinner ideas.

# Turkey Skewers with Mango Salsa[8]

Do you like to grill? You can prepare this on a stove-top grill as well as outside on a charcoal or gas grill. It makes four or five servings.

### INGREDIENTS

| 2½ | pounds turkey tenderloins |
| 1 | teaspoon minced garlic |
| 1 | teaspoon minced fresh ginger |
| ⅓ | cup GF soy sauce |
| ¼ | cup rice vinegar |
| 2 | teaspoons sugar |
| | Salt and pepper, to taste |
| | Lime juice |
| | Mango Salsa (page 216) |

### DIRECTIONS

1. Soak wooden skewers for about 10 minutes so that they will not catch fire on the grill.
2. Slice the turkey tenderloins lengthwise into 2" slices. Thread the turkey onto the skewers. Set aside.

3. Combine the garlic, ginger, soy sauce, vinegar, sugar, and salt and pepper, to taste, in a shallow baking dish.
4. Place the turkey skewers in the marinade and refrigerate, covered, for 60 minutes or overnight. (If you prefer, you can marinate the turkey before skewering it.)
5. Prepare the grill.
6. Grill over hot coals for 10 minutes per side, or until done, brushing with the marinade occasionally.
7. Sprinkle with the lime juice before serving.
8. Serve with the mango salsa.

*Tips: Instead of purchasing turkey tenderloins, buy a boneless turkey breast and cut it into tenderloin portions. Use what you need for this recipe and freeze the remainder for another meal.*

*Prepare the mango salsa from scratch (as indicated in the KISS lunches section of this chapter). Or use prepared GF mango or peach salsa.*

# Spicy Sesame Chicken Fajitas[9]

Many Mexican or Tex-Mex dishes call for flour fajitas. An easy substitute is corn tortillas, available in any supermarket.

The chicken (or turkey, if you prefer) in this recipe can be cooked over a grill, or you can cook it in a little olive oil on the stove top—whichever is easier. This recipe makes 4 to 6 servings.

### INGREDIENTS

| | |
|---|---|
| 2½ | pounds skinless, boneless chicken or turkey breasts |
| ¼ | cup sesame seeds |
| ¼ | teaspoon ground red pepper |
| | Salt, to taste |
| 2 | tablespoons olive oil (if you prefer to cook the chicken in a skillet instead of grilling it) |
| 18 | corn tortillas |
| 2 | cups chopped avocado |
| 4 | cups shredded lettuce |
| | Mango Salsa (page 216) |
| 2 | cups sour cream |

## DIRECTIONS

1. Pound the chicken breasts between two pieces of foil to a thickness of ⅛". (You want the pieces very thin to cook quickly.)
2. Sprinkle with the sesame seeds, red pepper, and salt before cooking. Press into the meat.
3. Grill over a charcoal fire for about 1½ minutes on each side, until the pink is just gone from the meat but the meat is still moist. (Or cook in a skillet with the olive oil.)
4. While the chicken is cooking, warm the tortillas on a cookie sheet in a 400°F oven for about 3 minutes.
5. Remove the cooked chicken from the grill or skillet.
6. Cut the chicken into strips.
7. Assemble the fajitas: Place about ¼ cup of the chicken in the center of a tortilla. Top with the avocado, lettuce, salsa, and sour cream. Fold and serve.

# Vegetable and Beef Salad

What do you do with leftover meat from a pork or beef roast? Use the leftovers in this salad, which makes a better cold-served main course than it does a side dish. It can be prepared ahead of time.

## INGREDIENTS

1    *cup GF elbow macaroni or rotini*

2    *cups fresh broccoli, cut up*

2    *cups bite-size pieces cooked pork or beef*

1    *medium carrot, shredded*

½    *cup sliced fresh mushrooms*

¾    *cup Creamy Cucumber Dressing (page 224)*

½    *cup cherry tomato halves or quartered medium tomato*

## DIRECTIONS

1. Cook the macaroni according to package directions. Do not overcook!
2. Drain the macaroni well in a colander.
3. In a large bowl, combine the macaroni, broccoli, pork or beef, carrot, and mushrooms. Toss to mix.

4. Add the dressing. Toss to coat all ingredients.
5. Chill for 30 minutes or overnight.
6. Add the tomatoes when you serve it.

*Tip: No pork or beef? Use chicken, turkey, shrimp, or scallops.*

# Creamy Cucumber Dressing[10]

This simple salad dressing will taste great on just about any salad.

## INGREDIENTS

| | |
|---|---|
| 1 | *cup plain yogurt* |
| ½ | *cucumber, peeled and finely chopped* |
| 1 | *teaspoon fresh lemon juice* |
| 1 | *clove garlic, minced* |
| ½ | *teaspoon salt* |
| ½ | *teaspoon ground white pepper* |

## DIRECTIONS

1. In a blender, combine the yogurt, cucumber, lemon juice, garlic, salt, and pepper.
2. Blend until smooth.
3. Refrigerate until chilled.

*Tip: If your diet excludes dairy products—but you can tolerate goat's milk—look for goat's yogurt at the health food store.*

# White Bean Soup with Ham and Greens[11]

This soup does not take long to prepare, but if you are pressed for time, you can make it a day or two ahead of time; it will keep well in the refrigerator. Serve it with a GF corn bread and a green salad for an easy, light supper.

## INGREDIENTS

| | |
|---|---|
| 2 | *tablespoons extra-virgin olive oil* |
| 8 | *ounces chopped country ham or honey ham* |

1   *cup finely chopped onion*

2   *cloves garlic, minced*

½   *teaspoon dried leaf thyme*

1   *can (15 ounces) Great Northern beans, rinsed and drained*

4   *cups GF chicken broth*

1   *cup chopped, trimmed mustard greens or spinach*

  *Salt and freshly ground black pepper, to taste*

## DIRECTIONS

1. Heat the oil in a heavy stockpot or kettle over medium-high heat.
2. Add the ham, onion, garlic, and thyme.
3. Stir well to combine and cook for about 7 minutes, or until the onion is tender and translucent but not browned.
4. Add the beans and chicken broth.
5. Simmer for about 20 minutes.
6. Add the greens and simmer for 8 to 12 minutes, or until the greens are tender and wilted.
7. Season with the salt and pepper, to taste. Serve with freshly baked GF corn bread or corn muffins.

# Spaghetti Squash Marinara[12]

I love Italian food! And, judging by the popularity of Italian restaurants, the chances are, you do, too. Being gluten-sensitive does not exclude you from eating Italian pasta. You can find various types of GF pasta online, in health food stores, and even in some neighborhood supermarkets.

But pasta—even GF pasta—is high in carbohydrates. If you are watching your carbs and want a healthier alternative, try this.

## INGREDIENTS

1   *medium spaghetti squash*

¼   *cup chopped onion*

2   *cloves garlic, minced*

1   *tablespoon olive oil*

1   *can (16 ounces) diced or whole tomatoes*

1   *teaspoon dried Italian seasoning, crushed*

¼   *teaspoon salt*

¼   *teaspoon ground pepper*

    *Grated Parmesan cheese (optional)*

**DIRECTIONS**

1. Preheat the oven to 350°F.
2. Cut the squash in half lengthwise.
3. Scoop out the seeds.
4. Place the squash, cut sides down, in a large baking dish. Prick the skin all over with a fork.
5. Bake in the oven for 30 to 40 minutes, or until tender.
6. As the squash is baking, cook the onion and garlic in the olive oil until the onion is tender.
7. Stir in the tomatoes (with juice), Italian seasoning, salt, and pepper.
8. Bring the sauce to a boil. Reduce the heat and simmer, uncovered, for 10 to 15 minutes, or to the desired consistency. Stir often.
9. To serve, remove the squash pulp from the shell. Spoon the sauce over the squash. Sprinkle with the cheese, if using.

## GF Bread Crumbs

To prepare GF bread crumbs, save slices of GF bread that have dried out. Freeze them, if necessary, until you have enough to make the bread crumbs.

1. Break the bread into small pieces.
2. Arrange in a single depth on a cookie sheet and place in the oven on low heat (250°F).
3. Bake until the bread is completely dry but not toasted. Remove from the oven.
4. Cool, then place the bread in a food processor or a blender and process it into crumbs.
5. Use the crumbs in recipes calling for bread crumbs, such as the one that follows.

# Pecan-Coated Catfish[13]

Traditional catfish recipes call for breading the catfish and frying. Here is a recipe that is lighter and uses GF bread crumbs and pecans.

## INGREDIENTS

| | |
|---|---|
| 1 | *pound fresh or frozen catfish fillets, thawed, ½"–¾" thick* |
| ¼ | *cup fine GF dried bread crumbs* |
| 2 | *tablespoons cornmeal* |
| 2 | *tablespoons grated Parmesan cheese or other cheese (such as a hard goat's cheese)* |
| 2 | *tablespoons ground pecans* |
| ¼ | *teaspoon salt* |
| ¼ | *teaspoon pepper* |
| ¼ | *cup GF flour* |
| ¼ | *cup milk or milk substitute* |
| 2–3 | *tablespoons olive oil or coconut oil* |
| ⅓ | *cup chopped pecans* |

## DIRECTIONS

1. Rinse the fish and pat dry.
2. Cut into 5 serving-size pieces. Set aside.
3. In a shallow bowl, mix the bread crumbs, cornmeal, cheese, ground pecans, salt, and pepper.
4. Coat each portion of the fish with flour, dip into the milk, then coat evenly with the bread crumb mixture. (Note: Dipping the fish with flour first helps the crumb mixture stick to it during the cooking process.)
5. Heat the oil in a large skillet. When the oil is hot, place the fish in the oil and cook for 4 to 6 minutes on each side, or until golden and the fish flakes easily with a fork. Keep warm.
6. Remove excess crumbs from the skillet. Add chopped pecans.
7. Cook and stir for about 2 minutes, or until toasted.
8. Sprinkle the pecans over the catfish.

# CHAPTER 18

## GLUTEN-FREE COOKING 301

Who doesn't like to sit down to a home-cooked meal? *Preparing* the meal, of course, is another matter. Fortunately, some people really like to cook. And if you are one of them, here are some recipes for you.

To be sure, most of these recipes require either more prep time, more ingredients, or more cooking time, so we consider them more advanced—although not really more difficult.

Get out your measuring cup and your wooden spoon, and enter the world of GF Cooking 301.

## GF COOKING 301: BREAKFASTS

## Breakfast Apple-Citrus Compote[1]

Fruit provides essential vitamins and minerals. The best way to eat fruit is fresh. But occasionally, you may want a change of pace. Here is a good way to start your day.

### INGREDIENTS

| | |
|---|---|
| 2 | *cups peeled and sliced tart apples (about 2 medium)* |
| 1½ | *cups (about 9 ounces) pitted prunes* |
| 1½ | *cups orange juice* |
| 2 | *tablespoons honey* |
| 1 | *tablespoon lemon juice* |
| ½ | *teaspoon ground cinnamon* |
| 2 | *navel oranges, peeled and cut into segments* |
| 2 | *pink grapefruits, peeled and cut into segments* |
| | *Mint sprigs (optional)* |

## DIRECTIONS

1. In a 2- to 3-quart saucepan, combine the apples, prunes, and orange juice and bring to a boil.
2. Reduce the heat and simmer for about 10 minutes, or until the apples are tender but not soft.
3. Remove from the heat and stir in the honey, lemon juice, and cinnamon.
4. Cool, cover, and chill.
5. Stir in the oranges and grapefruits.
6. To serve, spoon the fruits with their liquid into serving dishes. Garnish with the mint sprigs, if using.

# Broccoli Frittata[2]

Broccoli for breakfast? Why not? Who says breakfast has to be relegated to toast, cereal, and eggs? Give this a try—at least for a brunch.

## INGREDIENTS

| | |
|---|---|
| 2½ | tablespoons finely chopped onion |
| 2 | teaspoons butter |
| 1 | package (10 ounces) frozen chopped broccoli, cooked and drained |
| ½ | small clove garlic crushed (optional) |
| 1 | cup cooked rice |
| 2½ | tablespoons grated Parmesan cheese (or substitute) |
| 2 | eggs, slightly beaten |
| ¼ | cup milk |
| ½ | teaspoon salt (optional) |
| | Dash of ground black pepper |
| ⅓ | cup grated mozzarella cheese (or substitute) |

## DIRECTIONS

1. Sauté the onion in the butter, until tender but not brown.
2. Add the broccoli, garlic (if using), rice, and Parmesan and mix well.
3. Combine the eggs, milk, salt, and pepper.
4. Stir the egg mixture into the rice mixture.

5. Turn into a well-buttered, shallow 1-quart casserole.

6. Top with the mozzarella.

7. Bake at 350°F for 20 to 25 minutes, or until set.

## Red Flannel Hash[3]

Do you have leftover pork loin in your refrigerator? Use it, along with turkey bacon, in this breakfast hash. Serve with GF toast or a GF English muffin. This recipe serves six.

### INGREDIENTS

| | |
|---|---|
| 6 | *slices turkey bacon, cut into ½" pieces* |
| ½ | *cup sliced green onions* |
| ½ | *cup chopped green bell pepper* |
| 3 | *cups cooked, chopped red potatoes* |
| 2 | *teaspoons GF Worcestershire sauce* |
| ¼ | *teaspoon salt* |
| ⅛ | *teaspoon ground pepper* |
| 3 | *cups julienned cooked pork loin* |
| 1 | *cup drained, chopped pickled beets* |

### DIRECTIONS

1. Cook the turkey bacon until crisp in a large skillet.

2. Add the onions and bell pepper. Cook over medium-high heat for 1 minute.

3. Stir in the potatoes, Worcestershire sauce, salt, and ground pepper. Cook for 5 minutes, stirring occasionally.

4. Stir in the pork and beets. Cook until heated through.

## Blueberry Sauce

If your breakfast plans include waffles, pancakes (page 231), or French toast (made with GF bread, of course), then treat yourself to this blueberry sauce to dress them up.

### INGREDIENTS

| | |
|---|---|
| 2 | *cups fresh or frozen blueberries* |
| ¼ | *cup water* |

1    *cup orange juice*

¾    *cup sugar (A healthier choice: Instead of sugar, use xylitol, a natural sweetener. Follow directions on the package for substitution ratios.)*

¼    *cup cold water*

3    *tablespoons cornstarch*

½    *teaspoon almond extract*

⅛    *teaspoon ground cinnamon*

## DIRECTIONS

1. In a saucepan over medium heat, combine the blueberries, ¼ cup water, orange juice, and sugar.
2. Stir gently and bring to a boil.
3. In a cup or small bowl, mix together the cold water and cornstarch.
4. Gently stir the cornstarch mixture into the blueberries. Do not mash the berries.
5. Simmer gently for 3 to 4 minutes, or until thick enough to coat the back of a metal spoon.
6. Remove from the heat and stir in the almond extract and cinnamon.
7. Thin the sauce with water if it is too thick for your liking.

# Amaranth Pancakes[4]

Here's a GF pancake recipe that uses amaranth flour, which you may have to order online or buy at a health food store. This makes 6 servings.

## INGREDIENTS

1    *cup amaranth flour*

½    *cup arrowroot powder*

½    *cup ground almonds*

1    *teaspoon baking soda*

1    *teaspoon ground cinnamon*

1¼    *cups water*

2    *tablespoons lemon juice*

2   *tablespoons vegetable oil*

2   *tablespoons honey*

## DIRECTIONS

1. In a large bowl, combine the amaranth flour, arrowroot, almonds, baking soda, and cinnamon.
2. In a separate bowl, combine the water, lemon juice, oil, and honey and mix well.
3. Stir the liquid mixture into the flour mixture and mix well.
4. Heat a lightly oiled griddle or skillet over medium-high heat.
5. Drop the batter by spoonfuls onto the griddle, using approximately 2 tablespoons for each pancake.
6. Brown on both sides and serve hot.

## Cooked Rice Cereal

This cooked rice cereal is actually easy to prepare. To add additional zest, add fresh blueberries or other fruit.

### INGREDIENTS

1½   *cups white rice (uncooked)*

2   *cups low-fat milk or milk substitute, such as soy milk or rice milk*

¼   *cup sugar*

1½   *teaspoons ground cinnamon*

### DIRECTIONS

1. Prepare the rice according to the package directions.
2. Combine the warm cooked rice, milk, sugar, and cinnamon.
3. Stir and serve.

## Spinach Soufflé[5]

Have you ever prepared a soufflé? This one is easy.

### INGREDIENTS

1   *large egg*

⅓   *cup low-fat milk or milk substitute*

⅓   *cup grated Parmesan cheese (or substitute)*

1    teaspoon crushed garlic

     Salt and pepper, to taste

2    packages (10 ounces each) frozen leaf spinach, thawed

## DIRECTIONS

1. Preheat the oven to 350°F.
2. In a medium bowl, whisk together the egg, milk, cheese, garlic, salt, and pepper.
3. Fold in the spinach.
4. Place in a small casserole dish.
5. Bake for 20 minutes, or until lightly set.

## GF COOKING 301: LUNCHES

# Best Fresh Turkey Sandwiches

You don't have to wait until Thanksgiving to eat turkey sandwiches—just visit your supermarket deli. I recommend Boar's Head Turkey; it's free of unhealthy additives. Here's a wonderful turkey sandwich for home or on the go. I recommend using organic vegetables—tomatoes, lettuce, and avocado—if they are available and affordable.

## INGREDIENTS

2    slices GF bread
1    tablespoon GF mayonnaise
     Fresh deli turkey slices
1    avocado, sliced
1    tomato, sliced
1    romaine lettuce leaf
     Kosher salt and pepper, to taste

## DIRECTIONS

1. Toast the bread lightly.
2. Spread the mayonnaise, and add the turkey, avocado, tomato, lettuce, salt, and pepper.
3. Serve with fresh fruit and rice chips.

# Tuna Crepes

Crepes look exotic but are not difficult to make. And—more impor-tant—you can prepare them GF. Here's a nice recipe featuring tuna.

## INGREDIENTS

| | |
|---|---|
| 3 | eggs or egg substitute |
| 1 | cup brown rice flour |
| 1–2 | tablespoons olive oil |
| ¼–½ | cup water (The amount is determined by consistency. Add enough water to make a smooth and runny crepe batter.) |
| 1 | tablespoon vanilla extract |
| | Butter (or substitute) to oil the crepe pan |
| 1 | can white albacore tuna in water |
| 2 | tablespoons mayonnaise (regular GF or soy mayo) |
| 2 | tablespoons pickle relish |
| 1 | tablespoon curry powder |
| | Goat cheese, to taste |

## DIRECTIONS

1. In a medium bowl, beat the eggs.
2. Gradually add the flour, oil, and water, alternating a little of each, until all are incorporated and the proper crepe consis-tency is achieved.
3. Add the vanilla extract and stir to mix thoroughly.
4. Wipe the crepe pan with enough butter to allow the crepes to slide easily.
5. Use a ladle to pour a small amount of the batter into the hot crepe pan.
6. Pick the pan up, roll the batter around until it covers the pan, then cook until light golden brown.
7. Flip and cook until golden brown on both sides. Do not over-cook. Repeat to make remaining crepes.
8. Drain the tuna well.
9. Add the mayonnaise, relish, and curry powder and mix well.

10. Place the tuna mixture into the crepes and roll.
11. Top with the goat cheese.
12. Place under the broiler until the cheese melts, then serve with rice or kasha and pineapple slices or other fresh fruit.

# Chili Sweet-Potato Hash[6]

Tired of boring sandwiches or salads for lunch? Try this hash.

## INGREDIENTS

| | |
|---|---|
| 2 | tablespoons extra-virgin olive oil |
| ½ | pound bulk GF breakfast sausage (Look for fresh sausage without preservatives.) |
| 1 | medium sweet potato, scrubbed clean, cut in half lengthwise, thinly sliced into half moons |
| 1 | large red onion, chopped |
| 2 | teaspoons chili powder |
| 1 | teaspoon ground cumin |
| 2 | teaspoons ground coriander |
| | Salt and ground pepper, to taste |
| 3 | yellow ripe tomatoes, seeded and diced |
| 1 | small jalapeño pepper, seeded and chopped |
| 2–3 | tablespoons chopped fresh cilantro |
| 1 | lime, juiced |
| ½ | cup chopped flat-leaf parsley |
| 1 | cup grated extra-sharp Cheddar cheese (or substitute) |
| 1 | tablespoon butter |
| 4 | large eggs |

## DIRECTIONS

1. Preheat a large nonstick skillet over medium–high heat. Add enough of the oil to coat the pan in two turns.
2. Add the breakfast sausage and break it up with the back of a wooden spoon into little chunks.
3. Brown the sausage for 3 minutes.
4. Add the sweet potato and ¾ of the onion.

5. Season with the chili powder, cumin, coriander, salt, and ground pepper.

6. Stir frequently and cook for 10 to 12 minutes, or until the potato is tender.

7. While the hash is cooking, in a small bowl, combine the tomatoes, jalapeño pepper, the remaining onion, cilantro, lime juice, and a little salt and ground pepper. Set the salsa aside.

8. Once the hash is cooked, add the parsley, stir to combine, and transfer the hash to a serving platter.

9. Sprinkle with the cheese and cover with foil. The cheese will melt while you prepare the eggs.

10. Wipe clean the skillet you made the hash in, return it to the stove over medium-high heat, and add the butter.

11. Once the butter has melted, crack each of the eggs into the skillet, season with a little salt and ground pepper, and cook to desired doneness.

12. Transfer the eggs to the top of the hash, sprinkle with the tomato salsa, and serve.

Tip: Instead of fried eggs, try poached or scrambled.

## Avocado and Tomato Salsa

Eat this as a healthy snack with GF rice crackers or blue corn tortilla chips or as an open-faced sandwich on GF millet bread (or your favorite GF bread). Use organic tomatoes and avocados if they are available and within your budget.

### INGREDIENTS

1    avocado
1    tomato
     Juice from ½ fresh lemon
     Kosher salt and fresh pepper, to taste

### DIRECTIONS

1. Peel the avocado, remove the pit, and chop into small pieces.
2. Slice and dice the tomato into small pieces. (You can put the

tomato and avocado into a food processor and pulse until chopped into small pieces. Be careful not to overprocess.)

3. In a small bowl, mix the avocado and tomato with the lemon juice, and add the salt and pepper.

# Dave's Eggplant Caviar

If you don't tell people this is eggplant, they won't know it. Use this as a salsa or as a spread on GF bread, or just eat it as a salad.

## INGREDIENTS

| | |
|---|---|
| 2 | *eggplants* |
| ½ | *cup olive oil* |
| 2 | *brown onions* |
| ½ | *cup minced garlic* |
| 2 | *green bell peppers* |
| 4–6 | *finely chopped fresh jalapeño peppers (optional)* |
| 2 | *cans (16 ounces each) crushed plum tomatoes* |
| 1 | *small can tomato paste* |
| 3 | *tablespoons coarsely ground fresh black pepper* |
| | *Salt, to taste* |

## DIRECTIONS

1. Preheat the oven to 350°F.
2. Prick the eggplants repeatedly with a fork tine. Bake them for 1 hour.
3. Remove the skin from the eggplants and finely chop. Set aside.
4. Heat the oil to medium heat and sauté the onions and garlic until the onions are translucent.
5. Add the bell peppers, jalapeño peppers (if using), tomatoes with juice, tomato paste, and chopped eggplant. Add the ground pepper and salt.
6. Bring to a boil and simmer for 30 minutes.
7. Cool and serve.

# Tofu Salad[7]

This vegetarian lunch for four is similar to egg salad.

## INGREDIENTS

| | |
|---|---|
| 1 | pound firm tofu, mashed or crumbled |
| ¼ | cup chopped onion |
| ½ | cup sliced celery |
| 1 | clove garlic, pressed, or ¼ teaspoon garlic powder |
| 1 | tablespoon chopped parsley |
| 1 | teaspoon Spike seasoning |
| 3 | tablespoons soy mayonnaise or regular GF mayonnaise |
| ⅓ | cup sweet relish (optional) |
| ¼ | cup chopped red bell pepper (optional) |
| ¼ | cup chopped red cabbage (optional) |
| 1 | teaspoon mustard or mustard powder (optional) |

## DIRECTIONS

1. Mix the tofu, onion, celery, garlic, parsley, Spike seasoning, and mayonnaise together. Add the relish, pepper, cabbage, and mustard, if using.
2. Serve on GF bread with your favorite garnish, such as lettuce, tomato, or alfalfa sprouts. Or serve on a lettuce leaf.

# Veggie, Almond, and Feta Sandwich or Salad[8]

You can make this to use as a sandwich filling on your favorite GF bread, as lettuce wrap, or as a salad. It will serve four.

## INGREDIENTS

| | |
|---|---|
| 2 | small zucchini, chopped |
| 2 | roma tomatoes, diced |
| 10 | chopped kalamata olives |
| 1 | red or green bell pepper, chopped |

½   onion, preferably sweet Vidalia, chopped

½   cucumber, chopped

⅓   cup crumbled feta cheese

¼   cup sliced toasted almonds

2   tablespoons fresh basil, finely chopped

1   teaspoon fresh thyme

⅛   cup olive oil

⅛   cup balsamic vinegar

   Salt and freshly ground pepper, to taste

## DIRECTIONS

1. Mix the zucchini, tomatoes, olives, bell pepper, onion, and cucumber in a bowl.
2. Crumble the feta into the bowl, add the almonds, basil, and thyme and mix.
3. Mix together the oil and vinegar.
4. Pour the oil and vinegar mixture over the vegetable mixture and toss well. Add the salt and ground pepper, to taste.

# Mexican Chicken Soup[9]

Chef Sara Mouton created a "one size fits all" chicken soup, which she adapted to become Italian, Mexican, Asian, and Greek. Here is the GF Mexican version. This recipe will make about 2¾ cups.

## INGREDIENTS

1   large corn tortilla

1   can (14½ ounces) low-sodium GF chicken broth

½   cup shredded cooked chicken

½   cup rinsed, drained black or pinto beans

½   cup defrosted frozen corn

⅓   cup chopped canned Mexican tomatoes

   Salt, to taste

¼   cup shredded Monterey Jack cheese (or substitute)

**DIRECTIONS**

1. Preheat the oven to 350°F.
2. Prepare oven-baked tortilla chips by spraying a cookie sheet with nonstick cooking spray and placing the tortilla on it.
3. Cut the tortilla into 8 wedges. Bake for 10 minutes.
4. While the tortilla is baking, combine the chicken broth, chicken, beans, corn, and tomatoes (with juice) and heat until hot.
5. Add the salt, to taste.
6. Crumble the tortilla chips into the soup.
7. Sprinkle with the cheese.

## GF COOKING 301: DINNERS

# Fresh Tomato and Basil Pasta

Ah, Italian cooking! You can have Italian cooking, including pasta. Prepare this pasta dish using GF pasta, invite your friends over, and watch them rave over the dish, unaware that they are eating GF. As always, I recommend using organic vegetables whenever possible.

**INGREDIENTS**

| | |
|---|---|
| 5–10 | *plum tomatoes, diced* |
| 5–7 | *fresh basil leaves* |
| 2 | *large cloves garlic, minced* |
| 5 | *tablespoons extra-virgin olive oil* |
| | *Kosher salt and pepper, to taste* |
| 1 | *package GF spaghetti* |
| | *Fresh Parmesan cheese or cheese subsititue* |

**DIRECTIONS**

1. Mix the tomatoes, basil, and garlic together.
2. Let it stand at room temperature for at least 1 hour. (This allows the flavors to blend.)
3. Add the oil, and salt and pepper, to taste, and mix.

4. Cook the pasta according to the package directions. Do not rinse.
5. Combine the pasta with the tomatoes.
6. Grate the cheese over the top.

*Tips: You can warm the tomato sauce if desired. For a special treat, sauté jumbo shrimp in extra-virgin olive oil, and add to this recipe.*

## Chicken with Sesame Snow Peas in Apricot Sauce[10]

Chicken is a healthy dinner entrée. But if you prepare it often, it could become a little boring. Try this dish to give your healthy dinner new life.

### INGREDIENTS

2    *teaspoons olive oil*

3    *cloves garlic, peeled and minced*

1    *pound chicken or 1 medium package tofu, cubed*

1    *tablespoon sesame seeds*

1    *jar (8 to 10 ounces) all-fruit apricot preserves*

1    *tablespoon GF soy sauce*

1    *tablespoon Dijon mustard or regular mustard*

½    *teaspoon grated fresh ginger*

½    *pound snow peas, with ends trimmed*

### DIRECTIONS

1. In a large skillet over medium heat, warm the oil.
2. Add the garlic and cook for 1 minute.
3. Add the chicken and cook until no longer pink. (Or add cubed tofu and cook for 2 minutes.)
4. Add the sesame seeds and cook for 2 minutes.
5. Toss in the apricot preserves, soy sauce, mustard, and ginger. Bring to a boil.
6. Reduce the heat to low and simmer for 5 minutes.
7. Add the snow peas and simmer until tender-crisp, for about 5 minutes.
8. Serve with rice.

# Chicken Pepper Steak

This elegant and colorful dinner is fast and easy to prepare. If possible, buy organic chicken.

## INGREDIENTS

4    *tablespoons olive oil*

2    *large boneless, skinless chicken breasts, cut into chunks*

2–3  *large red, yellow, and green bell peppers, washed, seeded, and cut into thick strips*

    *Freshly ground black pepper, to taste*

1    *tablespoon GF Worcestershire sauce*

    *Jasmine rice*

1    *large clove garlic, minced*

1    *teaspoon kosher salt*

## DIRECTIONS

1. Pour 3 tablespoons of the olive oil into a large skillet to coat the bottom of the pan.
2. Over medium to high heat, combine the chicken, bell peppers, ground pepper, and Worcestershire sauce and cook for 20 to 30 minutes, or until the chicken is done.
3. Prepare the rice. Follow the package directions, and add the remaining 1 tablespoon olive oil, the garlic, and the salt.
4. Serve the chicken pepper steak over the rice.

# Sautéed Pork or Veal over Pasta

Here is another Italian dish to add to your recipe list. It is delicious, and although it looks great when you serve it, it is not terribly difficult to prepare.

## INGREDIENTS

1    *pound veal or lean pork tenderloin*

    *Rice flour (enough to coat the meat)*

| 1 | tablespoon olive oil and 4 tablespoons butter (You may use 5 tablespoons of olive oil instead of the olive oil and butter, if you prefer.) |
|---|---|
| 8–10 | large mushrooms |
| ½ | cup Marsala wine |
| | Salt and pepper, to taste |
| | GF penne pasta |
| | Freshly grated Parmesan cheese or cheese substitute |

1. Cut the veal into strips.
2. Coat the veal with the rice flour.
3. Pour the oil and butter into a skillet and heat on medium to high heat.
4. Place the veal into the skillet and cook.
5. Add the mushrooms, turning frequently to brown on all sides.
6. When the veal and mushrooms are cooked, turn up the heat and add the wine.
7. Let the alcohol in the wine cook down.
8. Add the salt and pepper, to taste.
9. Cook the pasta. Do not rinse.
10. Place the pasta into the skillet with the veal and mushroom mixture.
11. Sprinkle with the cheese.
12. Serve with fresh steamed broccoli.

# Wild Rice with Walnuts and Dates[11]

Broil your favorite fish (or a chicken breast), and serve this pilaf-style dish alongside it. It will take time to prepare—approximately 90 minutes total, because wild rice requires more cooking time than white rice does—but the results will be worth it. This makes 6 to 8 side-dish servings.

## INGREDIENTS

| 2 | cups chopped celery (4 ribs) |
|---|---|
| ¼ | cup chopped onion |
| 1 | tablespoon butter or butter substitute |

1    *cup uncooked wild rice, rinsed and drained*

1    *can (14½ ounces) GF chicken or beef broth*

1    *cup water*

⅓    *cup pitted whole dates, snipped*

¼    *cup chopped walnuts, toasted*

## DIRECTIONS

1. In a large skillet, cook the celery and onion in the butter for 10 minutes, or until tender but not brown.
2. Add the rice. Cook and stir for 3 minutes.
3. Add the broth and water and bring to a boil.
4. Reduce the heat. Cover and simmer for 50 to 60 minutes, or until the rice is tender and most of the liquid is absorbed.
5. Stir in the dates and walnuts.
6. Cook, uncovered, for 3 to 4 minutes, or until the mixture is thoroughly heated and the remaining liquid is absorbed.

# Spicy Cornmeal Cod[12]

Packaged breading for fish—even so-called cornmeal—found in the supermarket contains wheat flour. But you can easily prepare your own light breading. For a change of pace from broiled or grilled fish, try this oven-baked fish that has a crispy crust.

## INGREDIENTS

1½    *pounds cod, perch, or other lean fish fillets, about ½" thick*

¾    *cup cornmeal (pure cornmeal—not a packaged cornmeal mix)*

¼    *cup all-purpose GF flour*

½    *teaspoon salt*

½    *teaspoon garlic powder*

½    *teaspoon dried oregano*

½    *teaspoon ground red pepper*

½    *teaspoon ground black pepper*

2    *large eggs, beaten*

3    *tablespoons butter, melted, or olive oil or butter substitute*

## DIRECTIONS

1. Preheat the oven to 500°F.
2. Cut the fish fillets into 4" × 2" pieces.
3. Mix the cornmeal, flour, salt, garlic powder, oregano, red pepper, and black pepper.
4. Dip the fish into the eggs, then coat with the cornmeal mixture.
5. Place the fish on an ungreased cookie sheet.
6. Drizzle the butter over the fish.
7. Bake for 10 to 12 minutes, turning the fish once, or until golden brown.

# Grilled Vegetables[13]

They look and taste gourmet, but they are easy to prepare. The "trick" is to baste the veggies with olive oil and to watch the cooking time. You can use a charcoal fire or a gas grill.

## HERE ARE SOME VEGETABLES THAT LEND THEMSELVES TO GRILLING:

- Asparagus spears, whole
- Bell peppers, cut into 1" strips
- Broccoli spears, cut lengthwise in half
- Carrots, cooked for 10 minutes (or until crisp-tender) in boiling water before putting on the grill
- Cauliflowerets, cut lengthwise in half
- Cherry tomatoes
- Corn on the cob, husked and soaked in water before putting on the grill
- Eggplant, cut into ¼" slices
- Green beans, whole
- Mushrooms, whole
- Onions, cut into ½" slices
- Potatoes, cut into 1" wedges, partially cooked for 5 to 10 minutes before putting on the grill
- Zucchini, cut into ¾" pieces

## DIRECTIONS

1. Heat the coals or gas grill.
2. Grill the vegetables 4 to 5 inches from the heat.
3. Brush occasionally with olive oil or your favorite homemade salad dressing to add flavor and to keep them from drying out.
4. Cook for 10 to 15 minutes, depending upon the level of doneness you prefer.

# CHAPTER 19

## GIVE ME BREAD!

If I were to take a poll that asked gluten-sensitive people, "What do you miss on a gluten-free diet?" the answer would come back unanimously: *bread*.

We know that "man cannot live by bread *alone*." But it's hard to live *without* bread. You can take gluten out of almost all food and not miss it—except for bread. Bread as we have grown to know it and love it has a taste and texture unique to wheat flour. (Even specialty breads, such as potato, rye, and pumpernickel use wheat flour as a base.)

If you have purchased GF bread at the health food store, you have probably been disappointed. It is often dry or crumbly and lacks much taste.

The alternative is to bake your own bread. You may still hunger for the taste of wheat bread, but the bread you bake will tantalize you as it comes out of the oven or bread-making machine.

Many people avoid baking (regular) bread from scratch because of the time and effort. Bread-making machines have made baking bread simple—especially when packaged mixes are used.

The good news for GF bread bakers is that baking GF bread is actually easier than baking wheat bread. The easiest way—but rather pricey—to bake is to use a packaged bread mix (available in health food stores or online). A better alternative: Bake your bread from scratch.

If you have a bread-making machine, use it! But if you don't have one, you can still bake bread without a lot of effort.

So, what are you waiting for? Gather your ingredients and get to work. In a couple of hours, your mouth will start watering as the scent of baking bread fills your kitchen.

## FLOUR MIXES

If bread baking becomes a weekly routine, I recommend mixing large batches of all-purpose baking flour.

Most bakers agree that a mixture of several different types of flours produces the best results. Here are three different flour mixtures:

# Bette's Featherlight Rice Flour Mix[1]

This rice flour mix produces bread that has a nice texture and is very light. The rice flour gives the lightness; the tapioca flour and cornstarch help bind, and the potato flour helps keep moisture in the baked goods. This recipe makes 9 cups of flour.

### INGREDIENTS

4    *cups rice flour*

4    *cups tapioca flour*

4    *cups cornstarch*

4    *tablespoons potato flour (This is potato flour, not potato starch!)*

### DIRECTIONS

Thoroughly mix or sift all ingredients and keep in a dry area.

*Tip: You can adjust the recipe up or down; just keep the proportions the same. (For the potato flour, use 1 teaspoon per cup of flour mix.)*

# Quinoa Featherlight Flour Mix

Bette's Featherlight Rice Flour Mix can be easily adapted to use other flours, which give it a unique taste and texture. I especially like this flour mix, because of quinoa's slightly nutty flavor.

### INGREDIENTS

4    *cups quinoa flour*

4    *cups tapioca flour*

4    *cups cornstarch*

4    *tablespoons potato flour*

## DIRECTIONS

Mix or sift all ingredients and store in a dry container.

# Cole's Flour Blend[2]

This flour blend can be used in any bread recipe. It combines a number of different flours—rice, sweet rice, garfava, tapioca, amaranth, buckwheat, sorghum, and quinoa. The author of this flour recipe says that if she is out of amaranth, buckwheat, sorghum, or quinoa, she makes it up by increasing the amount of one (or more) of the other flours.

## INGREDIENTS

1½   *cups brown rice flour*

⅔    *cup potato starch flour (not potato flour)*

⅓    *cup white rice flour*

⅓    *cup sweet rice flour*

¼    *cup garfava*

¼    *cup tapioca flour (same as tapioca starch or tapioca starch flour)*

¼    *cup amaranth flour*

¼    *cup white buckwheat flour*

¼    *cup sorghum flour*

¼    *cup quinoa flour*

4    *teaspoons xanthan gum or guar gum*

## DIRECTIONS

Sift each flour several times to reduce sticking. Mix all ingredients and store in a dry container.

*Tip: You may wish to omit the xanthan gum or guar gum until you are ready to bake your bread, then add in the amount that the recipe calls for (in proportion to the amount of flour). By omitting this ingredient, the flour mixture can be used as an all-purpose flour for other baked goods.*

## BREAD RECIPES

Although we usually think of "bread" as a loaf that we slice up to use in sandwiches, bread includes biscuits and rolls, as well as crusty loaves. It even includes pizza crust!

Baking GF bread requires some experimentation—mainly with the flour mixture. When you find a flour mixture that you like, substitute it for the ones in the following recipes.

Here are recipes for several types of breads.

# Basic Featherlight Rice or Quinoa Bread[3]

This recipe will make a medium-size loaf, just right for a bread-making machine.

### INGREDIENTS

| | |
|---|---|
| 3 | cups featherlight rice flour mix (or quinoa flour mix) |
| 2¼ | teaspoons xanthan gum |
| 1½ | teaspoons unflavored gelatin |
| 1½ | teaspoons egg substitute |
| ¾ | teaspoon salt |
| 3 | tablespoons sugar |
| ⅓ | cup dry milk powder or nondairy substitute |
| 2¼ | teaspoons dry yeast granules |
| 1 | egg plus 2 whites |
| 4½ | tablespoons butter, cut into chunks, or coconut oil |
| ¾ | teaspoon dough enhancer or vinegar |
| 3 | teaspoons honey or molasses |
| 1½ | cups water |

### DIRECTIONS

1. Grease the bread pan(s) and dust with rice flour.
2. Combine the dry ingredients in a medium bowl and set aside.
3. In another bowl or the bowl of your mixer, whisk the egg and egg whites, butter, dough enhancer, and honey until blended.
4. Add most of the water to the egg mixture. Add the remaining water, as needed, after you start mixing the bread.

5. For hand mixing, turn the mixer on low and add the dry ingredients a little at a time and mix well.
6. Check to make sure the dough is the consistency of cake batter. Add more water, as necessary.
7. Turn the mixer to high and beat for 3½ minutes.
8. Spoon into the prepared pan(s), cover, and let rise in a warm place for about 35 minutes for rapid-rising yeast, or 60 or more minutes for regular yeast, until the dough reaches the top of the pan.
9. Preheat the oven to 400°F. Bake for 50 to 60 minutes, covering with foil after 10 minutes.
10. For a bread machine: Place the ingredients in the machine pan in the order suggested in the manual.
11. Use the setting for medium crust.

*Tip: This basic featherlight recipe is excellent. But if you find it is a little bland, increase the salt to 1 teaspoon. And for even more flavor, add 1 teaspoon coconut or almond extract.*

## Basic GF Bread[4]

As you look at the ingredients below, you will see that this recipe does not specify the type of GF flour mixture to use. Select one that appeals to you. I suggest that you try various bread recipes to find the one that you like best.

### INGREDIENTS

| | |
|---|---|
| 3 | *eggs* |
| 1 | *teaspoon vinegar* |
| ¼ | *cup olive oil* |
| 1⅛ | *cups water* |
| 3⅓ | *cups GF flour mix* |
| 3 | *tablespoons sugar* |
| 1½ | *teaspoons salt* |
| ⅔ | *cup dry milk or milk substitute* |
| 2¼ | *teaspoons active dry yeast* |

### DIRECTIONS

1. Combine the eggs, vinegar, oil, and water in a mixing bowl. Mix well and set aside.

2. Combine the flour mix, sugar, salt, dry milk, and yeast in another bowl and mix well.

3. Slowly add the flour mixture to the egg mixture, stirring constantly.

4. Beat for 5 to 7 minutes with a mixer or vigorously by hand to ensure complete mixing. The dough will be the consistency of very thick cake batter.

5. Place the dough in a lightly greased bowl, cover, and set in a warm place.

6. Allow the dough to rise until it's about double in size. Punch the dough down and fold out into a bread pan coated with nonstick cooking spray.

7. Smooth out any bumps on top of the dough ball with your finger.

8. Cover and allow to rise until it's about double.

9. Preheat the oven to 375°F. Bake for 35 minutes.

10. Cover the top of the bread with foil and bake for 20 minutes longer.

*Tips: This recipe also works well in bread machines. Set to normal cycle, large loaf size, and follow the directions for your machine.*

*Make sure that all the ingredients are blended well during the mixing stage by checking periodically and pushing any remaining dry ingredients downward with a rubber spatula. Be careful not to touch the mixing blade.*

## GF Biscuits[5]

### INGREDIENTS

½ cup garfava flour

4 tablespoons buttermilk powder

¼ cup potato starch

¼ cup cornstarch

8 teaspoons baking powder

¼ teaspoon xanthan gum

2 eggs

⅓ cup olive oil

¼ cup water, depending on batter consistency

## DIRECTIONS

1. In a medium bowl, mix the flour, buttermilk powder, potato starch, cornstarch, baking powder, and xanthan gum. In another bowl, mix the eggs and oil.
2. Add the egg mixture to the flour mixture and mix well. Add water as needed. The mixture should be stiff enough to make rounded spoonfuls.
3. Preheat the oven to 350°F.
4. On a greased cookie sheet, drop the biscuit mix by spoonfuls to make 10 to 12 biscuits.
5. Bake for 15 to 20 minutes.

# Egg Bread Loaf[6]

This is not a sandwich bread (it's too crumbly), but it tastes great and makes wonderful toast or can be eaten fresh out of the oven with your dinner. The nice thing about this bread is that it is fairly fast and easy to prepare.

## INGREDIENTS

| | |
|---|---|
| ¼ | cup shortening or coconut oil |
| 3 | tablespoons honey |
| 2 | eggs |
| 1 | cup plain yogurt or sour cream |
| 1 | teaspoon vinegar |
| 1 | packet yeast (about 1 tablespoon) |
| ½ | cup potato starch |
| 1½ | cups cornstarch |
| ½ | teaspoon baking soda |
| 1 | tablespoon baking powder |
| 2 | teaspoons xanthan gum |
| ¼ | teaspoon salt |

## DIRECTIONS

1. Preheat the oven to 350°F.
2. Grease a loaf pan and set aside.
3. In a large bowl, combine the oil, honey, eggs, yogurt, and vinegar. With an electric mixer, combine well to remove all lumps.

4. Gradually add the yeast, potato starch, cornstarch, baking soda, baking powder, xanthan gum, and salt. Mix by hand. The dough will be quite wet.

5. Place the dough in the prepared pan, and smooth the top with your wet hands.

6. Bake for 40 to 45 minutes, or until the loaf is lightly browned and a wooden pick inserted in the middle tests clean.

## Dinner Rolls[7]

### INGREDIENTS

| | |
|---|---|
| 2 | large eggs |
| ¾ | teaspoon cider vinegar |
| 3 | tablespoons olive oil |
| 1 | cup very warm water |
| 1⅓ | cups white rice flour |
| ⅓ | cup potato starch |
| ⅓ | cup tapioca flour |
| ¼ | cup cornstarch |
| 2 | tablespoons sugar |
| 2 | teaspoons xanthan gum |
| 1 | teaspoon salt |
| ½ | cup dry milk |
| 2¼ | teaspoons dry yeast |

### DIRECTIONS

1. In a large bowl, mix the eggs, vinegar, oil, and water.

2. In a separate bowl, combine the rice flour, potato starch, tapioca flour, cornstarch, sugar, xanthan gum, salt, dry milk, and yeast.

3. Add the flour mixture to the egg mixture a little at a time and mix well. The dough should be stiffer than a cake batter but not as stiff as a cookie dough.

4. If the dough appears to be too dry, add water, 1 tablespoon at a time.

5. Spoon the dough into a 12-muffin pan coated with nonstick cooking spray.
6. Preheat the oven to 350°F.
7. Let the dough rise approximately 30 minutes on top of the warm oven, or until the dough doubles in size.
8. Bake for 20 to 25 minutes.

# Pizza Crust[8]

According to the creator of this recipe, this crispy pizza crust tastes delicious and imitates "real" pizza crust so well that no one will guess it is gluten-free. The recipe makes one large pizza crust or four small individual pizzas.

## INGREDIENTS

1    *tablespoon GF dry yeast*
⅔    *cup brown rice flour or bean flour*
½    *cup tapioca flour*
2    *tablespoons dry milk powder or nondairy milk powder or sweet rice flour*
2    *teaspoons xanthan gum*
½    *teaspoon salt*
1    *teaspoon unflavored gelatin powder*
1    *teaspoon Italian herb seasoning*
⅔    *cup warm water (105°F)*
½    *teaspoon sugar or ¼ teaspoon honey*
1    *teaspoon olive oil*
1    *teaspoon cider vinegar or ¼ teaspoon unbuffered vitamin C crystals*

## DIRECTIONS

1. Preheat the oven to 425°F.
2. In a medium mixer bowl using regular beaters (not dough hooks), blend the yeast, flours, milk powder, xanthan gum, salt, gelatin powder, and Italian herb seasoning on low speed.
3. Add the water, sugar, oil, and vinegar.
4. Beat on high speed for 3 minutes. (*Tip:* If the mixer bounces around

the bowl, the dough is too stiff. Add water, if necessary, 1 tablespoon at a time, until the dough does not resist the beaters.)

5. The dough will resemble soft bread dough. (You can also mix it in a bread machine on the dough setting.)

6. Put the mixture onto a 12" pizza pan, a baking sheet (for thin, crispy crust), or an 11" × 7" pan (for a deep-dish version) that has been coated with nonstick cooking spray.

7. Liberally sprinkle rice flour onto the dough, then press the dough into the pan, continuing to sprinkle the dough with flour to prevent it from sticking to your hands.

8. Make the edges slightly higher to contain toppings.

9. Bake for 10 minutes.

10. Remove from the oven.

11. Spread the pizza crust with sauce (below) and toppings.

12. Bake for 20 to 25 minutes longer, or until the top is nicely browned.

## Pizza Sauce

Prepare this fat-free sauce while the pizza crust bakes. It fills the kitchen with a delicious aroma.

### INGREDIENTS

| | |
|---|---|
| 8 | *ounces tomato sauce* |
| ½ | *teaspoon dried oregano* |
| ½ | *teaspoon dried basil* |
| ½ | *teaspoon dried rosemary* |
| ½ | *teaspoon fennel seeds* |
| ¼ | *teaspoon gluten-free garlic powder* |
| 2 | *teaspoons sugar or 1 teaspoon honey (optional)* |
| ½ | *teaspoon salt* |

### DIRECTIONS

1. Combine the tomato sauce, oregano, basil, rosemary, fennel, garlic powder, sugar, and salt in a small saucepan and bring to a boil over medium heat.

2. Reduce the heat to low and simmer for 15 minutes (Letting the sauce simmer for 15 minutes thickens it, so it won't make the pizza crust soggy.)
3. Top a pizza crust with the sauce and your favorite toppings.

The best desserts are the ones that come straight from Mother Nature—fruits. They are sweet, nonprocessed, ready-to-eat, and delicious. Fresh strawberries, peaches, apples, blueberries . . . they satisfy a craving and are full of the wonderful nutrients essential for good health.

That said, I realize that *once in a while,* you will want to have something other than fruit for dessert. But before you indulge, realize that there is just as much gluten-free junk food available to tempt you as there is non-gluten-free. Please don't substitute one type of junk for another! Prepare and eat snacks and desserts sparingly.

In this chapter, we've given you a few dessert recipes to show you that you won't be *deprived* living a GF way of life. And for many recipes, you don't have to do anything special—just substitute your favorite GF all-purpose flour.

These are dessert recipes that were modified to be gluten-free. Remember, though: You can substitute coconut oil in equal amounts for butter in any recipe that calls for butter, if you want to use a healthier fat or are avoiding dairy. And there are many healthier, low-glycemic index sugar substitutes on the market that are preferable to refined sugar, so you do not have to use sugar in a recipe (see Chapter 16).

## Chocolate-Chip Cookies

Who doesn't like Toll House chocolate chip cookies? I've discovered that baking cookies usually only requires a slight adaptation of the recipe: Use an all-purpose GF flour mixture (as described in Chapter 19) and add a teaspoon of xanthan or guar gum. I think you'll be quite pleased with the result.

## INGREDIENTS

2¼   cups all-purpose flour

1   teaspoon baking soda

1   teaspoon xanthan or guar gum

1   teaspoon salt

1   cup butter, softened

¾   cup granulated sugar

¾   cup packed brown sugar

1   teaspoon vanilla extract

2   eggs

2   cups (12-ounce package) semisweet chocolate morsels

1   cup chopped nuts (optional)

## DIRECTIONS

1. Preheat the oven to 375°F.
2. Combine the flour, baking soda, xanthan or guar gum, and salt in a small bowl. Set aside.
3. Beat the butter, granulated sugar, brown sugar, and vanilla extract in a large mixer bowl.
4. Add the eggs one at a time, beating well after each addition.
5. Gradually add the flour mixture into the butter mixture.
6. Stir in the morsels and nuts, if using.
7. Drop by rounded tablespoonsful onto an ungreased baking sheet. (The cookies will spread out. Smaller dollops are better than large ones.)
8. Bake for 9 to 11 minutes.
9. Let stand for 2 minutes, then remove to a rack to cool completely.
10. Serve with milk or milk substitute.

# Yellow Cake[1]

Just because you have gone gluten-free doesn't mean that you have to give your cookbooks away! In most cases, you can follow regular recipes, with minor modifications: For this basic yellow cake recipe, I substituted the quinoa featherlight flour mixture for wheat flour, and I added xanthan gum to help the baked goods "stick" together better. I also used soy milk instead of cow's milk.

The quinoa flour and soy milk give the cake a slightly nutty (but delicious!) flavor. Once you find the all-purpose GF flour you like best, try substituting it for "regular" flour in your favorite recipes.

## INGREDIENTS

2¼    *cups GF all-purpose flour*
1½    *cups sugar*
3½    *teaspoons baking powder*
1     *teaspoon salt*
3     *large eggs*
½     *cup shortening*
1¼    *cups milk or milk substitute*
1     *teaspoon vanilla extract*
      *Topping of your choice*

## DIRECTIONS

1. Preheat the oven to 350°F. Grease the bottom and side of a 13" × 9" pan or two 9" × 1½" round pan, and lightly flour.
2. Mix the flour, sugar, baking powder, and salt together in a large bowl. Set aside.
3. Beat the eggs and shortening until fluffy.
4. Alternate adding the flour mixture and the milk and vanilla extract to the eggs until all are incorporated.
5. Beat with an electric mixer for 3 minutes, scraping the side of the bowl occasionally.
6. Pour into the pan(s).
7. Bake the rectangular pan for 45 to 50 minutes, the round pans for 30 to 35 minutes. Check doneness with a wooden pick.
8. Remove from the oven and cool on a rack.
9. Ice, if desired. (*Note:* Prepared canned icings from the supermarket contain wheat!)

*Tip: Drizzle the cake with GF chocolate syrup or sprinkle with powdered sugar.*

# Quinoa Applesauce Cake[2]

This is a recipe that does not require a flour mixture. Instead, it just uses quinoa flour. The author of this recipe says that this cake can be prepared with half of the maple sugar, plus ⅛ teaspoon stevia extract powder—a nice thing to know, because less sugar is better.

### INGREDIENTS

| | |
|---|---|
| 1¾ | cups quinoa flour |
| 1 | cup currants |
| ½ | cup chopped pecans |
| ½ | teaspoon baking soda |
| ½ | teaspoon baking powder |
| ½ | teaspoon salt |
| ½ | teaspoon ground cloves |
| ½ | cup unsalted sweet butter |
| 1 | cup maple sugar |
| 1 | large egg |
| 2 | cups unsweetened applesauce |

### DIRECTIONS

1. Preheat the oven to 350°F.
2. Sprinkle ¼ cup of the flour over the currants and pecans and set aside.
3. Blend the baking soda, baking powder, salt, and cloves with the remaining 1½ cups of flour.
4. In another bowl, mix together the butter, sugar, and egg.
5. Combine the flour mixture, the butter mixture, and the applesauce, and add the currants and nuts last.
6. Spoon into a greased 8" × 8" cake pan and bake for 40 to 45 minutes, or until a cake tester inserted into the center comes out clean.

# Traveler's Cereal Snack[3]

When you are traveling, it's almost a necessity to take a snack with you. Here's a gluten-free treat that is healthy, too.

## INGREDIENTS

| | |
|---|---|
| 4 | cups gluten-free crispy corn puff cereal |
| 1 | cup Spanish peanuts |
| 1 | cup raisins |
| 1 | cup dried banana chips |
| 3 | tablespoons butter or coconut oil |
| 3 | tablespoons honey |
| ¾ | teaspoon ground cinnamon |
| ½ | teaspoon salt |
| 1 | cup flaked coconut |

## DIRECTIONS

1. Preheat the oven to 325°F.
2. Mix the cereal, peanuts, raisins, and banana chips in a 15" × 10" ungreased pan. Set aside.
3. Heat the butter and honey in a 1-quart saucepan over low heat, until the butter is melted.
4. Stir in the cinnamon and salt.
5. Pour over the cereal mixture, tossing until evenly coated.
6. Bake for 15 minutes, stirring once.
7. Stir in the coconut.
8. Let stand for 5 minutes and loosen from the pan.

# GF Piecrust[4]

Would you like to have a pumpkin or apple pie with Sunday dinner? Here's a recipe for piecrust. Just fill with your favorite fruit filling and bake.

## INGREDIENTS

| | |
|---|---|
| 1 | cup butter or coconut oil |
| 1¾ | cups sugar |
| 4 | eggs |
| 1¾ | cups rice flour |
| ½ | cup sweet rice flour (from an Asian market) |
| 1 | teaspoon xanthan gum |

1½ teaspoons baking powder

¼ teaspoon salt

1 teaspoon vanilla extract

## DIRECTIONS

1. Cream together the butter, sugar, and eggs.
2. Add the flours, xanthan gum, baking powder, salt, and vanilla extract.
3. Mix well and spread about ¼" deep on the bottom and sides of an 8" or 9" pie pan. A deep dish pie pan is best, because this crust takes a little more room than regular piecrusts.
4. Fill shell immediately with pumpkin pie filling or fruit filling mixture, and bake according to the directions in the recipe you're using.

# Macadamia Piecrust[5]

Some pies call for a graham cracker crust. Graham crackers are off-limits to gluten-sensitive individuals. But this piecrust is a great substitute. The recipe makes enough for one 9" piecrust. The best part: It's quick (about 5 minutes to prepare and 5 minutes to bake).

## INGREDIENTS

6 ounces macadamia nuts

2 eggs

1½ cups soy flour

## DIRECTIONS

1. Preheat the oven to 350°F.
2. Place the nuts into a food processor and blend until they reach a peanut butter–like consistency.
3. Scrape into a bowl and stir in the eggs and flour until well blended.
4. Place the dough between two pieces of waxed paper.
5. Roll out into a 12" circle.

6. Remove the top piece of waxed paper and invert the dough into a 9" pie plate.
7. Press into the bottom and up the side of the plate. Remove any overhanging dough.
8. Bake for 5 minutes, or until light golden brown.
9. Use in any recipe calling for a prebaked piecrust.

## Lime Sherbet

If you have an ice cream maker, you can prepare this sherbet using milk or a milk substitute.

### INGREDIENTS

3    *cups milk or milk substitute*

1    *cup frozen limeade concentrate, thawed*

3    *tablespoons sweetener of your choice*

### DIRECTIONS

1. Combine the milk, limeade concentrate, and sweetener in a blender or food processor.
2. Pour the mixture into the ice cream maker, following manufacturer's instructions.
3. Mix until iced.
4. You can eat this immediately, or you can "age" it for a deeper flavor.

*Tip: Substitute frozen orange juice, lemonade, or piña colada concentrate for a variety of flavors.*

# CHAPTER 21

## A 14-DAY GF DIET

In the previous chapters in this section, you found mouthwatering recipes that could appeal to you, no matter what level of cooking skill (or interest) you have. And you found recipes for delicious breads, as well as desserts. (Don't overdo these, though! This is an ideal time to eat healthy to help your body get well as fast as possible—and then stay well.) So, this chapter aims to provide you with information and tips on healthy eating.

## GF "FRIENDLY" FOODS

When you are planning your daily menus, select a variety of proteins, vegetables, salads, GF carbohydrates, and fruits. Here is a listing of a wide variety of foods from which to select and incorporate into your recipes and meals.

### Protein Foods

- Canned tuna, salmon, or sardines (packed in water)
- Chicken, turkey, or Cornish hen (without the skin)
- Eggs or egg whites
- Fat-free cheese
- Fat-free soy cheese
- Fat-free yogurt, plain
- Fresh fish (salmon, tuna, sardines, flounder, snapper, trout, etc.)
- Lean veal
- Milk and milk substitutes

- Red meats, such as beef, pork, lamb, buffalo, or venison (once or twice a week, as you choose)
- Seafood (shrimp, scallops, clams, lobster, calamari, octopus, mussels, etc.)
- Tofu, firm or soft

## Vegetables and Salad Greens

- Alfalfa sprouts
- Artichokes
- Arugula
- Asparagus
- Bean sprouts
- Beets
- Bell peppers (red, green, or yellow)
- Bok choy
- Broccoli
- Brussels sprouts
- Cabbage (red or white)
- Carrots
- Cauliflower
- Celery
- Collard greens
- Cucumbers
- Dandelion greens
- Eggplant
- Endive
- GF tomato soup
- Green beans
- Hot peppers
- Jicama

- Kale
- Leeks
- Lettuce (all types)
- Mushrooms
- Okra
- Olives (limit 5)
- Onions
- Parsley
- Radishes
- Sauerkraut (no sugar added)
- Snow peas
- Spinach
- Tomato juice (no salt)
- Tomato paste
- Vegetable juice
- Vegetable soup (low-fat)
- Water chestnuts
- Watercress
- Yellow squash
- Zucchini

## Carbohydrates

- Beans (red, black, garbanzo, lima, pinto, black-eyed, soy)
- Buckwheat (pearled, hulled, kasha)
- Corn
- GF breads
- GF pastas
- Green peas
- Lentils
- Potatoes

- Quinoa
- Rice (white or brown)
- Rice noodles
- Wild rice
- Winter squash (acorn, butternut, spaghetti)
- Yams or sweet potatoes

## Fruits

- Apples
- Apricots
- Bananas
- Berries (blueberries, strawberries, raspberries, blackberries, boysenberries)
- Cantaloupe
- Cherries
- Currants
- Dates
- Figs
- Grapefruit
- Grapes
- Guava
- Honeydew melon
- Kiwifruit
- Kumquats
- Lemons
- Lychees
- Mandarin oranges
- Mangoes
- Nectarines
- Oranges

- Papayas
- Peaches
- Pears
- Pineapples
- Plums
- Pomegranates
- Raisins
- Watermelon

## Seasonings

- GF bouillon (chicken, vegetable, beef)
- GF soy sauce or tamari sauce
- Lemon juice, vinegar
- Natural extracts (vanilla, almond, orange)
- Spices and herbs (allspice, basil, bay leaf, cardamom, cinnamon, cloves, cumin, curry, dill, fennel, garlic, horseradish, mace, marjoram, mint, mustard, nutmeg, oregano, paprika, parsley, pepper, rosemary, saffron, sage, tarragon, thyme, turmeric)

## Special-Occasion Foods

I recognize that from time to time, you may want a treat, such as ice cream, a GF cookie, GF cake, or even french fries. Special treats are okay—as long as you don't overdo them! Please do not substitute GF "junk" in place of processed foods that you were eating regularly. Take this opportunity to eat healthy to get healthy.

## 14-Day GF Diet

We provided you with recipes to show you that you *can* eat well on a GF diet. Now, I'd like to give you a 14-day diet—selections for breakfast, lunch, and dinner—to get you started. Mix and match to satisfy your taste buds.

Here are some suggestions about how to use the meal-selection chart in this chapter:

1. **Review the food lists above.** You will find many protein, vegetable, carbohydrate, and fruit choices. Substitute whatever you like into any menu or recipe.

2. **Eat your favorites frequently.** Who says you have to eat a different menu every day? If you like a particular meal, feel free to have it more frequently. But it is better to rotate your foods and not eat the same thing all the time.

3. **Don't be stuck on conformities!** You can eat breakfast for dinner and lunch for breakfast! The kind of food we eat at a particular time of day is convention—nothing more.

4. **Don't forget to check out Chapter 16.** This is where you will find many substitutes for cheese and milk, if you also choose to go dairy-free.

5. **Order sauces on the side.** When in doubt while eating out, get your sauces on the side.

6. **Add a salad and/or a vegetable to *any* meal.** And for dessert or a snack, eat fruit.

7. **Experiment with herbs.** Herbs and spices perk up your food. Many have "hidden" health benefits. Don't be afraid to try them.

8. **Think tomato.** Use tomato sauces, salsa, and other sauces that are gluten-free to perk up your food.

9. **Drink plenty of water or mineral water throughout the day.** Avoid tap water. You can also have coffee (if it agrees with you), tea, herbal tea, and juice. I would recommend smaller amounts of juice, diluted with sparkling mineral water, seltzer, or water—usually half juice, half water. Keep away from sodas (both diet and regular) or any other intensely sweetened beverage.

10. **Plan ahead.** This is extremely important, especially when eating gluten-free for the first time, to make sure you have everything you need. It's also important to plan ahead when eating out. Familiarize yourself with local menus and substitutions. If you frequent a particular restaurant, ask if the cook would prepare a GF pasta that you provide or warm your GF bread.

# ON THE ROAD? HERE'S WHAT TO DO

One of the biggest fears that individuals with gluten sensitivity harbor is eating out. Their first thought is that there will be nothing that they can order, unless the restaurant has a special GF menu. Their second fear is that someone will "slip" them some gluten.

I am gluten-sensitive, and I can assure you that you *can* dine out! And if you communicate with your wait staff and the chef, the problems you encounter will be minimal. Restaurants are very accommodating. Tell the wait staff you have a "wheat allergy." You will be amazed. You will find that the wait staff (or at least the manager) will steer you away from items containing (or possibly containing) gluten. And they will advise the chef to prepare foods without gluten.

That said, here are some other tips on eating out, especially when you are traveling on vacation or business.

1. **Add a salad or vegetables.** Substitute these for the french fries that usually accompany a sandwich.

2. **Eat lunch for breakfast.** You can usually find eggs and potatoes on breakfast menus, and they make good choices (especially if you don't have any GF bread with you). But think outside of the breakfast box! Nothing says that you cannot have chicken, turkey, or any other protein for breakfast, along with a salad and/or vegetables.

3. **Take GF bread.** If you have bread, you can find a deli counter and buy enough turkey to make a sandwich. All supermarkets have bagged salad, carrots, and other vegetables that you can eat as snacks or add to a "take-out" meal.

4. **Eat fruit.** You can find fresh fruit in any convenience store or supermarket (and sometimes in the lobby at a hotel!). Eat it as a snack or add it to your meal as an easy dessert.

5. **Carry dry-roasted or raw nuts.** They make a good snack and can be purchased almost anywhere.

6. **Ask about sauces.** When dining out, ask about the ingredients in the sauce. It's unlikely that tomato sauce will have gluten in it. *Tip:* Most Chinese restaurants will steam your food without any sauce.

(continued on page 274)

## Breakfast: Week 1

| DAY 1 | DAY 2 | DAY 3 | |
|---|---|---|---|
| • Egg omelet with onions, tomatoes, mushrooms<br><br>• Add potatoes, sweet potatoes, or yams to the omelet or have GF toast<br><br>• Fresh fruit of your choice | • Buckwheat waffles<br><br>• Fresh strawberries<br><br>• All-fruit jam (no sugar added) | • Buckwheat pancakes<br><br>• Fresh blueberries<br><br>• Natural maple syrup or all-fruit jam | |

## Breakfast: Week 2 (See Chapters 16, 17, and 18 for recipes)

| | | | |
|---|---|---|---|
| • Hot Kasha Breakfast Cereal (Chap. 17) | • Peanut Butter and Banana Toast (Chap. 16) | • Orange Pink-Grapefruit Smoothie (Chap. 16) | |

## Lunch: Week 1

| | | | |
|---|---|---|---|
| • Tuna or chicken salad made with low-fat mayonnaise, chopped celery, and carrots<br><br>• Romaine lettuce, radish, tomato<br><br>• GF bread | • Grilled turkey burger with onion and tomato<br><br>• Steamed broccoli<br><br>• GF burger bun | • Grilled or broiled shrimp<br><br>• Mixed green salad with vegetable<br><br>• Spaghetti squash (tomato sauce optional) | |

## Lunch: Week 2 (See Chapters 16, 17, and 18 for recipes)

| | | | |
|---|---|---|---|
| • Turkey-Bacon Lettuce Wrap (Chap. 16) | • Chef Salad to Go (Chap. 16) | • Open-Faced Toasted Tuna Salad with Cheese (Chap. 16) | |

## Dinner: Week 1

| | | | |
|---|---|---|---|
| • Baked red snapper with onion, cherry tomatoes, red potatoes, extra-virgin olive oil<br><br>• Mixed salad<br><br>• Baked yam or sweet potato | • GF penne pasta<br><br>• Tomato sauce<br><br>• Grilled shrimp<br><br>• Grilled vegetables: zucchini, onion, red and green peppers | • Grilled chicken breast<br><br>• Steamed broccoli, snow peas, carrots<br><br>• Spaghetti squash | |

## Dinner: Week 2 (See Chapters 16, 17, and 18 for recipes. Add salad and/or vegetables to all meals.)

| | | | |
|---|---|---|---|
| • Tuna Crepes (Chap. 18) | • Chicken Pepper Steak (Chap. 18)<br><br>• Jasmine Rice | • Broiled Salmon with Mustard Sauce (Chap. 16) | |

| DAY 4 | DAY 5 | DAY 6 | DAY 7 |
|---|---|---|---|
| • Egg omelet with zucchini, broccoli, onion<br><br>• Add potatoes, sweet potatoes, or yams to the omelet or enjoy GF toast | • Low-fat or fat-free cheese melted on GF bread with a slice of tomato<br><br>• Fresh fruit on the side | • GF cereal (hot or cold)<br><br>• Raspberries and/or raisins<br><br>• Milk of your choice | • Low-fat or fat-free unsweetened yogurt<br><br>• Cucumber, radish, green and red peppers, onion<br><br>• GF bread |
| • Turkey on Toast (Chap. 16) | • Goat Cheese Omelet (Chap. 17) | • Cooked Rice Cereal (Chap. 18) | • Broccoli Frittata (Chap. 18) |
| • Roast chicken (or meat of your choice)<br><br>• Steamed snow peas, cabbage, and carrots<br><br>• Baked or boiled sweet potato | • Grilled salmon<br><br>• Mixed salad<br><br>• Lentils and brown rice | • Chicken breast breaded in GF flour or bread crumbs and baked in the oven (you can also melt cheese of your choice for chicken parmesan)<br><br>• Mixed salad<br><br>• GF pasta with tomato sauce | • Grilled scallops<br><br>• Steamed asparagus<br><br>• Acorn squash |
| • Chicken Salad Sandwich (Chap. 17) | • Egg Salad Sandwich (Chap. 16) | • Asian Salad and Dressing (Chap. 17) | • Best Fresh Turkey Sandwich (Chap. 18) |
| • Grilled salmon with lemon and herbs<br><br>• Mixed salad<br><br>• Wild rice | • (Chinese take-out) Steamed shrimp with Chinese vegetables<br><br>• Rice (brown or white)<br><br>• Spicy Chinese mustard, GF soy sauce | • (Italian restaurant) Veal or chicken pizaiola<br><br>• Tricolored salad with arugula, radicchio, endive<br><br>• Roasted potatoes<br><br>• Spinach with garlic and olive oil | • (Mexican restaurant) Chicken fajitas with corn tortillas<br><br>• Beans<br><br>• Guacamole, pico de gallo<br><br>• Rice |
| • Pad Thai with Vegetables (Chap. 16) | • Sautéed Pork or Veal over Pasta (Chap. 18) | • Turkey Skewers with Mango Salsa (Chap. 17) | • Spicy Chicken Sesame Fajitas (Chap. 17) |

7. **Take your own GF soy sauce.** Carry a small container of GF soy sauce with you when you intend to go to an Asian-foods restaurant. *Tip:* Spontaneous decision to eat Chinese or Japanese? Stop at a grocery and get La Choy soy sauce. It's gluten-free.

8. **Enjoy ethnic food!** Sure, the breads and pasta are tempting. But Italian restaurants offer many other fine items that you can eat, such as grilled fish, shrimp, and meat. If you can tolerate milk products, order risotto; if not, ask for rice. Mexican restaurants usually offer corn tortillas. You can order all types of dishes prepared with beans, rice, salad, and vegetables. Avoid sour cream and cheese if you are eating dairy-free, but ask if the restaurant offers nondairy alternatives; many do. *Tip:* Salsa and pico de gallo are just fine. Middle Eastern menus offer a lot of protein, salads, and vegetables, including items such as hummus (avoid the pita bread) and stuffed grape leaves.

# HELPFUL RESOURCES FOR GLUTEN-FREE LIVING

This book was written with the goal of empowering you to take action so that you can start feeling better. The answer is simple but not easy: Go gluten-free (GF).

Going gluten-free is admittedly a lifestyle change. It requires new shopping habits, some new cooking habits, and new eating habits. But that does not condemn you to a life of deprivation! You will find that by setting yourself free from the foods that harm you, you will have more freedom to be healthy and to live a full life.

Nevertheless, there will be times—especially in the beginning—when this lifestyle change seems so huge that you cannot manage it. Take heart. You can do it!

Becoming aware of and accepting your problem is a huge first step. Now, venture into changing your life. In the remainder of this chapter, you'll find many resources that can "hold your hand" as you take your baby steps toward a new healthy lifestyle. The list is not inclusive, but it will get you started!

## ADVOCACY

- **American Celiac Disease Alliance** (www.americanceliac.org) is a federation of celiac organizations that came together in 2003 to form an education and advocacy group for individuals with celiac disease.

## BREAD-MAKING COOKBOOKS

The one food item that people on a gluten-free diet miss most is bread. And the "guru" of bread baking is Bette Hagman. She taught herself how to bake gluten-free after she was diagnosed with celiac disease about 20 years ago. She continues to refine recipes, including developing flour mixes that are lighter and tastier than most.

Her most recent bread cookbook is *The Gluten-Free Gourmet Bakes Bread: More Than 200 Wheat-Free Recipes* (Henry Holt & Sons), although she has published a number of other cookbooks on desserts, light and fast cooking, and main dishes.

## DAIRY SUBSTITUTES

- **Go Dairy Free,** www.godairyfree.org. One of the best resources for dairy substitutes is Go Dairy Free. This Web site provides alternatives to cow's milk. It not only recommends products (based on their health attributes), but it also tells how to make some of the substitutes at home—something that can help you save money.

- **U.S. Soyfoods Directory,** www.soyfoods.com. This directory provides resources for using soy and tofu in place of dairy.

## GLUTEN-FREE BEER

If you are a beer drinker, going gluten-free means giving up the "suds." But you have options: Two breweries in the United States and one in Canada (and a number of them outside of North America) make gluten-free beers; some have retail outlets in states outside of their brewery sites. And you also have the option of bottling your own gluten-free beer.

- **Bard's Tale Beer,** gluten-free beer (www.bardsbeer.com). This gluten-free beer is available in a number of states; however, it is not sold nationwide nor by mail.

- **Gluten-Free Brewing** is a Web site dedicated to helping home-brewers concoct gluten-free beer. (www.fortunecity.com/boozers/brewerytap/555/gfbeer/gfbeer.htm).

- **La Messagère** is a Canadian gluten-free beer brewed from rice and buckwheat. The brewery is Les bières de la Nouvelle-France (www.lesbieresnouvellefrance.com). The beer is sold in Canada.

- **Mr. Goodbeer** (www.mrgoodbeer.com) gives advice and recipes on brewing your own beer.
- **Ramapo Valley Brewery** (www.rvbrewery.com).

## GLUTEN-FREE CERTIFICATION

- **Gluten-Free Certification Organization** (www.gfco.org) is an independent service of the Gluten Intolerance Group. In the absence of U.S. government standards, GFCO was formed to supervise gluten-free food production according to a consistent, defined, science-based standard that is confirmed by field inspections. Its goal is to increase consumer confidence in gluten-free food labeling.

## GLUTEN-FREE FOOD, DRUG, AND RESTAURANT GUIDES AND DATABASES

- Buying prepared foods in the grocery and (especially) enjoying a meal in a restaurant requires some research and planning. A number of resources are available to help you. **AllergyFree Passport,** www.allergyfreepassport.com, is a series of booklets developed around ethnic food themes, which guide readers into making safe choices when eating in restaurants.
- **Clan Thompson Celiac SmartLists** (www.clanthompson.com), a series of software programs available in all formats (including for use in PDAs), allow you to search for gluten-free foods by brand name and by restaurant.
- **Clan Thompson Pocket Guides** (www.clanthompson.com). These booklets are essentially a print version of the software programs.
- **Gluten Free Dining Guide,** www.goodhealthpublishing.com. This guide lists 70 restaurants that offer gluten-free menus.
- **Gluten Guard, On Guard Solutions,** www.onguardsolutions.com. This company has developed searchable databases of 100,000 gluten-free foods. The software is available for use with portable devices.

- **Gluten-Free Restaurant Awareness Program** is a searchable database of restaurants (www.glutenfreerestaurants.org/find.php). It is currently limited to only four states.

- **Triumph Dining Cards** (www.triumphdining.com). These cards clearly list hidden ingredients that might find their way into restaurant foods. The cards can be given to wait staff and chefs. They are available in six global cuisines.

## GLUTEN-FREE SHOPPING

Gluten-free foods are far from mainstream in the United States. However, you can find them in a number of natural food grocery or specialty stores. And some "regular" supermarkets are beginning to carry their own (or other) brands of gluten-free foods, although the selection is limited.

### "Brick and Mortar" Stores

- **Albertson's** (www.albertsons.com) is a grocery-store chain that includes the Albertson's, Jewel-Osco, Shaw's, and Sav-on names. It carries house brands that are gluten-free, with a list available from its headquarters.

- **Hannaford Supermarkets** (www.hannaford.com), located in Maine, New Hampshire, Vermont, Massachusetts, and New York, offer a variety of gluten-free brands.

- **Local health food stores.** Most communities have stores that specialize in organic and gluten-free foods. Some of these stores offer an extensive array of foods, including organic vegetables, fruits, and meats, as well as aisles of gluten-free-labeled processed foods.

- **Publix Supermarkets** (www.publix.com), a large grocery chain in the Southeast, carries a number of products under its house brand. It also has a natural and organic section in its grocery stores that includes gluten-free foods. A list of foods is available from the company's corporate headquarters.

- **Safeway.** Approximately 1,700 Safeway stores operate across the United States and Canada. These include 329 Vons stores in southern California and Nevada, 132 Randalls and Tom Thumb stores in

Texas, 42 Genuardi's stores in the Philadelphia area, and 21 Carrs stores in Alaska. The store provides a list of GF products it sells.

- **Trader Joe's.** Trader Joe's (www.traderjoes.com) has more than 200 stores in in Arizona, California, Connecticut, Delaware, Illinois, Indiana, Maryland, Massachusetts, Michigan, Missouri, Nevada, New Jersey, New Mexico, New York, Ohio, Oregon, Pennsylvania, Virginia, and Washington. It considers itself a specialty grocery store that carries more than 2,000 items under its own label. The chain publishes two lists of gluten-free products, one for the East/Midwest, the other for the West Coast.

- **Wal-Mart,** in the summer of 2005, began requiring its suppliers to identify whenever gluten is used in its private-label products in its Super Wal-Mart stores.

- **Wegmans** (www.wegmans.com) is a chain of supermarkets in the Northeast (from Virginia to New York). It carries its own brands of gluten-free foods.

- **Whole Foods Market** (www.wholefoodsmarket.com) is quite possibly the largest retailer of natural and organic foods, with 181 stores in North America and the United Kingdom.

- **Wild Oats Markets** (www.wildoats.com) is an organic and natural food market that has 110 stores in 25 states and Canada. It offers its own brand of gluten-free foods and has a product guide available for downloading.

- **Winn-Dixie Foods** (www.winndixie.com) has a number of house brands that are gluten-free. It also has a growing selection of organic and gluten-free foods in a special section in its stores. A list of gluten-free foods is available.

## Online Stores

In many parts of the country, the availability of gluten-free products, even in health food stores, is limited. Online shopping offers a variety of foods.

- Arico Natural Foods Company, www.aricofoods.com
- Blue Chip Group, Inc., and Country Fresh Farms, www.shop.bluechipgroup.net

- Ener-G, www.ener-g.com

- Gluten Smart, www.glutensmart.com

- Gluten Solutions, Inc., www.glutensolutions.com

- Gluten-Free Gourmet, www.glutenfreegourmet.com

- Gluten-Free Market, www.glutenfreemarket.com

- Gluten-Free Oats, www.glutenfreeoats.com. This company produces rolled oats that test less than 3 ppm as certified by the University of Nebraska FARRP.

- Gluten-Free Trading Company, www.gluten-free.net

- Glutino, www.glutino.com

- Josef's Gluten-Free, www.josefsglutenfree.com

- Market America, www.marketamerica.com

- Mona's Gluten Free, www.madebymona.com

- Shop by Diet, www.shopbydiet.com

- The Gluten-Free Pantry, www.glutenfree.com

- The Gluten-Free Mall, www.glutenfreemall.com

- Wellness Grocer, www.wellnessgrocer.com

## Online Suppliers of Flours

A number of online and brick-and-mortar stores carry wheat-flour substitutes. You may find that buying directly from the manufacturer is more convenient and less expensive.

- **Amazing Grains** (www.amazinggrains.com) is a cooperative that grows, mills, and markets flour from the seed of a native grass. Montina is the registered trade name for its flour, which is milled from the seed of a native grass called Indian ricegrass (*Achnatherum hymenoides*). This grass is not related to rice. The cooperative is located at 405 Main Street SW, Ronan, MT 59864; 877-278-6585.

- **Arrowhead Mills** (www.arrowheadmills.com) carries several gluten-free flours and mixes. The company is located at 4600 Sleepytime Drive, Boulder, CO 80301; 800-434-4246.

- **Bob's Red Mill** (www.bobsredmill.com), 5209 SE International

Way, Milwaukie, OR 97222; 800-349-2173. This company mills a variety of flours, including all the different types of gluten-free flours used in bread, cake, and cookie recipes.

- **Heartland's Finest** (www.heartlandsfinest.com) produces flours and flour products. Its products are carried in retail stores and can also be purchased online. The company can be reached at PO Box 313, Ubly, MI 48475; 888-658-8909.

- **Namaste Foods** (www.namastefoods.com) manufactures food mixes, such as mixes for pizza, brownies, waffles and pancakes, and cakes. It can be reached at PO Box 3133, Coeur d'Alene, ID 83816; 866-258-9493.

- **Northern Quinoa Corporation** (www.quinoa.com) grows, mills, and markets quinoa and other gluten-free grains. It can be reached at PO Box 519, 428 3rd Street, Kamsack, SK S0A 1S0, Canada; 306-542-3949 or toll-free 866-368-9304.

- **Quinoa Corporation** (www.quinoa.net), PO Box 279, Gardena, CA 90248; 310-217-8125. This company specializes in growing, milling, and marketing quinoa.

- **Special Foods** (www.specialfoods.com), 9207 Shotgun Court, Springfield, VA 22153; 703-644-0991. Special Foods offers a variety of specialized gluten-free flours.

- **Tom Sawyer Gluten-Free Flours** (www.glutenfreeflour.com), 2155 West Highway 89A, Suite 106, Sedona, AZ 86336; 877-372-8800. Carries a general all-purpose flour.

## GLUTEN HOME-TESTING KITS

- Elisa Technologies, www.elisa-tek.com. This company offers several different home-testing kits used to identify the presence of gluten.

## GOOGLE

Google, the Web search engine, can alert you when gluten makes the news. Click on "more," then enter the topic you want to monitor, such as "gluten sensitivity," "gluten intolerance," and "celiac disease."

## HEALTH-CARE PROFESSIONALS INTERVIEWED FOR THIS BOOK

- **Kenneth Bock,** MD, CNS (www.rhinebeckhealth.com), Rhinebeck Health Center, 108 Montgomery Street, Rhinebeck NY 12572; 845-876-7082. (Dr. Bock also has offices in Albany, N.Y.)

- **Jeanne Drisko,** MD, CNS (http://integrativemed.kumc.edu), Program in Integrative Medicine, University of Kansas Medical Center, 3901 Rainbow Boulevard, Mail Stop 2028, Suite 3018 Wescoe, Kansas City, KS 66160; 913-588-6208.

- **Melvyn Grovit,** DPM, MS, CNS, 45 Ludlow Street, Suite 618, Yonkers, NY 10705; 914-476-1544.

- **Ronald Hoffman,** MD, CNS (www.drhoffman.com), The Hoffman Center, 40 East 30th Street, New York NY 10016; 212-779-1744.

- **Stephen T. Sinatra,** MD, CNS, CBT, Preventive and Metabolic Cardiology, 257 East Center Street, Manchester, CT 06040; 860-643-5101.

- **Betty Wedman–St. Louis,** PhD, RD, LD (www.betty-wedman-stlouis.com), nutritionist, PO Box 86212, St. Petersburg, FL 33738; 727-391-6198

## LABORATORIES

These are the laboratories we reference in this book.

- **Enterolab** (www.enterolab.com or www.intestinalhealth.org), 10875 Plano Road, Suite 123, Dallas, TX 75238; 972-686-6869. Enterolab offers a variety of tests, including a stool test, to identify gluten sensitivity. It also provides genetic testing. All tests are at a reasonable cost and may be ordered without a doctor's order.

- **IBT Reference Laboratory** (www.ibtreflab.com), 11274 Renner Boulevard, Lenexa, KS 66219; 800-637-0370. This laboratory has been found to give excellent and consistent results for IgG food hypersensitivity.

- **Immunosciences Lab, Inc.** (www.immunoscienceslab.com), 8693

Wilshire Boulevard, Suite 200, Beverly Hills, CA 90211; 800-950-4686. Immunosciences offers saliva testing for gluten sensitivity.

- **Metametrix Clinical Laboratory** (www.metametrix.com), 4855 Peachtree Industrial Boulevard, Suite 201, Norcross, GA 30092; 770-446-5483 or 800-221-4640. This laboratory provides immuno-reactivity tests for food antibodies, using 91 antigens.

## NUTRITION CREDENTIALS

Many doctors and nutritionists have special training in nutrition. The initials "CNS" (Certified Nutrition Specialist) after a health-care professional's name indicate that the health-care professional has completed a graduate level of education in the field of nutrition.

Registered Dietitians (RD) are eligible to take the CNS examination after they have completed a master's degree level of education and 1,000 hours of appropriate experience. The CNS designation is one of the highest levels of certification that is presently available in the field of nutrition.

## ONLINE FORUMS AND LISTSERVS

When you first accept that you are gluten sensitive, you may feel "different" and isolated, or you may just want to be able to talk with others who are going through the same change in lifestyle as you are. A number of forums (message boards) and listservs are available to you. A forum allows you to post and read messages. Listservs are similar; however, the messages are sent to you by e-mail.

- BrainTalk Communities, http://brain.hastypastry.net/forums/
- Celiac Forums, www.celiacforums.com
- Celiac.com, celiac disease and gluten-free diet message board and forum, www.glutenfreeforum.com
- Celiac@listserv.icors.org, (listserv)
- Delphi Groups, http://forums.delphiforums.com/celiac. A number of different message boards are available for posting.
- Food Allergy Kitchen http://groups.yahoo.com/group/foodallergy kitchen

- Gluten-Free Kitchen, http://health.groups.yahoo.com/group/glutenfreekitchen

- iVillage, celiac disease and gluten-free diets, http://messageboards.ivillage.com/iv-bhceliac

- Living Wheat and Gluten-Free, http://health.groups.yahoo.com/group/livingwheatandglutenfree

- Self, http://boards.self.com/index.jspa

- Silly Yaks (http://health.groups.yahoo.com/group/SillyYaks), one of several Yahoo Groups. This is a listserv. In addition to being able to discuss gluten-sensitivity problems, you can download a comprehensive restaurant guide (PDF format, not searchable).

- USA Silly Yaks, http://health.groups.yahoo.com/group/USASillyYaks

## RESEARCH CENTERS

- **Columbia University**, Celiac Disease Center is dedicated to patient care, education, and research (www.celiacdiseasecenter.columbia.edu/CF-HOME.htm).

- **National Foundation for Celiac Awareness** is not a research center; however, it collaborates with researchers and helps fund research projects aimed at finding a cure for celiac disease (www.celiaccentral.org).

- **National Organization for Rare Diseases** (www.rarediseases.org) is a national charity devoted to supporting research on rare diseases. A number of gluten-intolerance and celiac groups belong to this organization.

- **The Foundation for Nutrition and Inflammatory Bowel Diseases in Children** (www.nibdinkids.com) is a nonprofit organization formed to raise awareness and foster research in the utilization of proper nutrition in the treatment of juvenile inflammatory bowel disease. This organization does not do research, but it funds research projects by individuals.

- **University of Chicago** (www.uchospitals.edu/specialties/celiac/) has a celiac disease program dedicated to education and research.

- **University of Maryland, Center for Celiac Research** (http://celiaccenter.org) uses a multidisciplinary approach to research and education in celiac disease. It is engaged in clinical care, diagnostic support, education, and clinical and basic science research in celiac disease.

- **William K. Warren Medical Research Center for Celiac Disease,** University of California, San Diego (UCSD) (http://celiaccenter.ucsd.edu). This research center opened its doors in 2006. The center aims to conduct state-of-the-art research and provide comprehensive medical care to individuals and families affected by celiac disease.

## SUPPORT GROUPS

Support groups provide resources, information, and (often) forums through which individuals can share stories, post questions, and ask for help. "Live" support groups are available in many communities throughout the country.

Although these groups are largely focused on celiac disease, they address the issues of gluten intolerance.

- **Canadian Celiac Association** (www.celiac.ca) is a national organization of local chapters of celiac groups in Canada. The organization has a mission of awareness, advocacy, education, and research.

- **Celiac Disease Foundation** (www.celiac.org) offers links to other resources, information for children with gluten sensitivity, books, and other information.

- **Celiac Sprue Association** (http://csaceliacs.org/index.php) is a nonprofit celiac support group with more than 95 chapters and 10,000 members worldwide.

- **Celiac.com** (www.celiac.com). Although this online resource is dedicated to the support of those who have celiac disease, it is a premier site, offering a wide array of information and resources for anyone who has gluten sensitivity.

- **Gluten Intolerance Group** (www.gluten.net) supports people with gluten intolerances, including celiac disease, dermatitis herpetiformis, and other gluten sensitivities. Its Web site has links to some state and local associations.

# NOTES

## Introduction

1 C. Matteoni, et al., "Celiac Disease Is Highly Prevalent in Lymphocytic Colitis," *Journal of Clinical Gastroenterology,* March 2001, 32(3):25-227.

## Chapter 1

1 Marion Zarkadas, et al., "Celiac Disease and the Gluten-Free Diet: An Overview," *Topics in Clinical Nutrition,* April/June 2005, 20(2):127-38.

2 A. Fasano, and C. Catassi, "Current Approaches to Diagnosis and Treatment of Celiac Disease: An Evolving Spectrum," *Gastroenterology* 120 (2001): 636-51.

3 A. Rostom, "Incidence and Prevalence of Celiac Disease," NIH Consensus Development Conference on Celiac Disease, June 28-30, 2004, http://consensus.nih.gov/2004/2004CeliacDisease118html.htm (accessed January 2, 8, 2006).

4 A. Fasano, and C. Catassi, "Current Approaches to Diagnosis and Treatment of Celiac Disease: An Evolving Spectrum," *Gastroenterology* 120 (2001): 636-51.

5 Alessio Fasano, et al., "Prevalence of Celiac Disease in At-Risk and Not-at-Risk Groups in the United States," *Archives of Internal Medicine* 163 (February 10, 2003): 286.

6 Kenneth Fine, "Early Diagnosis of Gluten Sensitivity: Before the Villi Are Gone," www.enterolab.com/essay/.

7 Kenneth Fine, "Early Diagnosis of Gluten Sensitivity: Before the Villi Are Gone," www.enterolab.com/essay/.

8 J. O'Keefe, and L. Cordain, "Cardiovascular Disease Resulting from a Diet and Lifestyle at Odds with Our Paleolithic Genome: How to Become a 21st-Century Hunter-Gatherer," *Mayo Clinic Proceedings* (2004): 79:101-8.

9 "History of Grains," *The Whole Grain,* University of Minnesota, www.wholegrain.umn.edu/history/index.cfm.

10 We should make clear: ERS (Economic Research Service) of the U.S. Department of Agriculture defines "consumption" in economic terms—"goods that are used up." It does not use the term to imply human consumption, although in the case of wheat, barley, and rye, most consumption is done by humans.

11 *Nutrient Content of the U.S. Food Supply, 1909-2000,* Economic Research Service, U.S. Department of Agriculture, p. 20.

12 S. Eaton, and L. Cordain, "Evolutionary Aspects of Diet: Old Genes, New Fuels," *World Review of Nutrition and Dietetics* (Basel, Karger, 1997): 81:27.

13 "About Dr. Weston A. Price," Weston A. Price Foundation for Wise Traditions, www. westonaprice.org.

14 Samantha Flower, "Nutritional Therapy, Learning from Native Cultures," The Kevala Centre, www.kevala.co.uk (accessed December 17, 2005).

15 Jimaima Lako, "Dietary Trends and Diabetes: Its Association among Indigenous Fijians 1952 to 1994," *Asia Pacific Journal of Clinical Nutrition* 10 (September 2001): 183.

16 J. O'Keefe, and L. Cordain, "Cardiovascular Disease Resulting from a Diet and Lifestyle at Odds with Our Paleolithic Genome: How to Become a 21st-Century Hunter-Gatherer," *Mayo Clinic Proceedings* (2004): 79:101-8.

17 Karen Michel, "Native Americans Discuss a Return to Traditional Natural Foods to Combat Health Problems," *The Washington Post*, September 22, 2004, republished by Organic Consumers Association, www.organicconsumers.org (accessed December 28, 2005).

18 Brenda Norrel, "Leading Degenerative Diseases in Indian Country Can Be Fought with Healthy Diets," *Indian Country Today,* March 1, 2005.

19 "Diabetes Statistics for Native Americans," American Diabetes Association, www.diabetes. org/diabetes-statistics/native-americans.jsp (accessed December 28, 2005).

20 "Diabetes Statistics for Native Americans," American Diabetes Association, www.diabetes. org/diabetes-statistics/native-americans.jsp (accessed December 28, 2005).

21 "Chronic Conditions: Making the Case for Ongoing Care, September 2004 Update," Partnership for Solutions (partnership between Johns Hopkins University and The Robert Woods Johnson Foundation), www.partnerships for solutions.com (accessed December 28, 2005).

## Chapter 2

1 "Food Allergen Labeling and Consumer Protection Act of 2004," Center for Food Safety and Applied Nutrition, U.S. Food and Drug Administration, www.cfsan.fda.gov.

## Part 2

1 M. Hadjivassiliou, C. Williamson, and N. Woodroofe, "The Immunology of Gluten Sensitivity: beyond the Gut," *TRENDS in Immunology* (November 2004) 25:11.

## Chapter 3

1 The Dermatitis Herpetiformis Online Community, www.dermatitisherpetiformis.org.uk/ whatisdh.html (accessed July 17, 2005).

2 American Osteopathic College of Dermatology (AOCD), Dermatologic Disease Database, Dermatitis Herpetiformis, www.aocd.org/skin/dermatologic_diseases/dermatitis_herpeti. html (accessed August 20, 2005).

3 American Osteopathic College of Dermatology (AOCD), Dermatologic Disease Database, Dermatitis Herpetiformis, www.aocd.org/skin/dermatologic_diseases/dermatitis_herpeti. html (accessed August 20, 2005).

4 The Dermatitis Herpetiformis Online Community, www.dermatitisherpetiformis.org.uk/whatisdh.html.

5 Medline Plus, U.S. National Library of Medicine and National Institutes of Health, www.nlm.nih.gov/medlineplus/druginfo/medmaster/a601102.html (accessed August 22, 2005).

6 National Institute of Neurological Disorders and Stroke (NINDS), NINDS Shingles Information Page, www.ninds.nih.gov/disorders/shingles/shingles_pr.htm (accessed July 24, 2005).

7 The Net Doctor, www.netdoctor.co.uk/medicines/100001109.html (accessed August 20, 2005).

8 Lionel Fry, MD, "What Is DH?" *Crossed Grain,* summer 2001, reprinted with permission on the Dermatitis Herpetiformis Online Community, www.dermatitisherpetiformis.org.uk/whatisdh.html (accessed August 25, 2005).

9 G. Michaëlson, et al., "Psoriasis Patients with Antibodies to Gliadin Can Be Improved by a Gluten-Free Diet," *British Journal of Dermatology* 142 (2000): 44–51.

10 W. K. Woo, et al., "Celiac Disease-Associated Antibodies Correlate with Psoriasis Activity," *British Journal of Dermatology* 151 (October 2004): (4):891–4, www.blackwell-synergy.com/links/doi/10.1111/j.1365-2133.2004.06137.x (accessed August 27, 2005).

11 G. Michaëlsson, et al., "Gluten-Free Diet in Psoriasis Patients with Antibodies to Gliadin Results in Decreased Expression of Tissue Transglutaminase and Fewer Ki67+ Cells in the Dermis," *Acta Dermato-Venereologica* 83 (2003): 425–9.

12 G. Michaëlson, et al., "Psoriasis Patients with Antibodies to Gliadin Can Be Improved by a Gluten-Free Diet," *British Journal of Dermatology* 142 (2000): 44–51.

13 F. Drago, et al., "Pemphigus Improving with Gluten-free Diet," *Acta Dermato-Venereologica* 85(1) (2005): 84–5.

14 M. B. Crawford, "Urticaria," www.emedicine.com.

15 E. Scala, et al., "Urticaria and Adult Celiac Disease," *Allergy* 54 (1999).

16 G. R. Powell, and W. L. Weston, "Dermatitis Herpetiformis Presenting as Chronic Urticaria," *Pediatric Dermatology* 21(5) (September 2004): 564.

17 L. Caminiti, et al., "Chronic Urticaria and Associated Celiac Disease in Children: A Case-Control Study," *Pediatric Allergy and Immunology* 16(5) (August 2005): 428.

# Chapter 4

1 National Ataxia Foundation, www.ataxia.org.

2 M. Hadjivassiliou, et al., "Gluten Ataxia in Perspective: Epidemiology Genetic Susceptibility and Clinical Characteristics," *Brain* 126 (2003): 685–91.

3 M. Hadjivassiliou, et al., "Gluten Sensitivity as a Neurological Illness," *Journal of Neurology, Neurosurgery, and Psychiatry* 72 (2002): 560–3.

4 National Institute of Neurological Disorders and Stroke (NINDS), NINDS Peripheral neuropathy fact sheet, www.ninds.nih.gov/disorders/peripheralneuropathy/peripheralneuropathy.htm.

5 M. Hadjivassiliou, et al., "Gluten Sensitivity as a Neurological Illness," *Journal of Neurology, Neurosurgery, and Psychiatry* 72 (2002): 560–3.

6 M. Hadjivassiliou, et al., "Gluten Sensitivity as a Neurological Illness," *Journal of Neurology, Neurosurgery, and Psychiatry* 72 (2002): 560-3.

7 M. Hadjivassiliou, et al., "Dietary Treatment of Gluten Ataxia," *Journal of Neurology, Neurosurgery, and Psychiatry* 74 (2003): 1221-4.

8 N. Zelnick, et al., "Range of Neurologic Disorders in Patients with Celiac Disease," *Pediatrics* 113(6): June 2004.

9 M. Hadjivassiliou, et al., "Headache and CNS White Matter Abnormalities Associated with Gluten Sensitivity," *Neurology* 56 (2001): 386-8.

10 Courier Press, "Gluten-Free Diet May Fight Migraines," www.courierpress.com (accesse October 17, 2005).

11 U.S. Department of Health and Human Services, Centers for Disease Control.

12 Centers for Disease Control, Fact Sheet, CDC Autism Research, May 4, 2006.

13 Centers for Disease Control, Fact Sheet, CDC Autism Research, May 4, 2006.

14 Centers for Disease Control, Fact Sheet, "Parental Report of Diagnosed Autism in Children Aged 4–17 Years, United States, 2003–2004," www.cdc.gov/od/oc/media/transcripts/ASDMMWRfactSheet.pdf.

15 Autism Research Institute, "Parent Ratings of Behavioral Effects of Biomedical Interventions," *Autism Research Institute Publication* 34 (March 2005).

16 "The GF/CF Diet, Success Stories: Dietary Intervention for Autistic Spectrum Disorders," the GF/CF diet support group information Web site, www.gfcfdiet.com/successstories.htm (accessed January 8, 2006).

17 A. M. Knivsberg, et al., "A Randomized, Controlled Study of Dietary Intervention in Autistic Syndromes," *Nutritional Neuroscience* 5(4) (2002): 251-61.

18 K. L. Reichelt, et al., "Can the Pathophysiology of Autism Be Explained by the Nature of the Discovered Urine Peptides?" *Neuroscience* 6(1) (February 2003): 19-28.

19 A. Vojdani, et al., "Immune Response to Dietary Proteins, Gliadin, and Cerebellar Peptides in Children with Autism," *Nutritional Neuroscience* 7(3) (June 2004): 151-61.

20 A. Vojdani, et al., "Immune Response to Dietary Proteins, Gliadin, and Cerebellar Peptides in Children with Autism," *Nutritional Neuroscience* 7(3) (June 2004): 151-61.

21 Attention Deficit Disorder Association, "Fact Sheet on Attention Deficit Hyperactivity Disorder (ADHD/ADD), www.add.org/articles/factsheet.html (accessed November 24, 2005).

22 National Institute of Mental Health, "Attention Deficit Hyperactivity Disorder," www.nimn.nih.gov/pulicat/adhd.cfm (accessed November 24, 2005).

23 Attention Deficit Disorder Association, "Fact Sheet on Attention Deficit Hyperactivity Disorder (ADHD/ADD), www.add.org/articles/factsheet.html (accessed November 24, 2005).

24 N. Zelnik, et al., "Range of Neurologic Disorders in Patients with Celiac Disease," *Pediatrics* 113 (2004): 1672-6.

25 National Institute of Mental Health, "Anxiety Disorders: Obsessive-Compulsive Disorder," www.nimh.nih.gov/publicat/anxiety.cfm (accessed November 24, 2005).

26 Päivi Pynnönen, et al., "Untreated Celiac Disease and Development of Mental Disorders in Children and Adolescents," *Psychosomatics* 43(4) (July-August 2002): 331-4.

27 Gluten-Free Celiac Disease Forum at Celiac.com, www.glutenfreeforum.com/.

# Chapter 5

1 "Health Topics: Handout on Health: Systemic Lupus Erythematosus," National Institute of Arthritis and Musculoskeletal and Skin Diseases, National Institutes of Health, Department of Health & Human Services, www.niams.nih.gov/hi/topics/lupus/slehandout/ (accessed August 28, 2005).

2 Lupus Foundation of America, www.lupus.org.

3 M. J. Rensch, et al., "The Prevalence of Celiac Disease Autoantibodies in Patients with Systemic Lupus Erythematosus," *American Journal of Gastroenterology* 96 (2001): 1113-5.

4 M. Hadjivassiliou, et al., "Gluten Sensitivity Masquerading As Systemic Lupus Erythematosus," *Annals of Rheumatic Diseases* 63 (2004): 1501-3 http://ard.bmjjournals.com (accessed August 4, 2005)

5 National Multiple Sclerosis Society, www.nationalmssociety.org.

6 National Multiple Sclerosis Society, www.nationalmssociety.org.

7 M. Hadjivassiliou, "Multiple Sclerosis and Occult Gluten Sensitivity," author reply, *Neurology* 64(5) (March 8, 2005): 933-4.

8 National Osteoporosis Foundation, www.nof.org.

9 W. Stenson, et al., "Increased Prevalence of Celiac Disease and Need for Routine Screening among Patients with Osteoporosis," *Archives of Internal Medicine* 165(4) (February 28, 2005).

10 W. Wright, "Personal Story," Osteoporosis Society of Canada, www.osteoporosis.ca (accessed September 22, 2005).

11 T. Valdimarsson, et al., "Reversal of Osteopenia with Diet in Adult Celiac Disease," *Gut* 38:322-7.

12 T. Kemppainen, et al., "Bone Recovery after a Gluten-Free Diet: A 5-Year Follow-Up Study," *Bone* 25(3) (September 1999): 355-60.

13 *The Merck Manual of Health & Aging*, "What Is Osteomalacia?" www.merck.com.

14 R.A. Basu, et al., "Celiac Disease Can Still Present with Osteomalacia!" *Rheumatology* 39 (2000): 335-6.

15 W. DeBoer, et al., "A Patient with Osteomalacia as Single Presenting Symptom of Gluten-Sensitive Enteropathy," Journal of Internal Medicine 232(1) (July 1992): 81-5.

16 A. J. Dorst, and J. D., Ringe, "Severe Osteomalacia in Endemic Sprue. An Important Differential Diagnosis in Osteoporosis," *MMW Fortschr Med* 116(8) (March 20, 1998): 42-5.

17 R. A. Basu, et al., "Celiac Disease Can Still Present with Osteomalacia!" *Rheumatology* 39 (2000): 335-6.

18 Centers for Disease Control, Arthritis, www.cdc.org (accessed September 26, 2005).

19 "Juvenile Rheumatoid Arthritis," *Kids Health for Parents,* http://kidshealth.org/parent/medical/arthritis/jra.html.

20 Arthritis Foundation, Disease Center, www.arthritis.org.

21 Arthritis Foundation, Disease Center, www.arthritis.org.

22 I. Alghafeer, et al., "Rheumatic Manifestations of Gastrointestinal Diseases," *Rheumatic Diseases* 51(2), Arthritis Foundation, www.arthritis.org (accessed September 26, 2005).

23 E. Lubrano et al., "The Arthritis of Celiac Disease: Prevalence and Pattern in 200 Adult Patients," *British Journal of Rheumatology* 35 (1996): 1314-8.

24 I. Hafström, et al., "A Vegan Diet Free of Gluten Improves the Signs and Symptoms of Rheumatoid Arthritis: The Effects on Arthritis Correlate with a Reduction in Antibodies to Food Antigens," *Rheumatology* 40 (2001): 1175-9, http://rheumatology.oxfordjournals.org (accessed September 25, 2005).

25 RemedyFind, www.remedyfind.com.

26 Home Schooler's Curriculum Swap, http://theswap.com/BBS/ForumHome/12798.html.

27 Scleroderma Foundation, "What Is Scleroderma?" www.scleroderma.org/medical/overview.shtm (accessed September 26, 2005).

28 Arthritis Foundation, "Sjögren's Syndrome," www.arthritis.org.

29 D. Slot, and H. Locht, "Arthritis as Presenting Symptom in Silent Adult Celiac Disease," *Scandinavian Journal of Rheumatology* 29 (2000): 260-3.

30 National Institute of Diabetes and Digestive and Kidney Diseases, "National Diabetes Statistics Fact Sheet: General Information and National Estimates on Diabetes in the United States" (2003), http://diabetes.niddk.nih.gov/dm/pubs/statistics/index.htm#7 (accessed September 11, 2005).

31 Vijay Kumar, et al., "Celiac Disease-Associated Autoimmune Endocrinopathies," *Clinical and Diagnostic Laboratory Immunology* (July 2001): 679.

32 M. Addison, "Type 1 Diabetes: New Perspectives on Disease Pathogenesis and Treatment," seminar, *The Lancet* 358 (July 21, 2001): 225.

33 M. Addison, "Type 1 Diabetes: New Perspectives on Disease Pathogenesis and Treatment," seminar, *The Lancet* 358 (July 21, 2001): 225.

34 O. I. Saadah, et. al., "Effect of Gluten-Free Diet and Adherence on Growth and Diabetic Control in Diabetics with Celiac Disease," *Archives of Disease in Childhood* 89 (2004): 871-876, www.abd.bmjournals.com (accessed July 8, 2005).

35 C. E. Counsell, et al., "Celiac Disease and Autoimmune Thyroid Disease," *Gut* 35:844-846 http://gut.bmjjournals.com/cgi/content/abstract/35/6/844 (accessed August 20, 2005).

36 U. Volta, et al., "Celiac Disease in Patients with Autoimmune Thyroiditis," *Digestion* 64 (2001): 61-5.

37 A. Ventura, et al., "Duration of Exposure to Gluten and Risk for Autoimmune Disorders in Patients with Celiac Disease," *Gastroenterology* 117 (1999): 297-303.

38 C. Sategna-Guidetti, et al., "Prevalence of Thyroid Disorders in Untreated Adult Celiac Disease Patients and Effect of Gluten Withdrawal: An Italian Multicenter Study," *American Journal of Gastroenterology* 96(3):75.

# Chapter 6

1 P. Green, et al., "Characteristics of Adult Celiac Disease in the USA: Results of a National Survey," *American Journal of Gastroenterology* 96(1) (2001).

2 A. Fasano, et al., "Prevalence of Celiac Disease in At-Risk and Not-at-Risk Groups in the United States," *Archives of Internal Medicine* 163(3) (February 10, 2003).

3 G. Corrao, et al., "Mortality in Patients with Celiac Disease and Their Relatives: A Cohort Study," *The Lancet* 358(9279) (August 4, 2001).

4 National Digestive Diseases Information Clearinghouse (NDDIC), "Irritable Bowel Syndrome," http://digestive.niddk.nih.gov/ddiseases/pubs/ibs/.

5 IBS Tales, "The Tale of Charlene," www.ibstales.com/happy_tales_five.htm (accessed October 6, 2005).

6 D. S. Sanders, et al., "Association of Adult Celiac Disease with Irritable Bowel Syndrome: A Case-Control Study in Patients Fulfilling ROME II Criteria Referred to Secondary Care," *The Lancet* 358 (9292) (November 3, 2001): 1504-8.

7 C. O'Leary, et al., "Celiac Disease and Irritable Bowel-Type Symptoms," *American Journal of Gastroenterology* 97(6) (June 2002): 1463-7.

8 B. Shahbazkhani, et al., "Celiac Disease Presenting with Symptoms of Irritable Bowel Syndrome," *Alimentary Pharmacology & Therapeutics* 18(2) (July 2003): 231.

9 Jen-Paul Achkar, MD, "Inflammatory Bowel Disease," American College of Gastroenterology, www.acag.gi.org/patients/gihealth/ibd.asp (accessed October 2, 2005).

10 A. R. Eurler, and M. E. Ament, "Celiac Sprue and Crohn's Disease: An Association Causing Severe Growth Retardation," *Gastroenterology* 72(4 Pt 1) (April 1977): 729-31.

11 R. Gillberg, et al., "Chronic Inflammatory Bowel Disease in Patients with Celiac Disease," *Scandinavian Journal of Gastroenterology* 17(4) (June 1982): 491-6.

12 E. G. Breen, et al., "Celiac Proctitis," *Scandinavian Journal of Gastroenterology* 22(4) (May 1987): 471-7.

13 A. Sha, et al., "Epidemiological Survey of Celiac Disease and Inflammatory Bowel Disease in First-Degree Relatives of Celiac Patients," *Quarterly Journal of Medicine* 74(275) (March 1990): 283-8.

14 A. Tursi, et al., "High Prevalence of Celiac Disease among Patients Affected by Crohn's Disease," *Inflammatory Bowel Diseases* 11(7) (July 2005): 662-6.

15 A. Kang, et al., "Celiac Sprue and Ulcerative Colitis in Three South Asian Women," Indian Journal of Gastroenterology 23 (2004): 24-5, www.indianjgastro.com (accessed October 8, 2005).

16 P. Iovino, et al., "Esophageal Impairment in Adult Celiac Disease with Steatorrhea," *American Journal of Gastroenterology* 93(8) (August 1998): 1243.

17 A. Cuomo, et al., "Reflux Oesophagitis in Adult Celiac Disease: Beneficial Effect of a Gluten-Free Diet," *Gut* 52 (2003): 514-7.

18 G. R. Corassa, et al., "Celiac Disease in Adults," *Baillieres Clinical Gastroenterology* 9(2) (June 1995): 329-50.

19 P. Collin, et al., "Endocrinological Disorders and Celiac Disease," *Endocrine Reviews* 23(4) (2002): 464-83.

20 I. de Freitas, et al., "Celiac Disease in Brazilian Adults," *Journal of Clinical Gastroenterology* 34 (April 2002): 4.

21 David Wray, "Gluten-Sensitive Recurrent Aphthous Stomatitis," *Digestive Diseases and Sciences (Historical Archive),* Springer Science+Business Media B.V. 26(8) (August 1981): 737-40.

22 Mayo Clinic, "Celiac Disease: Signs and Symptoms," www.mayoclinic.com.

23 Joseph Murray, MD, PhD, "The Widening Spectrum of Celiac Disease," summarized by Jim Lyles (Sprue-nik Press, November 1996).

24 Centers for Disease Control, "Giardiasis Fact Sheet," www.cdc.gov/ncidod/dpd/parasites/giardiasis/factsht_giardia.htm.

25 E. Mastropasqua, and A. Farruggio, "Giardia Duodenalis: A Confounding Factor for the Diagnosis of Celiac Disease," *Journal of Clinical Gastroenterology* 36(2) (2003): 185.

26 B. Landzberg, and B. Connor, "Persistent Diarrhea in the Returning Traveler: Think beyond Persistent Infection," *Scandinavian Journal of Gastroenterology* 40(1) (January 2005): 112-4.

# Chapter 7

1 Centers for Disease Control and Prevention, "Chronic Fatigue Syndrome," www.cdc.gov/ncidod/diseases/cfs/.

2 Department of Pain Medicine and Palliative Care, Beth Israel Medical Center, "Fibromyalgia," http://stoppain.org/pain_medicine/.

3 National Institute of Arthritis and Musculoskeletal and Skin Diseases (NIAMS), National Institutes of Health, "Questions and answers about fibromyalgia," www.niams.nih.gov/hi/topics/fibromyalgia/fibrofs.htm.

4 A. Skowera, M. Peakman, et al., "High Prevalence of Serum Markers of Celiac Disease in Patients with Chronic Fatigue Syndrome," Journal of Clinical Pathology 54 (2001): 335-6.

5 R. Zipser, et al., "Presentations of Adult Celiac Disease in a Nationwide Patient Support Group," Digestive Diseases and Sciences 48(4) (April 2003): 761-4.

6 National Library of Medicine, "Iron deficiency anemia," www.nlm.nih.gov/.

7 U. Schmitz, et al., "Iron-Deficiency Anemia as the Sole Manifestation of Celiac Disease," The Journal of Clinical Investigation 72(7) (July 1994): 519-21.

8 B. Annibale, et al., "Efficacy of Gluten-Free Diet Alone on Recovery from Iron Deficiency Anemia in Adult Celiac Patients," American Journal of Gastroenterology 96(1) (January 2001): 132.

9 U. Karnam, et al., "Prevalence of Occult Celiac Disease in Patients with Iron Deficiency Anemia: A Prospective Study," Southern Medical Journal 97(1) (January 2004).

10 National Center for Biotechnology Information, "Genes and Disease; Diseases of the Immune System: Asthma," www.ncbi.nlm.nih.gov.

11 U.S. Environmental Protection Agency, Aging Initiative, "Age Healthier, Breathe Easier: Solutions You Can Use to Control or Reduce Environmental Triggers," www.epa.gov/aging/solutions/index.html.

12 J. Kero, et al., "Could TH1 and TH2 Diseases Coexist? Evaluation of Asthma Incidence in Children with Celiac Disease, Type 1 Diabetes, or Rheumatoid Arthritis: A Register Study," Journal of Allergy and Clinical Immunology 108(5) (November 2001): 781-3.

13 K. Palosuo, et al., "Rye Gamma-70 and Gamma-35 Secalins and Barley Gamma-3 Hordein Cross-React with Omega-5 Gliadin, A Major Allergen in Wheat-Dependent, Exercise-Induced Anaphylaxis," Clinical & Experimental Allergy 31(3) (March 2001): 466-73.

14 G. Kanny, et al., "Chronic Urticaria to Wheat," Allergy 56(4) (April 2001): 356.

15 BrainTalk Communities, http://brain.hstypastry.net/forums (accessed October 19, 2005).

16 U.S. National Library of Medicine and National Institutes of Health, Medline Plus, "Unintentional Weight Loss," www.nlm.nih.gov/medlineplus/ency/article/003107.htm

17 S. Bode, and E. Gudmand-Hoyer, "Symptoms and Haematologic Features in Consecutive Adult Celiac Patients," Scandinavian Journal of Gastroenterology 31(1) (January 1996): 54-60.

18 J. L. Shaker, et al., "Hypocalcemia and Skeletal Disease As Presenting Features of Celiac Disease," Archives of Internal Medicine 157(9) (May 12, 1997): 1013-6.

19 American Heart Association, "Cardiomyopathy," www.americanheart.org.

20 National Library of Medicine and the National Institutes of Health, "Myocarditis," www.nlm.nih.gov/medlineplus/ency/article/000149.htm.

21 Alessio Fasano, and Carlo Catassi, "Current Approaches to Diagnosis and Treatment of Celiac Disease: An Evolving Spectrum," Gastroenterology 2001 120:636-51.

22 Andrea Frustaci, L. Cuoco, et al., "Celiac Disease Associated with Autoimmune Myocarditis," *Circulation 2002* 105:2611-8, originally published online May 13, 2002.

23 M. Curione, M. Barbato, et al., "Idiopathic Dilated Cardiomyopathy Associated with Celiac Disease: The Effect of a Gluten-Free Diet on Cardiac Performance," *Digestive and Liver Disease* 34(12) (December 2002): 866-9.

24 Nisheeth K. Goel, et al., "Cardiomyopathy Associated with Celiac Disease," *Mayo Clinic Proceedings* 80 (2005): 674-6.

25 Andrea Frustaci, L. Cuoco, et al., "Celiac Disease Associated with Autoimmune Myocarditis," *Circulation 2002* 105:2611-8, originally published online May 13, 2002.

26 A. Meini, et al., "Prevalence and Diagnosis of Celiac Disease in IgA-Deficient Children," *Annals of Allergy, Asthma, & Immunology* 77 (October 1996): 333-6.

27 F. Cataldo, et al., "Celiac Disease and Selective Immunoglobulin A Deficiency," *Journal of Pediatrics* 131(2) (August 1997): 306-8.

28 Peter Arkwright, et al., "Autoimmunity in Human Primary Immunodeficiency Diseases," *Blood* 99(8) (April 15, 2002): 2694-702.

29 M. Heneghan, et al., "Celiac Sprue and Immunodeficiency States: A 25-Year-Review," *Journal of Clinical Gastroenterology* 25(2) (September 1997): 421-5.

30 "Rice Study Shows Immune System Evolution Prevents Disease," Rice University, www.media.rice.edu/.

# Chapter 8

1 Bari Spielman, "Flatulence in Dogs," PetPlace.com, www.petplace.com/dogs/flatulence-in-dogs/page1.aspx (accessed February 18, 2006).

2 Tim Watson, "Diet and Skin Disease in Dogs and Cats," *American Society for Nutritional Sciences, Journal of Nutrition* 128 (1998): 2783S-9S.

3 Michael Day, "The Canine Model of Dietary Hypersensitivity," *Proceedings of the Nutrition Society* 64(4) (November 2005): 458-64.

4 W. Grant Guilford, et al., "Prevalence and Causes of Food Sensitivity in Cats with Chronic Pruritus, Vomiting, or Diarrhea," *Journal of Nutrition* 128 (1998): 2790S-1S, originally presented as part of the Waltham International Symposium on Pet Nutrition and Health in the 21st Century, Orlando, Florida, May 1997.

5 V.R.M. Batt, and E. J. Hall, "Gluten-Sensitive Enteropathy in the Dog," *Wiener Medizinische Wochenschrift* 79(8) (1992): 242-7.

6 Stanley Marks, "Advances in Dietary Management of Gastrointestinal Disease," presentation at the World Small Animal Veterinary Association, 2003, www.vin.com/proceedings/Proceedings.plx?CID=WSAVA2003&PID=6690&O=Generic (accessed February 18, 2006).

7 Stanley Marks, "Advances in Dietary Management of Gastrointestinal Disease," presentation at the World Small Animal Veterinary Association, 2003.

8 Purina Beneful, http://beneful.com/products/original.aspx.

9 PetSmart, Great Choice, food for dogs, with chunky chicken.

10 Iams, Food for Thought Technical Bulletin No. 38R, "Wheat: Ingredients and Their Use in Our Pet Foods," www.iams.com.

## Chapter 9

1 Autism Research Institute, www.autismwebsite.com/.

## Chapter 10

1 Kenneth D. Fine, MD, "Frequently Asked Questions about Results Interpretation," Enterolab, www.enterolab.com/What_Happens (accessed January 10, 2006).

2 Kenneth D. Fine, MD, "Frequently Asked Questions about Results Interpretation," Enterolab, www.enterolab.com/What_Happens (accessed January 10, 2006).

3 Dr. Fine is the medical director and director of operations of EnteroLab Reference Laboratory in Texas. He has been a part of the Dallas academic and clinical medical community for more than 15 years, holding staff positions at both Baylor University Medical Center and the University of Texas-Southwestern Medical School. His research has been published in prestigious medical journals, including *Gastroenterology, The New England Journal of Medicine, The Journal of Clinical Investigation,* and *The American Journal of Gastroenterology.*

4 K. D. Fine, and F. Ogunji, "A New Method of Quantitative Fecal Fat Microscopy and Its Correlation with Chemically Measured Fecal Fat Output," *American Journal of Clinical Pathology* 113(4):528–34.

5 Aristo Vojdani, PhD, MSc, MT, is the founder and chief executive officer of Immunosciences Lab, Inc. He is a graduate of Bar Ilan University in Israel, where he studied microbiology, biochemistry, and immunology. In addition to directing Immunosciences Lab, Dr. Vojdani is also assistant research neurobiologist in the Department of Neurobiology, David Geffen School of Medicine, at the University of California in Los Angeles.

## Chapter 11

1 Codex Alimentarius, "Understanding the Codex Alimentarius," www.codexalimentarius. net (accessed December 30, 2005).

2 Codex Alimentarius, "Codex Standard for Gluten-Free Foods: Codex Stan 118-1981 (amended 1983)."

3 Celiac.com, "Forbidden list," www.celiac.com.

4 Lone Star Celiac Support Group, www.dfwceliac.org.

5 Lone Star Celiac Support Group, www.dfwceliac.org.

6 Lieberman, S., *Dare to Lose: 4 Simple Steps to a Better Body,* Avery (2003).

7 Information about these flours came from various sources, including The Gluten-Free Pantry, www.glutenfree.com; Celiac.com, www.celiac.com; The Cook's Thesaurus, www.foodsubs.com/; Bob's Red Mill, www.bobsredmill.com.

8 Jeff Beavin, *The Gluten/Wheat-Free Guide to Eating Out,* Good Health Publishing, www.goodhealthpublishing.com.

9 Lists of restaurants came from Jeff Beavin, *The Gluten/Wheat-Free Guide to Eating Out,* Good Health Publishing, www.goodhealthpublishing.com; Lani Thompson, Clan Thompson Celiac Pocket Guide to Restaurants, www.clanthompson.com. Always discuss your dietary needs with your wait staff and verify that the items offered are gluten-free.

10 At the time of this book's publication, gluten-free nutrition information was available online.

11 No gluten-free nutrition information was available online at the time of publication.

12 Online gluten-free menu is available.

# Chapter 12

1 S. Lieberman, and N. Bruning, *The Real Vitamin & Mineral Book, 2003,* 3ʳᵈ ed., (Avery/ Penguin Putnam, New York).

2 J. A. Catanzaro, and L. Green, "Microbial Ecology & Probiotics in Human Medicine (Part II)," *Alternative Medicine Review 2001* 2(4):296-305.

3 J. A. Catanzaro, and L. Green, "Microbial Ecology & Probiotics in Human Medicine (Part II)," *Alternative Medicine Review 2001* 2(4):296-305.

4 James E. Williams, "Portal to the Interior: Viral Pathogens and Natural Compounds That Restore Mucosal Integrity and Modulate Inflammation," *Alternative Medicine Review 2003* 8(4):395-409.

5 Alan Miller, The Pathogens, Clinical Implications and Treatment of Intestinal Hyperpermeability. *Alternative Medicine Review 2001* 2(5):330-45.

6 Kathleen A. Head, and Julie S. Jurenka, "Inflammatory Bowel Disease Part I: Ulcerative Colitis—Pathophysiology and Conventional and Alternative Treatment Options," *Alternative Medicine Review 2003* 8(3):247-83.

7 Shari Lieberman, and Alan Xenakis, "The Mineral Miracle. 2005" Square One Publishers, New York.

8 H. J. Cornell, and F. A. Macrae, J. Melney, et al., "Enzyme Therapy for the Management of Celiac Disease," *Scandinavian Journal of Gastroenterology* 40 (2005): 1304-12.

# Chapter 13

1 National Digestive Diseases Information Clearinghouse, "Lactose intolerance," http:// digestive.niddk.nih.gov/ddiseases/pubs/lactoseintolerance/ (accessed February 4, 2006).

2 M. Boniotto, et al., "Variant Mannose-Binding Lectin Alleles Are Associated with Celiac Diseases," *Immunogenetics* 54(8) (November 2002): 596-8.

3 N. F. Childers, and M. S. Margoes, "An Apparent Relation of Nightshades (Solanaceae) to Arthritis," *Journal of Neurological and Orthopedic Medical Surgery* 12 (1993): 227-31, http:// noarthritis.com/research.htm.

4 Eric Orr, "Monsanto Re-engineers Nature," *Chattooga Quarterly News,* Chattooga Conservancy, www.chattoogariver.org/index.php?req=monsanto&quart=Su2005 (accessed February 5, 2006).

5 P. Montague, "2005 Was a Very Good Year for the Biotech Food Industry," Rachel's Democracy & Health News #837 (January 5, 2006), Environmental Research Foundation, www.rachel.org.

# Chapter 14

1 C. Matteoni, et al., "Celiac Disease Is Highly Prevalent in Lymphocytic Colitis," *Journal of Clinical Gastroenterology* 32(3) (March 2001): 25-227.

2 "A Brief History of Celiac Disease," Celiac Sprue Association, www.csaceliacs.org/ historyofcd.php.

3 James S. Steward, MD, West Middlesex University Hospital, Isleworth, Middlesex, England, "History of the Celiac Condition," University of Sunderland, http://osiris. sunderland.ac.uk.

4 William R. Treem, "Emerging Concepts in Celiac Disease," *Current Opinion in Pediatrics* 16:5 (October 2004), www.co-pediatrics.com.

5 S. Accomando, and F. Catoldo, "The Global Village of Celiac Disease," *Digestive and Liver Disease* 36(★7) (July 2004): 492-8, www.ncbi.nlm.nih.gov.

6 Codex Standard 118, www.codexalimentarius.net.

7 Rhonda R. Kane, "International Perspective on Gluten-Free," presented July 14, 2005, to the Food Advisory Committee on Approaches to Establish Thresholds for Food Allergens, U.S. Food and Drug Administration, www.fda.gov/ohrms/dockets/ac/05/slides/2005-4160s2_05_rkane.ppt (accessed January 28, 2006).

8 Australia New Zealand Food Standards, Standard 1.2.8, Nutrition Information Requirements, www.foodstandards.gov.au/foodstandardscode/ (accessed January 28, 2006).

9 L. Soliah, "A Survey of Nutrition in Medical School Curricula," *Today's Dietitian* 6(2), www.todaysdietitian.com/archives/td_204p.20.shtml (accessed February 7, 2006).

10 D. Nelsen, "Gluten-Sensitive Enteropathy (Celiac Disease): More Common Than You Think," *American Family Physician* 66(12) (December 15, 2002).

11 R. Zipser, et al., "Physican Awareness of Celiac Disease: A Need for Further Education," *Journal of General Internal Medicine* 20(7) (July 2005): 644.

12 American College of Physicians, "The Impending Collapse of Primary Care Medicine and Its Implications for the State of the Nation's Health Care: A Report from the American College of Physicians January 30, 2006 (accessed February 11, 2006).

13 New York State Public Health Law, Title V, Clinical Laboratory and Blood Banking Services, www.wadsworth.org/labcert/regaffairs/clinical/title5.pdf (accessed February 11, 2006).

14 National Institutes of Health, www.nih.gov.

15 NIH News, "NIH Announces Final Ethics Rules," (August 25, 2005), www.nih.gov/news/pr/aug2005/od-25.htm.

16 K. Mangan, "Medical-Research Ethics under the Microscope: Schools Try to Plot the Fine Line between Commercial Links and Conflicts of Interest," *The Chronicle of Higher Education* (July 25, 2003), http://chronicle.com (accessed January 31, 2006).

17 David Hamilton, "Illness of the Intestines Gets Late Notice in the U.S.," *The Wall Street Journal* (December 9, 2005) www.post-gazette.com/pg/05343/620030.stm (accessed February 12, 2006).

18 A. Fasano, and C. Catassi, "Current Approaches to Diagnosis and Treatment of Celiac Disease: An Evolving Spectrum," *Gastroenterology 2001* 120:636-51.

19 Stanford University, "Stanford Researchers Find Cause, Possible Cure for Gluten Intolerance," http://mednews.stanford.edu/releases/2002/september/gluten.html.

20 Reuters, "Non-Toxic Wheat Possible Option for Future Celiac Disease Treatment," October 28, 2005.

# Chapter 15

1 Bette Hagman, *The Gluten-Free Gourmet Bakes Bread* (Owl Books, 1999), 40.

2 This recipe, as well as others for dairy substitutes (unless otherwise noted), come from Go Dairy Free, www.godairyfree.org.

3 Ray Peat, "Coconut Oil: You Want a Food Loaded with Real Health Benefits? You Want Coconut Oil," www.mercola.com/2001/mar/24/coconut_oil.htm.

4 Go Dairy Free, www.godairyfree.org/guide/eat/substitutes/sourcream.htm.

# Chapter 16

1 Wholehealth MD, www.wholehealthmd.com.

2 McCann's Irish Oatmeal, www.mccanns.ie/pages/faq.html.

3 Wegmans, www.wegmans.com/greatMeals/recipes/.

4 RecipeZaar, www.recipezaar.com/150978.

5 RecipeZaar, www.recipezaar.com/157201.

6 RecipeZaar, www.recipezaar.com/106530.

7 Cooks.com, www.cooks.com.

8 All Recipes, http://salad.allrecipes.com/az/EggSalad.asp.

9 Alaska Smokehouse, www.alaskasmokehouse.com.

10 *Rachael Ray's 30-Minute Meals,* Food TV, www.foodnetwork.com.

# Chapter 17

1 Epicurious, Classic Omelet, www.epicurious.com/recipes/recipe_views/views/15068.

2 Zoe Quinta, Bed & Breakfast Inns Online, www.bbonline.com/recipe/quintazoe_qt_recipe2.html.

3 Adapted from Thurston House, Bed and Breakfast, Bed & Breakfast Inns Online, www.bbonline.com/recipe/thurston_fl_recipe1.html.

4 Recipe Zaar, Gluten-Free Waffles, www.recipezaar.com/40362.

5 *Rachael Ray's 30 Minute Meals,* Food TV, www.foodnetwork.com.

6 Bob Blumer, *The Surreal Gourmet,* Food TV, www.foodnetwork.com.

7 Bob Blumer, *The Surreal Gourmet,* Food TV, www.foodnetwork.com.

8 Cooks.com, Turkey Skewers with Mango Salsa, www.cooks.com.

9 RecipeZaar, Spicy Sesame Chicken Fajitas, www.recipezaar.com/92972.

10 Michele O'Sullivan, Creamy Cucumber Dressing, All Recipes, http://salad.allrecipes.com/az/CreamyCucumberDressing.asp.

11 Southern U.S. Cuisine, About.com, http://southernfood.about.com/od/beansoups/r/bl00927c.htm.

12 *Better Homes and Gardens New Home Cook Book* (Meredith Corp., 1996).

13 *Better Homes and Gardens New Home Cook Book* (Meredith Corp., 1996).

# Chapter 18

1 5 A Day, Recipe America.com, www.recipeamerica.com.

2 Cooks.com, www.cooks.com.

3 Recipe America, www.recipeamerica.com.

4 Amaranth pancakes, All Recipes, http://brunch.allrecipes.com/az/mrnthPncks.asp.

5 Mr. Breakfast, Spinach Soufflé, www.mrbreakfast.com.

6 *Rachael Ray's 30 Minute Meals,* Food TV, www.foodnetwork.com.

7 Fun Lunch Recipes for Vegetarian Kids and their Parents, Better Health USA, www.betterhealthusa.com/public/269.cfm.

8 Fabulous Foods, www.fabulousfoods.com/recipes/main/sandwiches/veggiefetasand.html.

9 Sara Moulton, *Good Morning America,* ABC News, http://i.abcnews.com/GMA/Springtime/story?id=412924&page=1.

10 Tanya Paulsen, Cooks.com, www.cooks.com.

11 *Better Homes and Gardens New Home Cook Book* (Meredith Corp., 1996).

12 *Betty Crocker's New Cookbook* (McMillan, 1996).

13 *Betty Crocker's New Cookbook* (McMillan, 1996).

## Chapter 19

1 Bette Hagman, *The Gluten-Free Gourmet Bakes Bread* (Owl Books, 1999).

2 Rhonda Johnson, Cole's Flour Blend, New Diets.com, www.newdiets.com.

3 Adapted from Bette Hagman's Basic Featherlight Rice Bread, *The Gluten-Free Gourmet Bakes Bread* (Owl Books, 1999).

4 Cory Bates, GF Banana Bread, Celiac.com, www.celiac.com.

5 JoAnn Garcia, Authentic Foods.com, www.authenticfoods.com/recipes/biscuits.htm.

6 Grit.com, www.grit.com/articles/RecipeBox0506/.

7 Amber Lee, Dinner Rolls, gfutah.org.

8 Carole Fenster, Pizza Crust, Living Without, www.livingwithout.com/special_pizza.htm.

## Chapter 20

1 Starlight Yellow Cake, *Betty Crocker's New Cook Book* (McMillan, 1996).

2 Peter J. D'Adamo, *Eat Right 4 Your Type*, RecipeNet, www.recipenet.org/health/recipes/recipkit/quinoa_applesauce_cake.htm.

3 Fitness and Freebies, www.fitnessandfreebies.com/celiac/cerealsnack.html.

4 Azspirit, GF Pie Crust Recipe, SpiritKeep, http://spiritkeep.net/recipebox/azgfpiecrust1.html.

5 Crystal Elizabeth Teed, "Gluten Free Macadamia Pie Crust," All Recipes, http://pie.allrecipes.com/az.76516.asp.

The facts that support gluten sensitivity and a gluten-free diet are supported by research published in renowned scientific journals. We have included in this section abstracts of some of the major studies confirming the problems of gluten intolerance. These abstracts have been taken directly from the published papers, with full credit given to the authors and publication, as noted. The abstracts are organized by the chapters of the book devoted to the various conditions and diseases.

## CHAPTER 3: GLUTEN AND SKIN DISEASES

**Journal:** *Acto Dermato-Venereologica,* 2003;83(6):425-9
**Paper:** "Gluten-free Diet in Psoriasis Patients with Antibodies to Gliadin Results in Decreased Expression of Tissue Transglutaminase and Fewer Ki67+ Cells in the Dermis"
**Authors:** Michaelsson G, Ahs S, Hammarstrom I, Lundin IP, Hagforsen E. Department of Medical Sciences/Dermatology and Venereology, University Hospital, Uppsala, Sweden.
**Abstract:** Previous studies have shown that 16 percent of patients with psoriasis vulgaris have IgA and/or IgG antibodies to gliadin, but few have antibodies to endomysium. The increase in duodenal intraepithelial lymphocytes was mild. Still, highly significant clinical improvement was observed after 3 months on a gluten-free diet. This study surveys certain immunohistological aspects of involved and non-involved skin in 28 AGA-positive psoriasis patients before and after 3 months of a gluten-free diet. Staining was performed for CD4+ T lymphocytes, Langerhans' cells, endothelium, proliferating (Ki67) cells, and tissue transglutaminase. In the entire group of patients, as well as in those on a gluten-free diet as the only treatment, Ki67+ cells in involved dermis were highly significantly decreased after the diet.

There was a significant decrease in Ki67+ cells even in patients without increased intraepithelial lymphocytes. Tissue transglutaminase was highly overexpressed in involved skin in the papillary endothelium, and decreased by 50 percent after gluten-free diet. The possible role of tissue transglutaminase in the pathogenesis of psoriasis needs further investigation.

**Journal:** *Pediatric Allergy and Immunology,* 2005 Aug;16(5):428–32
**Paper:** "Chronic Urticaria and Associated Coeliac Disease in Children: A Case–Control Study"

**Authors:** Caminiti L, Passalacqua G, Magazzu G, Comisi F, Vita D, Barberio G, Sferlazzas C, Pajno GB. Department of Pediatrics, Allergy Unit, University of Messina, Via Consolare Valeria, 98125 Messina, Italy.

**Abstract:** Celiac disease (CD) and chronic urticaria (CU) are both sustained by immune mechanisms, but there are so far few data on their clinical association. We performed a case–control study to determine the occurrence of CD in urticaria and matched control children, and to assess the clinical relevance of this association. Children and adolescents were diagnosed to have severe chronic idiopathic urticaria in the presence of hives for more than 6 weeks poorly or not responsive to oral antihistamines. Other known causes of urticaria had to be excluded. A matched control group without urticaria was enrolled. In both groups, the presence of CD was searched by assaying antitransglutaminase and anti-edomysial antibodies, and confirmed with endoscopic intestinal biopsy.

CD was diagnosed and confirmed in 4/79 (5.0 percent) of children with CU and in 17/2545 (0.67 percent) of the controls (p = 0.0003). In the four children with urticaria and CD the gluten free diet (GFD) lead to complete remission of urticaria within 5 to 10 weeks, whereas the disappearance of serological markers occurred in longer times (5 to 9 months).

The presence of CD in children with CU was significantly more frequent than in controls. GFD resulted in urticaria remission. CD may be regarded in such subjects as a cause of CU.

## CHAPTER 4: NEUROLOGICAL DISORDERS

**Journal:** *Journal of Neurology, Neurosurgery, and Psychiatry,* 2003;74:1221–1224

**Paper:** "Dietary Treatment of Gluten Ataxia"

**Authors:** M Hadjivassiliou1, G A B Davies-Jones, D S Sanders, and R A Grünewald.

**Abstract:** Gluten ataxia is an immune mediated disease, part of the spectrum of gluten sensitivity, and accounts for up to 40 percent of cases of idiopathic sporadic ataxia. No systematic study of the effect of gluten-free diet on gluten ataxia has ever been undertaken.

To study the effect of gluten-free diet on patients presenting with ataxia caused by gluten sensitivity.

Forty-three (43) patients with gluten ataxia were studied. All were offered a gluten-free diet and monitored every six months. All patients underwent a battery of tests to assess their ataxia at baseline and after one year on diet. Twenty six patients (treatment group) adhered to the gluten-free diet and had evidence of elimination of antigliadin antibodies by 1 year. Fourteen patients refused the diet (control group). Three patients had persistently raised antigliadin antibodies despite adherence to the diet and were therefore excluded from the analysis.

After one year there was improvement in ataxia reflected in all of the ataxia tests in the treatment group. This was significant when compared with the control group. The diet associated improvement was apparent irrespective of the presence of an enteropathy.

Gluten ataxia responds to a strict gluten-free diet even in the absence of an enteropathy. The diagnosis of gluten ataxia is vital as it is one of the very few treatable causes of sporadic ataxia.

**Journal:** *Nutritional Neuroscience*, 2004;Jun;7(3):151-61
**Paper:** "Immune Response to Dietary Proteins, Gliadin, and Cerebellar Peptides in Children with Autism"

**Authors:** Vojdani A, O'Bryan T, Green JA, Mccandless J, Woeller KN, Vojdani E, Nourian AA, Cooper EL. Section of Neuroimmunology, Immunosciences Lab., Inc., 8693 Wilshire Blvd., Ste. 200, Beverly Hills, CA 90211. drari@msn.com.

**Abstract:** The mechanisms behind autoimmune reaction to nervous system antigens in autism are not understood. We assessed the reactivity of sera from 50 autism patients and 50 healthy controls to specific peptides from gliadin and the cerebellum. A significant percentage of autism patients showed elevations in antibodies against gliadin and cerebellar peptides simultaneously.

For examining cross-reaction between dietary proteins and cerebellar antigens, antibodies were prepared in rabbits, and binding of rabbit anti-gliadin, anti-cerebellar peptides, anti-MBP, anti-milk, anti-egg, anti-soy, and anti-corn to either gliadin- or cerebellar-antigen-coated wells was measured. In comparison to anti-gliadin peptide binding to gliadin peptide at 100 percent, the reaction of anti-cerebellar peptide to gliadin peptide was 22 percent, whereas the binding of anti-myelin basic protein (MBP), anti-milk, anti-egg, and anti-soy to gliadin was less than 10 percent.

Further examination of rabbit anti-gliadin (EQVPLVQQ) and anti-cerebellar (EDVPLLED) 8 amino acid (AA) peptides with human serum albumin (HSA) and an unrelated peptide showed no binding, but the reaction of these antibodies with both the cerebellar and gliadin peptides was greater than 60 percent.

This cross-reaction was further confirmed by DOT-immunoblot and inhibition studies. We conclude that a subgroup of patients with autism produce antibodies against Purkinje cells and gliadin peptides, which may be responsible for some of the neurological symptoms in autism.

**Journal:** *Pediatrics*, Vol. 113 No. 6 June 2004, pp. 1672-1676
**Paper:** "Range of Neurologic Disorders in Patients With Celiac Disease"

**Authors:** Nathanel Zelnik, MD, Avi Pacht, MD, Raid Obeid, MD, and Aaron Lerner, MD. From the Department of Pediatrics, Carmel Medical Center, The Bruce Rappaport Faculty of Medicine, Technion-Israel Institute of Technology, Haifa, Israel.

**Abstract:** During the past two decades, celiac disease has been recognized as a multisystem autoimmune disorder. A growing body of distinct neurologic conditions such as cerebellar ataxia, epilepsy, myoclonic ataxia, chronic neuropathies, and dementia have been reported, mainly in middle-aged adults. There still are insufficient data on the association of CD with various neurologic disorders in children, adolescents, and young adults, including more common and "soft" neurologic conditions, such as headache, learning disorders, attention-deficit/ hyperactivity disorder (ADHD), and tic disorders. The aim of the present study is to look for a broader spectrum of neurologic disorders in CD patients, most of them children or young adults.

Patients with CD were asked to fill in a questionnaire regarding the presence of neurologic disorders or symptoms. Their medical charts were reviewed, and those who were reported as having neurologic manifestations underwent neurologic examination and brain imaging or electroencephalogram if required. Their neurologic data were compared with that of a control group matched for age and gender.

Patients with CD were more prone to develop neurologic disorders (51.4 percent) in comparison with control subjects (19.9 percent). These disorders include hypotonia, developmental delay, learning disorders and ADHD, headache, and cerebellar ataxia. Epileptic disorders were only marginally more common in CD. In contrast, no difference was found in the prevalence of tic disorders in both groups. Therapeutic benefit, with gluten-free diet, was demonstrated only in patients with transient infantile hypotonia and migraine headache.

This study suggests that the variability of neurologic disorders that occur in CD is broader than previously reported and includes "softer" and more common neurologic disorders, such as chronic headache, developmental delay, hypotonia, and learning disorders or ADHD. Future longitudinal prospective studies might better define the full range of these neurologic disorders and their clinical response to a gluten-free diet.

## CHAPTER 5: OTHER AUTOIMMUNE DISEASES

**Journal:** *American Journal of Gastroenterology*, 2001 Apr;96(4):1113-5.
**Paper:** "The prevalence of celiac disease autoantibodies in patients with systemic lupus erythematosus."
**Authors:** Rensch MJ, Szyjkowski R, Shaffer RT, Fink S, Kopecky C, Grissmer L, Enzenhauer R, Kadakia S. Department of Medicine, Brooke Army Medical Center, Fort Sam Houston, TX 78234-6200.
**Abstract:** Systemic lupus erythematosus has been associated with false positive autoantibodies for primary biliary cirrhosis, chronic active hepatitis, Sjogren's syndrome, rheumatoid arthritis, thyroid disorders, syphilis, and scleroderma. An increased prevalence of autoantibodies are found in celiac disease and systemic lupus erythematosus, which share the human lymphocyte HLA-B8 and HLA-DR3 histocompatibility antigens. This study examines the prevalence of celiac disease autoantibodies in systemic lupus erythematosus patients.

Patients observed in the Department of Rheumatology at our institutions in San Antonio, Texas, with known systemic lupus erythematosus were offered participation in the study. One hundred three of the 130 patients contacted agreed to participate.

Patients were excluded if they were pregnant or medically unable to undergo endoscopy. All volunteers were tested for the serological presence of IgA and IgM antigliadin and IgA antiendomysial antibodies. Those with positive serology underwent esophagogastroduodenoscopy with duodenal mucosal biopsy.

Twenty-four of 103 (23.3 percent) systemic lupus erythematosus patients tested positive for either antigliadin antibody, whereas none of the 103 patients tested positive for antiendomysial antibody. None of the 24 antigliadin positive patients were found to have endoscopic or histological evidence of celiac disease, making the false positive rate of antigliadin antibody 23 percent.

The presence of false positive antigliadin antibodies in patients with systemic lupus erythematosus is common. Despite shared human lymphocyte antigen loci there does not seem to be an association between celiac disease and systemic lupus erythematosus.

**Journal:** *Archives of Internal Medicine,* 2005 Feb 28;165(4):393-9
**Paper:** "Increased Prevalence of Celiac Disease and Need for Routine Screening among Patients with Osteoporosis"
**Authors:** Stenson WF, Newberry R, Lorenz R, Baldus C, Civitelli R. Divisions of Gastroenterology, Washington University School of Medicine, St Louis, MO 63110.

**Abstract:** There is an increased prevalence of osteoporosis among patients with celiac disease. However, the relative prevalence of celiac disease among osteoporotic and nonosteoporotic populations is not known, and the benefit of screening the osteoporotic population for celiac disease remains controversial.

We evaluated 840 individuals, 266 with and 574 without osteoporosis, from the Washington University Bone Clinic by serologic screening for celiac disease. Individuals with positive serologic test results for antitissue transglutaminase or antiendomysial antibody were offered endoscopic intestinal biopsy to confirm the diagnosis of celiac disease. Individuals with biopsy-proven celiac disease were treated with a gluten-free diet and followed up for improvement in bone mineral density.

Twelve (4.5 percent) of 266 patients with osteoporosis and 6 (1.0 percent) of 574 patients without osteoporosis tested positive by serologic screening for celiac disease. All but 2 serologically positive individuals underwent in-testinalbiopsy. Nine osteoporotic patients and one nonosteoporotic patient had positive biopsy results. The prevalence of biopsy-proven celiac disease was 3.4 percent among the osteoporotic population and 0.2 percent among the nonosteoporotic population. All biopsy-positive individuals tested positive by antitissue transglutaminase and antiendomysial antibody. The antitissue transglutaminase levels correlated with the severity of osteoporosis as measured by T score, demonstrating that the more severe the celiac disease the more severe the resulting osteoporosis. Treatment of the patients with celiac disease with a gluten-free diet resulted in marked improvement in T scores.

The prevalence of celiac disease among osteoporotic individuals (3.4 percent) is much higher than that among nonosteoporotic individuals (0.2 percent). The prevalence of celiac disease in osteoporosis is high enough to justify a recommendation for serologic screening of all patients with osteoporosis for celiac disease.

**Journal:** *Rheumatology* (Oxford); 2001 Oct;40(10):1175-9
**Paper:** "A Vegan Diet Free of Gluten Improves the Signs and Symptoms of Rheumatoid Arthritis: The Effects on Arthritis Correlate with a Reduction in Antibodies to Food Antigens"

**Authors:** Hafstrom I, Ringertz B, Spangberg A, von Zweigbergk L, Brannemark S, Nylander I, Ronnelid J, Lassonen L, Klareskog L. Department of Rheumatology, Karolinska Institutet at Huddinge University Hospital, Stockholm, Sweden.

**Abstract:** Whether food intake can modify the course of rheumatoid arthritis (RA) is an issue of continued scientific and public interest. However, data from controlled clinical trials are sparse. We thus decided to study the clinical effects of a vegan diet free of gluten in RA and to quantify the levels of antibodies to key food antigens not present in the vegan diet.

Sixty-six patients with active RA were randomized to either a vegan diet free of gluten (38 patients) or a well-balanced non-vegan diet (28 patients) for 1 year. All patients were instructed and followed-up in the same manner. They were analysed at baseline and after 3, 6, and 12 months, according to the response criteria of the American College of

Rheumatology (ACR). Furthermore, levels of antibodies against gliadin and beta-lactoglobulin were assessed and radiographs of the hands and feet were performed.

Twenty-two patients in the vegan group and 25 patients in the non-vegan diet group completed 9 months or more on the diet regimens. Of these diet completers, 40.5 percent (nine patients) in the vegan group fulfilled the ACR20 improvement criteria compared with 4 percent (one patient) in the non-vegan group.

Corresponding figures for the intention to treat populations were 34.3 and 3.8 percent, respectively. The immunoglobulin G (IgG) antibody levels against gliadin and beta-lactoglobulin decreased in the responder subgroup in the vegan diet-treated patients, but not in the other analysed groups. No retardation of radiological destruction was apparent in any of the groups.

The data provide evidence that dietary modification may be of clinical benefit for certain RA patients, and that this benefit may be related to a reduction in immunoreactivity to food antigens eliminated by the change in diet.

## CHAPTER 6: DIGESTIVE DISORDERS

**Journal:** *Archives of Internal Medicine*, 2003 Feb 10;163(3):286-92
**Paper:** "Prevalence of Celiac Disease in At-Risk and Not-At-Risk Groups in the United States: a Large Multicenter Study"
**Authors:** Fasano A, Berti I, Gerarduzzi T, Not T, Colletti RB, Drago S, Elitsur Y, Green PH, Guandalini S, Hill ID, Pietzak M, Ventura A, Thorpe M, Kryszak D, Fornaroli F, Wassermann SS, Murray JA, Horvath K. Center for Celiac Research, University of Maryland School of Medicine, 22 S Greene St, N5W70, PO Box 140, Baltimore, MD 21201-1595.

**Abstract:** Celiac disease is an immune-mediated enteropathic condition triggered in genetically susceptible individuals by the ingestion of gluten. Although common in Europe, CD is thought to be rare in the United States, where there are no large epidemiologic studies of its prevalence. The aim of this study was to determine the prevalence of CD in at-risk and not-at-risk groups in the United States.

Serum antigliadin antibodies and anti-endomysial antibodies (EMA) were measured. In EMA-positive subjects, human tissue transglutaminase IgA antibodies and CD–associated human leukocyte antigen DQ2/DQ8 haplotypes were determined. Intestinal biopsy was recommended and performed whenever possible for all EMA-positive subjects. A total of 13,145 subjects were screened: 4508 first-degree and 1275 second-degree relatives of patients with biopsy-proven CD, 3236 symptomatic patients (with either gastrointestinal symptoms or a disorder associated with CD), and 4126 not-at-risk individuals.

In at-risk groups, the prevalence of CD was 1:22 in first-degree relatives, 1:39 in second-degree relatives, and 1:56 in symptomatic patients. The overall prevalence of CD in not-at-risk groups was 1:133. All the EMA-positive subjects who underwent intestinal biopsy had lesions consistent with CD.

Our results suggest that CD occurs frequently not only in patients with gastrointestinal symptoms, but also in first- and second-degree relatives and patients with numerous common disorders even in the absence of gastrointestinal symptoms. The prevalence of CD in symptomatic patients and not-at-risk subjects was similar to that reported in Europe. Celiac disease appears to be a more common but neglected disorder than has generally been recognized in the United States.

**Journal:** *Alimentary Pharmacology & Therapeutics*, 2003 Jul 15;18(2):231-5
**Paper:** "Coeliac Disease Presenting with Symptoms of Irritable Bowel Syndrome"
**Authors:** Shahbazkhani B, Forootan M, Merat S, Akbari MR, Nasserimoghadam S, Vahedi H, Malekzadeh R., Digestive Disease Research Center, Tehran University of Medical Sciences, Tehran, Iran.

**Abstract:** Coeliac disease may easily mimic symptoms which are parts of the criteria used for diagnosing irritable bowel syndrome. *Aim:* To find the frequency of coeliac disease among patients diagnosed as irritable bowel syndrome.

During a period of one year, irritable bowel syndrome patients referred to a university clinic in Tehran were studied. For each patient, an asymptomatic sibling was enrolled as control. Serological tests for coeliac disease were performed in all patients and controls. If positive, duodenal biopsy was performed to confirm the diagnosis. Patients subsequently diagnosed as coeliac disease were placed on a gluten free diet and re-evaluated after 6 months.

One hundred five cases of irritable bowel syndrome and 105 controls were enrolled. Coeliac disease was diagnosed in 12 of the irritable bowel syndrome patients and none of the controls. Eleven coeliac disease patients adhered to a gluten free diet. After 6 months, all 11 patients had significant improvement in symptoms and three were totally asymptomatic. Six allowed repeated endoscopy after 6 months of gluten free diet, of which five showed improvement in histological findings.

Coeliac disease is a common finding among patients labeled as irritable bowel syndrome. In this sub-group, a gluten free diet may lead to a significant improvement in symptoms. Routine testing for coeliac disease may be indicated in all patients being evaluated for irritable bowel syndrome.

**Journal:** *Inflammatory Bowel Disease*, 2005 Jul;11(7):662-6
**Paper:** "High Prevalence of Celiac Disease among Patients Affected by Crohn's Disease"
**Authors:** Tursi A, Giorgetti GM, Brandimarte G, Elisei W. Digestive Endoscopy Unit, "Lorenzo Bonomo" Hospital, Andria, Italy.

**Abstract:** Recent literature has shown a correlation between Crohn's disease and celiac disease, but a prospective study has not been performed. Our aim was to evaluate the prevalence of celiac disease in a consecutive series of patients affected by Crohn's disease, in whom the disease was diagnosed for the first time.

From January to December 2004, we diagnosed 27 patients affected by Crohn's disease (13 men and 14 women; mean age, 32.3 years; range, 16-69 years). In all patients, we performed antigliadin, antiendomysium, and antitransglutaminase antibody tests, and the sorbitol H2 breath test evaluation. In case of antibodies and/or sorbitol positivity, esophagogastroduodenoscopy was performed for a small bowel biopsy.

Antigliadin, antiendomysium, and antitransglutaminase antibody tests were positive in 8/27 (29.63 percent), 4/27 (14.81 percent), and 5/27 (18.52 percent) patients, respectively, whereas the sorbitol H2 breath test was positive in 11/27 (40.74 percent) patients: All of them underwent esophagogastroduodenoscopy. Nine of 11 patients showed signs of duodenal endoscopic damage, and 5/9 (55.55 percent) showed histologic features of celiac disease (18.52 percent of overall Crohn's disease population studied): 2 showed Marsh IIIc lesions (1 patient affected by ileal Crohn's disease and 1 affected by ileo-colonic Crohn's disease), 2 showed Marsh IIIb lesions (all of them affected by ileo-colonic Crohn's disease), 1 showed a Marsh IIIa lesion (1 patient affected by colonic Crohn's disease).

Prevalence of celiac disease seems to be high among patients affected by Crohn's disease, and this finding should be kept in mind at the time of the first diagnosis of Crohn's disease; a gluten-free diet should be promptly started.

**Journal:** Gut, 2003 Apr;52(4):514-7
**Paper:** "Reflux Oesophagitis in Adult Coeliac Disease: Beneficial Effect of a Gluten Free Diet"
**Authors:** Cuomo A, Romano M, Rocco A, Budillon G, Del Vecchio Blanco C, Nardone G. Dipartimento di Internistica Clinica e Sperimen-tale-Gastroenterologia and CIRANAD, Seconda Universita di Napoli, Napoli, Italy.

**Abstract:** Coeliac disease patients show a number of gastrointestinal motor abnormalities, including a decrease in lower oesophageal sphinc-ter pressure. The prevalence of endoscopic oesophagitis in these sub-jects however is unknown. Aim: To evaluate whether untreated adult coeliac patients had an increased prevalence of reflux oesophagitis and, if so, to assess whether a gluten free diet exerted any beneficial effect on gastro-oesophageal reflux disease (GORD) symptoms.

We retrospectively studied 205 coeliac patients (females/males 153/52, median age 32 years) who underwent endoscopy for duodenal biopsy and 400 non-coeliac subjects (females/males 244/156, median age 37 years) referred for endoscopy for upper gastrointestinal symp-toms. Each patient was given a questionnaire for evaluation of GORD symptoms prior to and 4 to 12 months after endoscopy. Coeliac patients were given a gluten free diet. Oesophagitis patients of both groups, fol-lowing an eight-week course of omeprazole, were re-evaluated for GORD symptoms at 4-month intervals up to one year. Significance of differences was assessed by Fisher's exact test.

Oesophagitis was present in 39/205 (19 percent, 95 percent confidence interval (CI) 13.8-25.0 percent) coeliac patients and in 32/400 (8 percent, 95 percent CI 5.5-11.1 percent) dyspeptic subjects. At the 1-year follow-up, GORD symptoms relapsed in 10/39 (25.6 percent, 95 percent CI 13-42.1 percent) coeliacs with oesophagitis and in 23/32 (71.8 percent, 95 percent CI 53.2-86.2 percent) non-coeliac subjects with oesophagitis.

Coeliac patients have a high prevalence of reflux oesophagitis. That a gluten free diet significantly decreased the relapse rate of GORD symptoms suggests that coeliac disease may represent a risk factor for development of reflux oesophagitis.

## CHAPTER 7: UNDIAGNOSED DISEASES AND CONDITIONS

**Journal:** *Journal of Clinical Pathology.* Vol. 54, pp: 335-336 April 2001

**Paper:** [Correspondence], "High Prevalence of Serum Markers of Celiac Disease in Patients with Chronic Fatigue Syndrome"

**Authors:** A Skowera, M Peakman, A Cleare, E Davies, A Deale, and S Wessely. Department of Immunology, Guy's King's and St. Thomas's School of Medicine, Denmark Hill Campus, London SE5 9RS, UK; Department of Psychological Medicine, Guy's King's and St. Thomas's School of Medicine.

**Abstract:** There has been recent interest in the possibility that undiagnosed coeliac disease might be the cause of diverse clinical symptoms, most particularly "tired all the time."[1] A recent study reported a prevalence of three in 100 cases in a primary care environment in which samples were taken from patients with a range of symptoms and signs.[2] The second most frequent symptom reported by the endomysial antibody (EMA) positive patients was "being tired all the time." We decided to examine the prevalence of EMA in patients attending our tertiary referral centre with the diagnosis of chronic fatigue syndrome (CFS).

We tested serum from 100 consecutive patients (47 men, 53 women; median age, 40 years; range, 18-57) referred to our specialist clinic and satisfying the standard CDC criteria for a diagnosis of CFS, and from 100 healthy control subjects (45 men, 55 women; median age, 40 years; range, 18-68) who were blood donors at the South East Thames Blood Transfusion Service. The CFS samples had been stored as part of other studies, and were analysed retrospectively. EMA of the IgA class were detected by indirect immunofluorescence (IF) using cryostat sections of distal primate oesophagus as substrate (Binding Site, Birmingham, UK). Positive samples were confirmed using an enzyme linked immunosorbant assay (ELISA) for the detection of antitissue transglutaminase antibodies[3] (Menarini Diagnostics, Wokingham, UK), tissue transglutaminase being the autoantigen responsible for the IF pattern of EMA. To exclude selective IgA deficiency, serum IgA concentrations were measured by laser nephelometry using specific antisera according to the manufacturer's instructions (Behring Laser Nephelometer II; Dade Behring, Dortmund, Germany).

Two of the 100 CFS samples were positive for EMA using IF, and this was confirmed by ELISA, but none of the 100 control samples was positive. None of the subjects had selective IgA deficiency. Mean (SD) serum IgA concentrations among patients with CFS were 2.1 g/litre (0.98). Neither of the positive cases, both women aged 27 and 54, had reported symptoms typical of CD, although one had a history of constipation. Routine blood tests including serum proteins and full blood count were normal, and both had been seen by consultant physicians before referral. Both had histories of hypothyroidism, were taking long term thyroxine, and were currently euthyroid. Before the diagnosis of CD was made retrospectively, both had received cognitive behaviour therapy (CBT), a standard treatment for CFS. In both cases, CBT led to a substantial improvement in the quality of life and physical activity, but neither patient was symptom free at the end of treatment or at six months follow up. In both cases, CD was subsequently confirmed on jejunal biopsy after the retrospective identification.

In general, it remains true that although a wide range of physical illnesses can be misdiagnosed as CFS (see Wessely et al for review[4]), in practice this is uncommon. In particular, if basic physical examination, investigations, and history are unremarkable, misdiagnosis of CFS and other physical illnesses is very unusual. Until now there have only been two reports concerning three cases of CD being misdiagnosed as CFS.[5,6] However, there is now evidence from primary care of a surprisingly high frequency of unsuspected positive EMA tests in people with non-specific symptoms and a suggestion that a higher index of suspicion is needed when assessing such patients.[7] We now extend that observation to our CFS clinic.

Indeed, given our prevalence of 2 percent, and the fact that there is a treatment for CD, we now suggest that screening for CD should be added to the relatively short list of mandatory investigations in suspected cases of CFS.

**Journal:** *American Journal of Gastroenterology,* 2001 Jan;96(1):132-7
**Paper:** "Efficacy of Gluten-Free Diet Alone on Recovery from Iron Deficiency Anemia in Adult Celiac Patients"

**Authors:** Annibale B, Severi C, Chistolini A, Antonelli G, Lahner E, Marcheggiano A, Iannoni C, Monarca B, Delle Fave G. Department of Gastroenterology, La Sapienza University, Rome, Italy.

**Abstract:** Iron deficiency anemia has been reported as the most frequent extraintestinal symptom in adult celiac disease. Prospective studies on the effect of gluten-free diet on recovery from iron deficiency anemia are lacking. The aim of this study was to verify in adult patients with celiac disease the efficacy of and the time course of recovery from iron deficiency anemia by a gluten-free diet alone.

We studied 190 consecutive adult patients with iron deficiency anemia, screened for celiac disease by duodenal biopsies. New diagnosed celiac patients were invited to follow a gluten-free diet alone without iron supplementation. After 6 months of diet, duodenal biopsies were performed and hematological tests were repeated at 6, 12, and 24 months.

Celiac disease was diagnosed in 26 (24 women, 2 men; 13.7 percent) adult patients. After 6 months of gluten-free diet 14 of 18 (77.8 percent) female patients recovered from anemia, but only 5 of 18 (27.8 percent) reversed from iron deficiency. At 12-month control all but one patient (94.4 percent) recovered from anemia and 9 patients (50 percent) from iron deficiency. After 24 months of diet, only the patient who did not recover from anemia at 12-month control was still anemic, whereas 10 patients (55.5 percent) reversed from iron deficiency. A significant inverse correlation ($r = -0.7141$, $p = 0.0003$) between increase of Hb concentrations and decrease of individual histological scores of duodenitis was observed.

A screening for celiac disease should be carried out in adult patients with iron deficiency anemia. Recovery from anemia occurs between 6 and 12 months on a gluten-free diet alone as a consequence of normalization of histological alterations of the intestinal mucosa.

**Journal:** *Circulation,* 2002 Jun 4;105(22):2611-8
**Paper:** "Celiac Disease Associated with Autoimmune Myocarditis"

**Authors:** Frustaci A, Cuoco L, Chimenti C, Pieroni M, Fioravanti G, Gentiloni N, Maseri A, Gasbarrini G. Department of Cardiology, Catholic University, Rome, Italy.

**Abstract:** Both celiac disease and myocarditis can be associated with systemic autoimmune disorders; however, the coexistence of the 2 entities has never been investigated, although its identification may have a clinical impact.

We screened the serum of 187 consecutive patients with myocarditis (118 males and 69 females, mean age 41.7+/-14.3 years) for the presence of cardiac autoantibodies, anti-tissue transglutaminase (IgA-tTG), and anti-endomysial antibodies (AEAs). IgA-tTG-positive and AEA-positive patients underwent duodenal endoscopy and biopsy and HLA analysis. Thirteen of the 187 patients were positive for IgA-tTG, and 9 (4.4 percent) of them were positive for AEA. These 9 patients had iron-deficient anemia and exhibited duodenal endoscopic and histological evidence of CD. CD was observed in 1 (0.3 percent) of 306 normal controls (P<0.003).

In CD patients, myocarditis was associated with heart failure in 5 patients and with ventricular arrhythmias (Lown class III-IVa) in 4 patients. From histological examination, a lymphocytic infiltrate was determined to be present in 8 patients, and giant cell myocarditis was found in 1 patient; circulating cardiac autoantibodies were positive and myocardial viral genomes were negative in all patients. HLA of the patients with CD and myocarditis was DQ2-DR3 in 8 patients and DQ2-DR5(11)/DR7 in 1 patient. The 5 patients with myocarditis and heart failure received immunosuppression and a gluten-free diet, which elicited recovery of cardiac volumes and function. The 4 patients with arrhythmia, after being put on a gluten-free diet alone, showed improvement in the arrhythmia (Lown class I).

A common autoimmune process toward antigenic components of the myocardium and small bowel can be found in >4 percent of the patients with myocarditis. In these patients, immunosuppression and a gluten-free diet can be effective therapeutic options.

## REFERENCES

[1] Feighery F. "Coeliac disease." BMJ 1999;19:236-9.

[2] Hin H, Bird G, Fisher P, et al. "Coeliac disease in primary care: case finding study." BMJ 1999;318:164-7.

[3] Lock R, Gilmore J, Unsworth D. "Anti-tissue transglutaminase, anti-endomysum and anti-R1-reticulin autoantibodies—the antibody trinity of coeliac disease." Clin Exp Immunol 1999;116:258-62.

[4] Wessely S, Hotopf M, Sharpe M. "Chronic fatigue and its syndromes." Oxford: Oxford University Press, 1998.

[5] Watson R, McMillan S, Dickey W, et al. "Detection of undiagnosed celiac disease with atypical features using antiretulcin and antigliadin antibodies." Q J Med 1992;84:713-18.

[6] Empson M. "Celiac disease or chronic fatigue syndrome—can the current CDC working case definition discriminate?" Am J Med 1998;104:79-80.

[7] Hin H, et al.

# INDEX

Underscored page references indicate boxed text and tables.

## A

Acidophilus, 130–31
Acne, 28
Acne rosea, 28
Actonel, 45
ADD, 37–38
ADHD, 37–38
Adrenalin, 17–18
Adult-onset diabetes, 51–52
Advair, 71
AGA, 15, 19, 24, 27–28, 75, 94–95, 100
Agave cactus, 113, 170
Alaska natives and gluten, 13
Albertson's, 173, 278
Alcohol, 179, 276–77
Allergans, 172–73
Allergies. *See* Food allergies
AllergyFree Passport, 277
Almonds
    Almond Milk, 166
    meal or flour, 115
    Veggie, Almond, and Feta Sandwich or
        Salad, 238–39
Amaranth flour
    Amaranth Pancakes, 231–32
    as flour substitute, 115
Amazing Grains, 280
American Celiac Disease Alliance, 275
Amino acids, 14
Anaphylaxis, 17–19
Anemia, 69–70
Ankylosing spondylitis, 50
Antibiotics, 27
Antibodies, 15, 17, 19, 24, 27–28, 98–101
Antiendomysial antibody (EMA), 15, 19,
    94–95
Antigens, food, 14–15
Antigliadin (IgA) antibody (AGA), 15, 19, 24,
    27–28, 75, 94–95, 100
Antihistamines, 17, 20, 29, 71
Anti-inflammatories, 133
Antioxidants, 129

Antitissue transglutaminase antibody
    (ATTA), 15, 19, 94, 100
Aphthous stomatitis, 64
Arrowhead Mills, 280
Arthritis, 47–51
Artificial sweeteners, avoiding, 111, 113
Aspartame, 111
Asthma, 70–71
Ataxia, 20, 31–34
Atrophy, 94–95
ATTA, 15, 19, 94, 100
Attention deficit disorder (ADD), 37–38
Attention deficit hyperactivity disorder
    (ADHD), 37–38
Autism, 35–37
Autoimmune diseases
    arthritis, 47–51
    celiac disease and, 54
    diabetes, 51–52
    gluten sensitivity and, 40, 42–44, 46,
        51–54, 75
    infections and, chronic, 75
    lupus, 40–42
    multiple sclerosis, 42–43
    osteomalacia, 46–47
    osteopenia, 43–46
    osteoporosis, 43–46
    rickets, 46
    thyroid disease, 52–54
Autoimmune thyroid disease, 53–55

## B

Back pain, 47
Bard's Tale Beer, 276
Barley, 106, 113, 133, 178
Beans
    as pasta substitute, 119
    Red Beans and Rice with Sausage, 194–95
    White Bean Soup with Ham and Greens,
        224–25
Beer, gluten-free, 179, 276

**Shari Lieberman, PhD, CNS, FACN,** has been in private practice as a clinical nutritionist for more than 20 years. She earned a master of science degree in nutrition, food science, and dietetics from New York University and a doctoral degree in clinical nutrition and exercise physiology from The Union Institute in Cincinnati. She is a certified nutrition specialist (CNS), a fellow of the American College of Nutrition (FACN), a member of the New York Academy of Science, a member of the American Academy of Anti-Aging Medicine, a former officer and present board member of the Certification Board for Nutrition Specialists, and president of the American Association for Health Freedom. In 2003, she received the Clinician of the Year Award from the National Nutritional Foods Association.

Dr. Lieberman is the founding dean of the master of science program in clinical nutrition at New York Chiropractic College, a contributing editor to the American Medical Association's *5th Edition of Drug Evaluations*, a peer reviewer for scientific publications, a published scientific researcher, and a presenter at numerous scientific conferences. She is a member of the nutrition team for the New York City Marathon.

Dr. Lieberman's bestseller *The Real Vitamin and Mineral Book* is now in its third edition. She also is the author of *Mineral Miracle, User's Guide to Brain-Boosting Supplements, Dare to Lose: 4 Simple Steps to a Better Body, Get Off the Menopause Roller Coaster, Maitake Mushroom and D-Fraction, Maitake: King of Mushrooms,* and *All About Vitamin C.* Dr. Lieberman is a frequent guest on television and radio, and she often is cited in magazine articles as an authority on nutrition.

To learn more about Dr. Lieberman and her work, visit her Web site at www.drshari.net.